FREE MONEY™
WHEN YOU'RE UNEMPLOYED

Other Books By Laurie Blum

Childcare/Education

Free Money for Day Care
Free Money for Private Schools
Free Money for Foreign Study
Free Money for College
Free Money for College from the Government
Free Money for Athletic Scholarships
Free Money from Colleges and Universities
Free Money for Graduate School (revised)
Free Money for Children's Medical Expenses
Free Money for Childhood Behavioral and Genetic Disorders

Healthcare

Free Money for Heart Disease and Cancer Care
Free Money for Diseases of Aging
Free Money for Infertility Treatments
Free Money for Mental/Emotional Disorders

The Arts

Free Money for People in the Arts

Business

Free Money for Small Business and Entrepreneurs
How to Invest in Real Estate Using Free Money
Free Money from the Federal Government for Small Businesses
    and Entrepreneurs

Other

Free Dollars from the Federal Government
The Complete Guide to Getting a Grant

FREE MONEY™ WHEN YOU'RE UNEMPLOYED

Laurie Blum

John Wiley & Sons, Inc.

New York · Chichester · Brisbane · Toronto · Singapore

I would like to briefly but sincerely thank Jung Cho, Cybèle Fisher, Walter Goldenberg, Shira Levin, Ken Rose, my wonderful editor P. J. Dempsey, Chris Jackson, and Ron Stone.

Free Money is a trademark of The Free Money Co.

Cover art: Evangelia Philippidis

This text is printed on acid-free paper.

Library of Congress Cataloging-in-Publication Data:

Blum, Laurie.
    Free money when you're unemployed / Laurie Blum.
        p.   cm.
    Includes index.
    ISBN 0-471-59944-1 (acid-free paper).   ISBN 0-471-59945-X (pbk. acid-free paper)
    1. Economic assistance. Domestic—United States.   2. Grants-in-aid—United States.   I. Title.
    HC110.P63B58   1993
    336.1′85—dc20   93-13317

Contents

Introduction

Maybe you are one of the unfortunate victims of a corporate restructuring. Or perhaps you are a middle- or even upper-management executive unemployed for the first time, losing your job as well as your pension and retirement benefits. Maybe you have been a wife and homemaker and because of a divorce or the death of your spouse, you just don't know how you are going to be able to manage financially.

Over and over, I am asked the same question on the radio and television broadcasts I do or in the thousands of letters I receive about my other *Free Money* books: Are there really monies to help me if I lose my job or run into tough financial circumstances? Happily, the answer is yes.

Free Money When You're Unemployed identifies private, corporate, and government sources that have millions of dollars to give to those who find themselves unemployed or in tough financial circumstances. These monies can be used to pay for everything from the grocery bill to a mortgage payment. This is "free money," money that is given simply because an individual needs financial help— and money that never needs to be paid back.

Remember, however, that funding sources are not without restrictions. Do you just walk up, hold out your hand, and expect someone to put money in it? Of course not. It takes time, effort, and thought on your part. You are going to have to fill out applications. You may experience frustration or rejection at some point, but the odds are in your favor that you will qualify for some sort of funding.

The hardest part has always been finding the sources of money. That is why I wrote this book. Though I have written books on grant monies available for almost every conceivable need—from monies to pay for college to start-up capital for small businesses—over and over in my research I'd come across grants available for individuals in tough financial circumstances. Much of the information in this book has never been made available to the general public.

The book is divided into four sections:

1. Private Foundation Funding. This section covers the easiest and most accessible funding sources for the average individual seeking a grant.

2. Flow-Through Funding. This section provides information about foundation monies that are given to individuals through nonprofit organizations.

3. Federal Grants. This section identifies agencies that offer direct funding and/or essential referral information.

When possible, listings within each chapter are arranged state by state to make this book easy to use. Check your state's listings in all chapters to see which grants apply to you. You'll find funding parameters and an address and phone number to contact for further information (and application forms).

By the time this book is published, some of the information it contains will have changed. No reference book can be as up-to-date as the reader or the author would like. Names, addresses, dollar amounts, telephone numbers, and other data are always in flux; however, most of the information will not have changed.

On the next few pages is a concise guide to applying for a grant and writing a proposal. Follow my instructions and you should be successful in obtaining some sort of assistance.

Good luck.

How to Apply for a Grant

Thousands of resources are available from private foundations, corporations, and government sources throughout the country. Applying for this aid is the challenging part; it requires diligence, thought, and organization.

First is the sorting-out or research-gathering phase. Look through each chapter of this book and make a list of the potential assistance sources that meet your needs. When compiling your list, pay close attention to the restrictions and qualifications.

Then, politely contact each of the sources you listed by mail or phone to verify all current information, such as address, telephone number, name of the proper contact (in cases where the contact's name is not listed, begin your letter, "To Whom It May Concern"), and his or her title. At this time, you can also arrange to get a copy of the source's most current assistance guidelines and an application form (if one is required). Use this opportunity to find out about any application deadlines and where you are in the funding cycle (i.e., if there is no deadline, when the best time to apply is; also be sure to ask when awards will be announced and funds distributed). However, do not "grill" or cross-examine the person you reach on the phone. Always be prepared to explain why you are applying and what you are applying for—in case you ring through to the key decision maker, who decides to interview you on the spot!

Second is the application phase. Most often you will be asked to submit a formal application rather than a proposal. Always be sure to read (and follow!) the instructions for completing the application. Usually the material you use for one application can be applied with a little restructuring to most, if not all, of the other applications you fill out. Make sure you answer each question as asked, in a manner appropriate to the application you are completing.

Grant applications take time (and thought) to fill out, so make sure you give yourself enough time to thoroughly complete the application before the deadline. Filling out the application can be a lengthy process, because you may be required to write one or more essays. Often, what is required is a "statement of purpose" explaining what you will use the money for and why you need the assistance for which you are applying. You may also need to assemble required attachments, such as tax returns and other financial records. You may also be required to include personal references. Be sure to get strong references. Call all the people you plan to list, and ask them if they feel comfortable giving you references. Remember, you have to convince the grantors to give money to you rather than someone else.

Be clear, concise, and neat! You may very well prepare a top-notch application, but it won't look good if it's sloppy. Applications and proposals should always be typed double-spaced. Make sure you keep a copy after you send the original. I have learned the hard way that there is nothing worse than having to reconstruct your application if problems arise simply because you didn't keep a copy.

Because no one application is guaranteed to win you a grant or an award, you should apply to a number of funding sources. Although none of the sources listed in this book requires an application fee, the effort you will have to put into the endeavor will probably limit you to a maximum of eight applications. (If you are ambitious and want to apply to more than eight sources, go right ahead.) Remember, the more sources you apply to, the greater your chances for success. (For a more detailed explanation of applying for a grant, please refer to my book, *The Complete Guide to Getting a Grant* [Possedion Press, 1993].)

Components of a Successful Proposal

One of the largest categories of grants that are given to individuals is grants for general welfare, that is, "free money" for emergency or long-term personal, medical, or living expenses. Applying for these grants is generally a much simpler process than applying for other kinds of grants. Most, if not all, of the foundations you apply to will require the following in order to consider your request for funding:

1. A brief but concise letter outlining the circumstances that caused your financial difficulty. In the final paragraph of your letter you should specify a dollar amount that you feel confident would ease your financial burden (i.e., "I request a grant in the amount of $2,500 to help me through this difficult period."). Remember to carefully look at the money given in the foundation listing to which you are applying. If you need $20,000 but the foundation only gives grants ranging from $5,000 to $15,000, the most you can request is $15,000.

2. Some foundations may ask you to fill out an application form. Don't panic. These forms are usually self-explanatory. (Again, for a more detailed explanation, please refer to my book, *The Complete Guide to Getting a Grant.*)

3. A copy of your tax return. Don't panic! You won't be penalized for showing excellent earnings or having savings. The issue is how the costs associated with your present medical problems or care needs have altered your financial stability. If you are in financial need you will certainly be given every consideration.

4. A personal interview. This may take place by phone or in person. Foundations are run by people committed to their mission of helping those in need or in trouble. Simply state the facts of your case and needs and all will go well.

Remember, the information in your application should be clear and concise. Your letter should not exceed two pages. Be sure to include any attachments the foundation might require. Follow my instructions and you should qualify for some sort of "free money."

Private Foundation Funding

The listings in this chapter are probably the most accessible funding sources for the average individual seeking a grant. Until now, this information has not been made readily available to the general public. And yet thousands of foundations give away millions of dollars to individuals to help them get through tough financial times.

The information is organized by state. Wherever possible, each listing includes a description of what cases the foundation will fund, any restrictions (i.e., residency in a particular town or city), the total amount of money awarded annually, the range of money given, the average size of the award, information on how to apply, deadline date(s), and name(s) of contact person(s).

Private Foundation Funding

ALABAMA

Cambodian Association of Mobile
P.O. Box 160812
Mobile, AL 36616
(205) 957-2096

Description: Grants for Cambodian immigrants who are residents of Alabama, to help pay for health services.
$ Given: N/A
Application Information: Write for guidelines.
Deadline: N/A
Contact: Sanh Suon, President

The Dixon Foundation
1625 Financial Center
Birmingham, AL 35203
(205) 252-2828

Description: Grants for residents of Alabama, to help pay for prescription medicines and health supplies.
$ Given: $215,152 for 62 grants; average range: $200–$25,000
Application Information: Write letter; formal application required.
Deadline: None
Contact: Carol D. Dixon, Secretary, or Joy Levio

Kate Kinloch Middleton Fund
P.O. Drawer 2527
Mobile, AL 36601

Description: Grants for residents of Mobile County, to help pay medical expenses.
$ Given: $108,286 for 63 grants; average range: $81–$8,094
Application Information: Write letter; an interview is required, in which the applicant must disclose the financial problem and burden.
Deadline: None
Contact: Joan Sapp

La Nelle Robson Foundation
25612 E. J. Robson Boulevard
Sun Lakes, AL 35248

Description: Grants for residents of Alabama, to pay for higher education and medical expenses.
$ Given: $145,400 for 15 grants
Application Information: Write proposal.
Deadline: None
Contact: Steven S. Robson, Vice President

McWane Foundation
P.O. Box 43327
Birmingham, AL
35243
(205) 991-9888

Description: Grants for residents of Alabama, to help pay medical expenses.
$ Given: $373,400 for varying number of grants
Application Information: Write letter; formal application not required.
Deadline: None
Contact: J. R. McMahon, Trustee

The William H. and Kate F. Stockham Foundation, Inc.
c/o Stockham Valves and Fittings, Inc.
4000 North Tenth Avenue
P.O. Box 10326
Birmingham, AL
35202

Description: Grants for present and former employees who reside in Alabama or in a southeastern state, to help pay for education or general living expenses.
$ Given: $18,000 for 21 grants; average range: $225–$3,500
Application Information: Write for guidelines.
Deadline: None
Contact: Richard J. Stockham, Jr.

ARIZONA

Jewish Family and Children's Service
2033 North Seventh Street
Phoenix, AZ 85006
(602) 257-1904

Description: Grants for immigrants and refugees who are residents of Arizona, to help pay general living expenses.
$ Given: N/A
Application Information: Write for guidelines.
Deadline: N/A
Contact: Patricia M. Brouard, Trustee

Lorraine Mulberger Foundation, Inc.
c/o Burch & Cracciolo
702 East Osborn
Phoenix, AZ 85014
(602) 274-7611

Description: Grants for residents of Arizona who can demonstrate financial need.
$ Given: $22,236 for 11 grants; average range: $300–$3,436
Application Information: Formal application required.
Deadline: None
Contact: Andrew Abraham

The Wallace Foundation
3370 North Hayden Road
Suite 123-287
Scottsdale, AZ 85251
(602) 962-4059

Description: Grants for residents of Arizona, to help pay general living expenses.
$ Given: $184,530 for 28 grants
Application Information: Write letter; formal application required.
Deadline: March 15, September 15
Contact: Nancy Shaw, Executive Director

ARKANSAS

Arkansas Department of Human Services
Refugee Resettlement Program
P.O. Box 1437
Little Rock, AR 72203
(501) 682-8263

Description: Grants for immigrants and refugees who are residents of Arkansas, to help pay medical and living expenses.
$ Given: N/A
Application Information: Write for guidelines.
Deadline: N/A
Contact: Walt Patterson, Director

Lyon Foundation, Inc.
65th and Scott
Hamilton Drive
Little Rock, AR 72204

Application Address:
P.O. Box 4408
Little Rock, AR 72214

Description: Grants for residents of Arkansas who can demonstrate financial need.
$ Given: $35,730 in grants awarded to individuals
Application Information: Write letter and proposal; include background information.
Deadline: None
Contact: Ralph Cotham, Secretary-Treasurer

CALIFORNIA

All Culture Friendship Center Refugee and Immigration Services
5250 Santa Monica Boulevard
Los Angeles, CA 90029
(213) 667-0489

Description: Grants for immigrants and refugees who are residents of California, to help pay general living expenses; also provides educational and social services.
$ Given: N/A
Application Information: Write or call for guidelines.
Deadline: None
Contact: N/A

Arrillaga Foundation
2560 Mission College Boulevard
Room 101
Santa Clara, CA 95050
(408) 980-0130

Description: Grants for residents of California, to help pay for education and living expenses.
$ Given: $364,255 for 40 grants
Application Information: Write proposal; formal application required.
Deadline: None
Contact: John Arrillaga, President

Avery–Fuller Children's Center
251 Kearny Street, No. 301
San Francisco, CA 94108
(415) 930-8292

Description: Grants for handicapped and disabled children who are residents of California, to help pay medical and educational expenses.
$ Given: $151,667; average: $1,500
Application Information: Write letter; formal application required.
Deadline: February 14, May 14, August 14, November 14
Contact: Bonnie Van Manen Pinkel, Executive Director

William Babcock Memorial Endowment
305 San Anselmo Avenue
Suite 219
San Anselmo, CA 94960
(415) 453-0901

Description: Grants for residents of Marin County, to help pay exceptional medical, surgical, and hospital expenses.
$ Given: $407,020 for 480 grants
Application Information: Call; formal application required.
Deadline: None
Contact: Alelia Gillin, Executive Director

Brotman Foundation of California
c/o Robert D. Hartford
433 North Camden Drive, No. 600
Beverly Hills, CA 90210
(213) 271-2910

Description: Grants for child welfare and residents of California, to help pay health and medical expenses.
$ Given: $302,200 for 36 grants
Application Information: Write letter; formal application required.
Deadline: None
Contact: Michael B. Sherman, President

California Department of Social Services Office of Refugee Services
744 P Street
Sacramento, CA 95814
(916) 324-1576

Description: Grants for immigrants and refugees who are residents of California, to help pay resettlement expenses; medical assistance is also provided.
$ Given: N/A
Application Information: Write for guidelines.
Deadline: N/A
Contact: Walter Barnes, Chief

Cambodian Association of America
602 Pacific Avenue
Long Beach, CA 90802
(213) 432-5849

Description: Grants for Southeast Asian immigrants and refugees who are residents of California, to help pay for general living expenses and integration within the United States.
$ Given: N/A
Application Information: Write or call for guidelines.
Deadline: None
Contact: Nil Hul, Executive Director

Catholic Social Service Refugee Resettlement Project
5890 Newman Court
Sacramento, CA 95819
(916) 452-1445

Description: Grants for refugees who are residents of Sacramento, to help pay resettlement expenses; various social services are also provided.
$ Given: N/A
Application Information: Write or call for guidelines.
Deadline: None
Contact: Cau Lao, Director

Clinica Monsigneur Oscar A. Romero
2675 West Olympic
Boulevard
Los Angeles, CA
90006
(213) 389-0288

Description: Grants for Central American and Caribbean immigrants and refugees who are residents of California, to help pay living expenses; educational, cultural, and basic social services are also available.
$ Given: N/A
Application Information: Write for guidelines.
Deadline: None
Contact: Ana Zeledon Friendly, Administrator

Coalition for Immigrant and Refugee Rights and Services
2111 Mission Street
San Francisco, CA
94110
(415) 626-2360

Description: Grants for immigrants and refugees who are residents of San Francisco, to help pay medical expenses; legal assistance and other social services are also provided.
$ Given: N/A
Application Information: Write for guidelines.
Deadline: N/A
Contact: Emily Goldfarb, Executive Director

Ebell of Los Angeles Rest Cottage Associations
743 South Lucerne
Boulevard
Los Angeles, CA
90005
(213) 931-1277

Description: Grants for residents of Los Angeles, to help pay medical expenses.
$ Given: $90,000 for 3 grants of $30,000 each
Application Information: Write letter; formal application required.
Deadline: None
Contact: Alberta Burke, Chair

Myrtle V. Fitschen Charitable Trust
380 Eddy Street
San Francisco, CA
94102
(415) 558-4161

Description: Grants for residents of San Francisco and San Francisco County, especially the elderly, to help pay for health and related services, including medical, dental, hospital, psychological, educational, and social assistance.
$ Given: $67,650 for 10 grants; average range: $2,400–$10,000
Application Information: Write letter; formal application required.
Deadline: September 1
Contact: Richard Livingston, Executive Director

German Ladies Benevolent Society
P.O. Box 27101
San Francisco, CA
94127
(415) 391-9947

Description: Grants for women and children of German heritage who reside in San Francisco and can demonstrate financial need.
$ Given: $83,813 for grants to individuals
Application Information: Write for guidelines; formal application required.
Deadline: Second Tuesday of every month
Contact: Inge Byrnes, Secretary-Treasurer

Clorinda Giannini Memorial Benefit Fund
P.O. Box 37121
San Francisco, CA
94137

Application Address:
Bank of America
Bank of America Center
San Francisco, CA
94104
(415) 622-4915

Description: Grants for employees of Bank of America with financial needs due to illness, accident, loss of income, or other emergency.
$ Given: $20,699 for 25 grants to individuals; average range: $14–$3,785
Application Information: Write letter.
Deadline: None
Contact: Susana Morales, Assistant Vice President, Bank of America

**Hattie Givens
Testamentary Trust**
1017 West 18th Street
Merced, CA 95340
(209) 722-7429
Application Address:
1810 M Street
Merced, CA 95340

Description: Grants for residents of
California, to cover costs of health care.
$ Given: $9,150 for 3 grants; average
range: $650–$5,000
Application Information: Formal
application required.
Deadline: None
Contact: Trustees

**The Goodman
Family Foundation**
700 South Flower
Street
Los Angeles, CA
90017-4101

Description: Grants for residents of Los
Angeles, to help pay health-related
expenses.
$ Given: $136,240 for 82 grants
Application Information: Write for
guidelines.
Deadline: None
Contact: Lawrence M. Goodman, Jr.,
President and Secretary-Treasurer

**Good Samaritan
Community Center**
1292 Portrero Avenue
San Francisco, CA
94110
(415) 824-3500

Description: Grants for Central American
and Caribbean refugees who are residents
of San Francisco; a variety of cultural and
advocacy programs are also provided.
$ Given: N/A
Application Information: Write or call for
guidelines.
Deadline: None
Contact: Will Wauters, Executive Director

Hmong Council
4670 East Butler
Avenue
Fresno, CA 93702
(209) 456-1220

Description: Grants for Southeast Asian
immigrants and refugees who are
residents of Fresno, to help pay medical,
legal, and living expenses.
$ Given: N/A
Application Information: Write for
guidelines.
Deadline: None
Contact: Phen Vue, Executive Director

Hoefer Family Foundation
100 Pine Street
Fifth Floor
San Francisco, CA
94111
(415) 342-7111

Description: Grants for residents of California, to help pay for higher education and general living expenses.
$ Given: $54,070 for 66 grants; average range: $20–$10,000
Application Information: Write letter or proposal; formal application not required.
Deadline: None
Contact: Alan Hoefer, President

International Institute of Los Angeles Refugee Relocation and Placement Program
164 West Valley Blvd.
San Gabriel, CA
91776
(818) 307-1084

Description: Grants for immigrants and refugees who are residents of California, to help pay housing, medical, and living expenses; other social services are provided.
$ Given: N/A
Application Information: Write or call for guidelines.
Deadline: N/A
Contact: Thongsy Chen, Director

International Institute of San Francisco
2209 Van Ness Avenue
San Francisco, CA
94109
(415) 673-1720

Description: Grants for immigrants and refugees who are residents of California, to help pay living expenses; other social services are also provided.
$ Given: N/A
Application Information: Write or call for guidelines.
Deadline: None
Contact: Don Eiten, Executive Director

John Percival and Mary C. Jefferson Endowment Fund
114 East De La Guerra
Santa Barbara, CA
93102
(805) 963-8822

Description: Grants for residents of Santa Barbara, to help pay medical, dental, or living expenses.
$ Given: $62,977 for 29 grants; average range: $106–$6,500
Application Information: Write letter; formal application required.
Deadline: N/A
Contact: Patricia M. Brouard, Trustee

**The Trustees of
Ivan V. Koulaieff
Educational Fund**
651 11th Avenue
San Francisco, CA
94118

Description: Grants for Russian
immigrants.
$ Given: $208,500 for 27 grants; average
range: $100–$43,200
Application Information: Write letter and
proposal.
Deadline: None
Contact: W. W. Granitow, Secretary

**Lao Family
Community**
855 West 15th Street
Merced, CA 95340
(209) 384-7384

Description: Emergency assistance for
Southeast Asian immigrants and refugees
who are residents of California, including
housing, medical care, educational
programs, and legal assistance.
$ Given: N/A
Application Information: Write or call for
guidelines.
Deadline: None
Contact: Houa Yang, Executive Director

**New Horizons
Foundation**
700 South Flower
Street
Suite 1122
Los Angeles, CA
90017-4160
(213) 626-4481

Description: Grants for Christian
Scientists with financial needs who live in
Los Angeles and are over 65.
$ Given: $26,347 for 11 grants; average
range: $200–$6,000
Application Information: Call or write for
guidelines; interview required.
Deadline: None
Contact: G. Grant Gifford, President

**Peninsula
Community
Foundation**
1700 South El
Camino Real, No. 300
San Mateo, CA
94402-3049
(415) 358-9817

Additional Address:
P.O. Box 6729
San Mateo, CA 94403
Fax: (415) 358-9817

Description: Grants for residents of San
Mateo County and northern Santa Clara
County who need emergency assistance.
$ Given: $112,584 for 161 grants; average
range: $50–$100
Application Information: Write letter and
proposal.
Deadline: None
Contact: John D. Taylor, Executive Director

Pfaffinger Foundation
Times Mirror Square
Los Angeles, CA
90053
(213) 237-5743

Description: Grants for current and former employees of the Times Mirror Company who can demonstrate financial need.
$ Given: $2.5 million in grants awarded to individuals; average range: $1,000–$10,000
Application Information: Formal application required.
Deadline: Submit proposal between July and September; deadline October 1.
Contact: James C. Kelly, President

Charles E. Saak Trust
c/o Wells Fargo Bank
2222 West Shaw Avenue
Suite 11
Fresno, CA 93711
(209) 442-6230

Description: Grants for disadvantaged residents of the Poplar, California area under 21, to help pay for dental and emergency medical expenses and scholarships for higher education.
$ Given: $40,935 for 170 grants; average range: $67–$960
Application Information: Write letter; formal application required.
Deadline: March 31
Contact: Wells Fargo Bank, N.A.

Virginia Scatena Memorial Fund for San Francisco School Teachers
c/o Bank of America, N.A.
555 California Street
Seventeenth Floor
San Francisco, CA
94104

Description: Grants for retired San Francisco public school teachers who are sick, disabled, or in financial need.
$ Given: $7,800 for 44 grants; average range: $125–$400
Application Information: Formal application required.
Deadline: None
Contact: Advisory Committee

Sequoia Trust Fund
555 California Street
Thirty-sixth Floor
San Francisco, CA
94104
(415) 393-8552

Description: Grants for residents of the San Francisco Bay area, to help pay general living expenses.
$ Given: $31,400 for 4 grants; average range: $2,400–$12,000
Application Information: Write letter; formal application not required.
Deadline: N/A
Contact: Walter M. Baird, Secretary

The Sonoma County Foundation
1260 North Dutton Avenue
Suite 280
Santa Rosa, CA 95401
(707) 579-4073

Description: Grants for residents of Sonoma County, to help pay for education and living expenses.
$ Given: $10,000 for 10 grants
Application Information: Write letter; formal application not required.
Deadline: June 1, September 1
Contact: Virginia Hubbell, Executive Director

Sunnyvale Community Services
810 West McKinley Avenue
Sunnyvale, CA 94086
(408) 738-4321

Description: Grants for immigrants and refugees who are residents of California, to help pay emergency expenses; other social services are also provided.
$ Given: N/A
Application Information: Write for guidelines.
Deadline: None
Contact: Janet Gundrum, Executive Director

Vietnamese Community of Orange County
3701 West McFadden Avenue
Suite M
Santa Ana, CA 92704
(714) 775-2637

Description: Grants for Southeast Asian immigrants and refugees who are residents of Orange County, to help pay living expenses; other social services are also provided.
$ Given: N/A
Application Information: Write for guidelines.
Deadline: N/A
Contact: Tuong Nguyen, Executive Director

Winnett Foundation
c/o Bullocks
Executive Offices
800 South Hope Street
Los Angeles, CA 90017-4684

Description: Grants for residents of California who have financial needs and medical expenses.
$ Given: $47,203 for 22 grants; average range: $2,229–$5,279
Application Information: Formal application required.
Deadline: None
Contact: N/A

COLORADO

Jane Nugent Cochems Trust
c/o Colorado
National Bank of
Denver
P.O. Box 5168
Denver, CO 80217
Application Address:
Colorado State
Medical Society
6061 Willow Drive
Suite 250
Englewood, CO 80111

Description: Grants for doctors in Colorado who can demonstrate financial need.
$ Given: $11,147 for 2 grants; average range: $5,000–$6,147
Application Information: Write for guidelines.
Deadline: N/A
Contact: President, Colorado State Medical Society

Colorado Masons Benevolent Fund Association
1770 Sherman Street
Denver, CO 80203
(303) 837-0367
Application Address:
1130 Panorama Drive
Colorado Springs, CO
80904
(719) 471-9589

Description: Grants for Colorado Masonic lodge members and their families who are in financial distress.
$ Given: $592,994 for grants awarded
Application Information: Write or call local members' lodge.
Deadline: N/A
Contact: Local lodge in Colorado

Colorado Refugee and Immigrant Services Program
190 East Ninth
Avenue
Room 390
Denver, CO 80203
(303) 863-8211

Description: Grants for refugees who are residents of Colorado, to help pay living expenses; medical assistance and other services are also provided.
$ Given: N/A
Application Information: Write or call for guidelines.
Deadline: None
Contact: Laurel Bagan, State Refugee Coordinator

Fort Collins Area Community Foundation
215 West Oak Street
Suite 102
Fort Collins, CO 80521
(303) 224-3462

Description: Grants for residents of Larimer and Weld counties who can demonstrate financial need.
$ Given: $265,679 for 75 grants; average range: $1,000–$5,000
Application Information: Write letter and proposal; six copies of proposal required.
Deadline: February 1, May 1, August 1, November 1
Contact: Diane M. Hogerty, Executive Director

A. V. Hunter Trust, Inc.
633 Seventeenth Street
Suite 1780
Denver, CO 80202
(303) 292-2048

Description: Grants for residents of Colorado who have financial needs and bills not covered by Medicare or Medicaid.
$ Given: $58,757 in grants awarded
Application Information: Formal application and interview required; social case worker must apply for applicant.
Deadline: None
Contact: Sharon Holt, Secretary

Henry W. Stoddard Trust
P.O. Box 1365
Arvada, CO 80001
Application Address:
7910 Ralston Road, Suite 1
Arvada, CO 80001-1365

Description: Grants for parents or caretakers of handicapped children, to support and care for the children or to help improve the parents' quality of life.
$ Given: $67,202 for grants of $1,000 each
Application Information: Write for guidelines.
Deadline: N/A
Contact: Wallis L. Campbell, Trustee

CONNECTICUT

Charitable Society in Hartford
c/o Robinson & Cole
One Commercial Plaza
Hartford, CT 06103
(203) 725-8200
Application Address:
Connecticut National Bank
777 Main Street
Hartford, CT 06115

Description: Grants for Hartford residents, to help pay for food, shelter, clothing, heat, etc.
$ Given: $40,693 for 158 grants; average range: $15–$350
Application Information: Churches, schools, and social service organizations must apply for individuals.
Deadline: None
Contact: Raymond S. Andrews, Jr., President

Marion Isabelle Coe Fund
c/o Colonial Bank & Trust Co.
P.O. Box 2210
Waterbury, CT 06722

Description: Grants for residents of Goshen, Litchfield, Morris, and Warren, for medical, car, insurance, and other expenses.
$ Given: $16,834 for grants awarded; average: $100/month
Application Information: Write for guidelines.
Deadline: None
Contact: Mrs. Speers

Connecticut Department of Human Resources State Refugee Coordinator
1049 Asylum Avenue
Hartford, CT 06115
(203) 566-4329

Description: Grants for refugees who are residents of Connecticut, to help pay resettlement expenses; medical assistance and support services are also provided.
$ Given: N/A
Application Information: Write or call for guidelines.
Deadline: N/A
Contact: Elliot Ginsberg, Coordinator

James Crocker Testamentary Trust
P.O. Box 1045
Canaan, CT 06018

Description: Grants for residents of Winchester who can demonstrate financial need.
$ Given: $2,368 for 9 grants; average range: $70–$450
Application Information: Write letter describing needs and providing background information.
Deadline: None
Contact: Kevin F. Nelligan

The de Kay Foundation
c/o Manufacturers Hanover Trust Company
600 Fifth Avenue
New York, NY 10020
(212) 957-1668

Description: Grants for the elderly in New York, New Jersey, and Connecticut with financial and medical needs.
$ Given: $202,540 for 83 grants; average range: $1,000–$5,000
Application Information: Write letter; formal application required.
Deadline: None
Contact: Lloyd Saltus, II, Vice President

Larrabee Fund Association
c/o Connecticut National Bank
777 Main Street
Hartford, CT 06115
(203) 728-2664

Description: Grants for female residents of Hartford who can demonstrate financial need.
$ Given: $203,285 in grants awarded
Application Information: Write for guidelines.
Deadline: None
Contact: N/A

W. J. Munson Foundation
c/o Colonial Bank & Trust Co.
P.O. Box 2210
Watertown, CT 06722
(203) 574-4575

Application Address:
71 Scott Road
Watertown, CT 06795

Description: Grants for residents of Watertown, to cover the cost of medical care.
$ Given: $68,863 for 172 grants; average range: $4–$1,563
Application Information: Write letter and proposal.
Deadline: None
Contact: William H. Eppehimer, Chair

**The Westport–
Weston Foundation**
c/o The Westport
Bank & Trust Co.
P.O. Box 5177
Westport, CT 06881
(203) 222-6988

Description: Grants for residents of
Westport and Weston, to help pay medical
and other expenses.
$ Given: $10,061 for 29 grants; average
range: $100–$400
Application Information: Write for
guidelines.
Deadline: N/A
Contact: Susanne M. Allen, Trust Officer

Widow's Society
c/o Connecticut
National Bank
777 Main Street
Hartford, CT 06115
Application Address:
20 Bayberry Lane
Avon, CT 06001
(203) 687-9660

Description: Grants for female residents
of Connecticut who can demonstrate
financial need.
$ Given: $122,824 for 117 grants; average
range: $75–$4,800
Application Information: Write letter or
apply through a public or private social
service agency.
Deadline: N/A
Contact: Dorothy Johnson, President

DELAWARE

**Borkee–Hagley
Foundation, Inc.**
P.O. Box 230
Wilmington, DE
19899
(302) 652-8616

Description: Grants for the elderly and
for individuals who are residents of
Delaware, to help pay for education and
housing expenses.
$ Given: $93,200 for 25 grants; average
range: $100–$15,000
Application Information: Write letter;
formal application required.
Deadline: November 1
Contact: Henry H. Silliman, Jr., President

Delaware Department of Health and Social Services Division of Economic Services
P.O. Box 906
CP Building
New Castle, DE 19720
(302) 421-6153

Description: Grants for refugees who are residents of Delaware, to help pay resettlement expenses; medical assistance and other services are also provided.
$ Given: N/A
Application Information: Write for guidelines.
Deadline: N/A
Contact: Thomas P. Eichler, Refugee Coordinator

Milton and Hattie Kutz Foundation
101 Garden of Eden Road
Wilmington, DE 19803
(302) 478-6200

Description: Grants for residents of Delaware, to help pay for child welfare, higher education, and living expenses.
$ Given: $44,500
Application Information: Write for guidelines.
Deadline: March 15 (for scholarships)
Contact: Robert N. Kerbel, Executive Secretary

DISTRICT OF COLUMBIA

Buchly Charity Fund of Federal Lodge No. 1
1212 Wisconsin Avenue, NW
Washington, DC 20007
Application Address:
7015 Leesville Road
Springfield, VA 22151

Description: Grants for widows and orphans of deceased former members of Federal Masonic Lodge No. 1.
$ Given: $27,000 for 12 grants; average range: $500–$6,700
Application Information: Write letter to Trustees showing financial needs upon death of husband.
Deadline: None
Contact: Willard E. Griffing

FLORIDA

Alfred I. duPont Foundation
P.O. Box 1380
Jacksonville, FL 32201
(904) 396-6600

Description: Grants for older residents of the southeastern United States with financial, health, or educational needs.
$ Given: $375,424 for 162 grants; average range: $2,400–$3,000
Application Information: Formal application required; write initial letter.
Deadline: None
Contact: Rosemary C. Wills, Assistant Secretary

Robert and Eugenie Friedman Foundation
76 Isla Bahia Drive
Fort Lauderdale, FL 33316

Description: Grants for residents of Florida who can demonstrate financial need.
$ Given: $4,300 for 5 grants to individuals
Application Information: Write for guidelines.
Deadline: None
Contact: N/A

Gore Family Memorial Foundation
501 East Las Olas
Fort Lauderdale, FL 33302

Description: Grants for residents of Broward County with financial, medical, housing, or other needs.
$ Given: $526,187 for 504 grants
Application Information: Write for guidelines; formal application required.
Deadline: None
Contact: N/A

The Ryan Foundation
1511 West Broadway
Oviedo, FL 32765
(407) 365-8390

Description: Emergency assistance and grants for needy residents of Florida.
$ Given: $62,203 for 77 grants to individuals; average range: $13–$7,479
Application Information: Application required; call or write first.
Deadline: None
Contact: Jean Beede

Roy M. Speer Foundation
1803 U.S. Highway 19
Holiday, FL
34691-5536

Description: Grants for residents of Florida who have financial and medical needs.
$ Given: $4,000 for 1 grant to an individual
Application Information: Write for guidelines; send initial letter of intent and purpose.
Deadline: None
Contact: Richard W. Baker, Trustee

Vero Beach Foundation for the Elderly
c/o First National Bank
255 South County Road
Palm Beach, FL 33480
(407) 770-0044

Application Address:
2800 Indian River Boulevard
Apartment U-2
Vero Beach, FL 32960

Description: Grants for residents of Vero Beach who are at least 65 and can demonstrate financial need.
$ Given: $86,774 for grants to individuals
Application Information: Application required through Indian River County Council on Aging.
Deadline: None
Contact: Richard Mead, Chair of the Board of Governors

GEORGIA

Pine Mountain Benevolent Foundation, Inc.
P.O. Box 2301
Columbus, GA 31902

Description: Grants for residents of Georgia who can demonstrate financial need.
$ Given: $2,200 for 2 grants; average range: $550–$1,650
Application Information: Write for guidelines.
Deadline: None
Contact: Cason J. Callaway, Jr.

Savannah Widows' Society
P.O. Box 30156
Savannah, GA 31410
(912) 232-6312

Description: Grants for female residents of Chatham County who are single and 55 or older.
$ Given: $1,400 for 4 grants, average range: $200–$500; $99,931 for 104 grants to individuals, average range: $10–$8,400.
Application Information: Application form required.
Deadline: None
Contact: Becky Traxler, President

HAWAII

The Hawaii Community Foundation
222 Merchant Street
Honolulu, HI 96813
(808) 537-6333

Description: Assistance for residents of Hawaii who can demonstrate financial need. (Winifred D. Robertson Fund—one-time assistance to adult residents of Oahu; Alice M. G. Soper Fund—one-time assistance to adults 50 or older with illness or disability)
$ Given: $1.6 million for 115 grants; average range: $100–$1,000
Application Information: Call first; formal application required.
Deadline: None
Contact: Suzanne Toguchi, Program Officer

The May Templeton Hopper Foundation
1412 Whitney Street
Honolulu, HI 96822
(808) 944-2807

Description: Grants for elderly individuals in Hawaii who have been residents for at least five years, to help with payments for general costs, boarding home or day care costs, rent, transportation, drug bills, etc.
$ Given: $473,988 for 287 grants; average range: $360–$9,600
Application Information: Call or write for guidelines and program information; formal application required.
Deadline: Submit the fifth day of the month if application is to be considered
Contact: Diana H. Lord, President

ILLINOIS

The Clara Abbott Foundation
One Abbott Park Road
Abbott Park, IL 60064
(708) 937-1091

Description: Grants for current and former employees of Abbott Laboratories or members of their families who are in financial hardship and disadvantaged.
$ Given: $3 million for 2,470 grants; average range: $100–$50,000
Application Information: Application form required.
Deadline: March 16
Contact: David C. Jeffries, Executive Director

Crane Fund for Widows and Children
222 West Adams Street
Room 849
Chicago, IL 60606

Description: Grants for residents of Illinois who can demonstrate financial need.
$ Given: $15,576 for 3 grants; average range: $1,500–$11,760
Application Information: Write for guidelines.
Deadline: N/A
Contact: Trustees

The Cultural Society, Inc.
P.O. Box 1374
Bridgeview, IL 60455
(312) 434-6665

Description: Grants for Muslims who can demonstrate financial need.
$ Given: $125,050 for grants to individuals
Application Information: Write for guidelines.
Deadline: None
Contact: Mohammad Nasr, Treasurer

Reade Industrial Fund
c/o Harris Trust & Savings Bank
P.O. Box 755
111 West Monroe Street
Chicago, IL 60690
(312) 461-2609

Description: Grants or emergency loans for individuals who have been or are employed in industries in Illinois and who by reasons beyond their control, such as job loss, illness, injury, etc., cannot care for themselves or their families.
$ Given: $161,939 for 51 grants; average range: $373–$5,000
Application Information: Write for guidelines; formal application required.
Deadline: None
Contact: Ronald F. Tuite, Jr.

The Shifting Foundation
8000 Sears Tower
Chicago, IL 60606

Description: Aid for social services, the disadvantaged, the homeless, women, and minorities among others.
$ Given: $48,000 for 6 grants to individuals; average range: $4,000--$10,000
Application Information: Application required; submit one copy of proposal.
Deadline: None
Contact: Pat Culver

Swiss Benevolent Society of Chicago
P.O. Box 2137
Chicago, IL 60690

Description: Grants for the elderly and individuals of Swiss descent in the Chicago area who can demonstrate financial need.
$ Given: $53,450 for 53 grants to individuals
Application Information: Formal application required; write for guidelines.
Deadline: N/A
Contact: Alan Weber, President

Tallman Boys Fund Trust
c/o First of America Trust Co.
189 East Court Street
Kankakee, IL 60901
(815) 937-3687

Description: Grants for boys of Protestant faith in Kankakee County who are under 21 and are either homeless or in need of training or general assistance.
$ Given: $4,020 for grants to individuals
Application Information: Formal application required; interview suggested; individuals must have nonprofit organizations apply on their behalf.
Deadline: None
Contact: Glen F. Rewerts, II, Trust Officer

INDIANA

Mary Jane Luick Trust
c/o American National Bank & Trust Co.
110 East Main Street
Muncie, IN 47305
(317) 747-7510

Description: Grants for elderly women of Delaware County with financial needs and medical expenses.
$ Given: $4,760 for 5 grants; average range: $300–$2,100
Application Information: Write for guidelines.
Deadline: None
Contact: July Polson

Allen and Rose Mills Trust
c/o Irwin Union Bank & Trust Co.
500 Washington Street
Columbus, IN 47201

Description: Grants for residents of Bartholomew County with financial or medical needs, including children, the deaf, the blind, or the elderly.
$ Given: $2,763 for 5 grants to individuals; average range: $100–$1,639
Application Information: Write for guidelines; social agencies can request applications on behalf of their clients.
Deadline: None
Contact: Stephen Kirts

Frank L. and Laura L. Smock Foundation
c/o Lincoln National Bank & Trust Co.
P.O. Box 960
Fort Wayne, IN
46801-0960
(219) 461-6477

Description: Grants for Indiana residents of Presbyterian faith who have medical or financial needs, including nursing care needs, and whose assets do not exceed $3,000.
$ Given: $148,804 for 33 grants; average range: $108–$24,783
Application Information: Write for guidelines.
Deadline: N/A
Contact: Alice Kopfer, Assistant Vice President

IOWA

Human Aid Society of Iowa
400 First Interstate Bank Building
Des Moines, IA 50309
Application Address:
550 39th Street
Des Moines, IA 50312
(515) 274-1450

Description: Grants for individuals with financial needs or who need food, clothing, and other material goods.
$ Given: $7,294 for 200 grants to individuals
Application Information: Write for guidelines; include information on applicant's need and situation.
Deadline: None
Contact: Joseph S. Brick, President

KANSAS

Brown Memorial Foundation
300 North Cedar
P.O. Box 187
Abilene, KS 67410
(913) 263-2351

Description: Operating foundation helping needy families and individuals.
$ Given: $10,000 for 20 grants to individuals ($500 each)
Application Information: Write for guidelines.
Deadline: N/A
Contact: N/A

**Charlotte Hill
Charitable Trust**
P.O. Box 754
Winfield, KS 67156
(316) 221-4600

Description: Grants for single women over 60 in Winfield or Arkansas City with financial needs and limited assets.
$ Given: $75,697 for 62 grants; average range: $40–$5,915
Application Information: Formal application required.
Deadline: None
Contact: Kay Roberts, Trustee

**Victor Murdock
Foundation**
c/o Bank IV Wichita, N.A.
P.O. Box 1122
Wichita, KS 67201
(316) 261-4361

Description: Grants for general charitable giving and health services, primarily in Wichita.
$ Given: $500 for a grant to one individual
Application Information: Write letter.
Deadline: None
Contact: Ted W. Schupp

**Topeka Community
Foundation**
5100 SW 10th
P.O. Box 4525
Topeka, KS 66604
(913) 272-4804

Description: Grants for family services, child welfare, and general charitable giving in Topeka and Shawnee County.
$ Given: $1,415 for 2 grants to individuals, average range: $415–$1,000; $159,585 for 38 grants, average range: $500–$5,000
Application Information: Application required; five copies of proposal required.
Deadline: February 15
Contact: Karen Welch, Executive Director

LOUISIANA

**Joe W. and Dorothy
Dorsett Brown
Foundation**
1801 Pere Marquette
Building
New Orleans, LA
70112
(504) 522-4233

Description: Grants for hospitals, community funds, and residents of Louisiana who can demonstrate financial need.
$ Given: $42,953 for grants to individuals
Application Information: Submit proposal.
Deadline: None
Contact: D. P. Spencer, President

MAINE

Camden Home for Senior Citizens
66 Washington Street
Camden, ME 04843
(207) 236-2087
Application Address:
Belfast Road
Camden, ME 04843
(207) 236-2014

Description: Grants for residents of Camden, Rockport, Hope, and Lincolnville, for heating, food, medical bills, drugs, rent, real estate, taxes, etc.
$ Given: $42,350 for 201 grants; average range: $50–$300
Application Information: Write for guidelines.
Deadline: None
Contact: Charles Lowe, President

Lena P. Frederick Trust Fund
c/o Key Trust Co.
of Maine
P.O. Box 1054
Augusta, ME
04332-1054
(207) 623-5527

Description: Grants for individuals of Belfast with financial, medical, or other needs.
$ Given: $7,361 in total grants awarded
Application Information: Write or call for guidelines; formal application required.
Deadline: None
Contact: Cristina L. Cook, Assistant Trust Officer

Anita Card Montgomery Foundation
20 Mechanic Street
Camden, ME
04843-1707

Description: Grants for residents of Camden, Rockport, Lincolnville, and Hope with financial or medical needs.
$ Given: $14,820 for 16 grants; average range: $40–$4,058
Application Information: Write for guidelines; formal application required.
Deadline: None
Contact: Robert C. Perkins

Portland Female Charitable Society
c/o Janet Matty
20 Noyes Street
Portland, ME 04103

Application Address:
142 Pleasant Street, No. 761
Portland, ME 04101

Description: Grants for residents of Portland for medical or dental care, health or food needs, or care for the ill, elderly, or children.
$ Given: $9,553 for 33 grants; average range: $20–$850
Application Information: Write for guidelines; social workers, nurses, or counselors may apply on behalf of individuals; interview required.
Deadline: None
Contact: Janet Matty

Portland Seamen's Friend Society
14 Lewis Street
Westbrook, ME 04092

Description: Grants to seamen with financial needs who live in Maine.
$ Given: Grants totaling $36,000 for 50 individuals in the form of a monthly stipend
Application Information: Write for guidelines; interview required.
Deadline: None
Contact: Lewis G. Emery

MARYLAND

The Baltimore Community Foundation
The Latrobe Building
Two East Read Street
Ninth Floor
Baltimore, MD 21202
(301) 332-4171

Description: Grants for widows and children of B&O Railroad employees.
$ Given: $153,900 for 50 grants to individuals
Application Information: Write for guidelines.
Deadline: N/A
Contact: Timothy D. Armbruster, Executive Director

The Eaton Fund, Inc.
c/o Mercantile-Safe
Deposit & Trust Co.
Two Hopkins Plaza
Baltimore, MD 21201
(301) 237-5521

Description: Grants for female residents of Baltimore who are 60 or older and can demonstrate financial need.
$ Given: $17,400 for 9 grants; average range: $900–$2,400
Application Information: Write for guidelines.
Deadline: None
Contact: Patricia Bentz, Assistant Vice President

NFL Alumni Foundation Fund
c/o Sigmund M. Hyman
P.O. Box 248
Stevenson, MD 21153-0248
(301) 486-5454

Description: Grants for former National Football League alumni with physical or mental disabilities, to help provide additional income or pay medical expenses. Also monies provided for death benefits.
$ Given: $144,426 for 24 grants; average range: $250 monthly minimum up to $12,000 annually
Application Information: Write letter providing background and income information.
Deadline: None
Contact: Sigmund M. Hyman

Steeplechase Fund
400 Fair Hill Drive
Elkton, MD 21921

Description: Grants for injured jockeys or their widows who can demonstrate financial need.
$ Given: $38,995 for grants to individuals
Application Information: Write letter describing disability and medical needs.
Deadline: N/A
Contact: Charles Colgan

Anna Emory Warfield Memorial Fund, Inc.
103 West Monument Street
Baltimore, MD 21201
(301) 547-0612

Description: Grants for elderly female residents of Baltimore.
$ Given: $150,050 for 42 grants; average range: $900–$3,925
Application Information: Write for guidelines; formal application and interview required.
Deadline: None
Contact: Thelma K. O'Neal, Secretary

MASSACHUSETTS

Boston Fatherless and Widows Society
c/o Goodwin, Proctor & Hoar
Exchange Place
Room 2200
Boston, MA
02109-2881
(617) 570-1130

Description: Grants for widowed or orphaned residents of Boston, for medical costs, food, clothing, or housing.
$ Given: $91,231 for 52 grants; average range: $325–$1,950
Application Information: Write for guidelines; formal application required; agencies or nonprofit organizations may apply on behalf of individuals.
Deadline: N/A
Contact: George W. Butterworth, III

Edwin S. Farmer Trust
133 Portland Street
Boston, MA
02114-9614

Description: Grants for women or married couples from Arlington who can demonstrate financial need.
$ Given: $11,280 for 7 grants; average range: $100–$2,840
Application Information: Write letter including information on marital status, finances, and gender.
Deadline: None
Contact: Harold E. Magnuson

German Ladies Aid Society of Boston, Inc.
2222 Centre Street
West Roxbury, MA
02132

Description: Grants for residents of West Roxbury who can demonstrate financial need.
$ Given: $2,498 in grants awarded
Application Information: Write for guidelines.
Deadline: None
Contact: N/A

Howard Benevolent Society
14 Beacon Street
Room 507
Boston, MA 02108
(617) 742-2952

Description: Grants for residents of Boston who are ill or have financial needs.
$ Given: $123,914 for 225 grants; average range: $550
Application Information: Call or write for guidelines.
Deadline: None
Contact: Marcia T. Burley

Howland Fund for Aged Women
c/o Child and Family Service
1061 Pleasant Street
New Bedford, MA
02740
(508) 993-4232

Description: Grants for elderly women in New Bedford who can demonstrate financial need.
$ Given: $7,950 for 10 grants; average range: $1,000–$1,200
Application Information: Formal application and interview required.
Deadline: None
Contact: Sally Ainsworth, President of the Trustees

Lend A Hand Society
34½ Beacon Street
Boston, MA 02108

Description: Grants for residents of Boston who can demonstrate financial need.
$ Given: $130,029 for unspecified number of grants.
Application Information: Write for guidelines.
Deadline: N/A
Contact: N/A

Lotta Theatrical Fund
294 Washington Street
Room 636
Boston, MA 02108
(617) 451-0698

Description: Grants for members of the theatrical profession and for theatrical schools and cultural institutions on behalf of applicants with financial needs.
$ Given: $19,500 for 12 grants; average range: $500–$3,000
Application Information: Write for guidelines; interview required.
Deadline: N/A
Contact: Claire M. McCarthy, Trust Manager

Newburyport Howard Benevolent Society
P.O. Box 9
Newburyport, MA 01950

Description: Grants for low-income families residing in Newburyport.
$ Given: $14,573 for grants awarded to individuals
Application Information: Write for guidelines.
Deadline: N/A
Contact: N/A

The Perpetual Benevolent Fund
c/o BayBank Middlesex
300 Washington Street
Newton, MA 02158
(617) 894-6500

Description: Grants for individuals with financial needs, especially residents of Newton and Waltham, who have no other resources for income, for rent payments, emergency assistance, clothing, day care or food costs, etc.
$ Given: $88,000 for 280 grants; average range: $400–$600
Application Information: Call or write for guidelines and formal application; nonprofit institutions (such as hospitals or social agencies) must apply on applicants' behalf.
Deadline: None
Contact: Marjorie M. Kelley, Administrator

Katherine C. Pierce Trust
c/o State Street Bank & Trust Co.
P.O. Box 351
Boston, MA 02101
(617) 654-3357

Description: Grants for women with financial needs "so that their lives may be made more comfortable."
$ Given: $33,550 for grants awarded; average range: $250–$5,000
Application Information: Write letter that includes description of applicant, needs, and financial status.
Deadline: None
Contact: Robert W. Seymour, Trust Officer

The Pilgrim Foundation
478 Torrey Street
Brockton, MA
02401-4654
(617) 586-6100

Description: Grants for families with financial needs residing in Brockton.
$ Given: $54,831 in grants awarded to individuals
Application Information: Formal application required.
Deadline: N/A
Contact: Executive Director

Charlotte M. Robbins Trust
c/o State Street Bank & Trust Co.
P.O. Box 351
Boston, MA 02101
(617) 654-3360

Application Address:
c/o State Street Bank
225 Franklin Street
Boston, MA 02110

Description: Grants for elderly couples or elderly women who are residents of Groton, Ayer, Harvard, Shirley, or Litteton.
$ Given: Unspecified number of grants totaling $6,006 are awarded
Application Information: Write letter including information on applicant's income, expenses, and financial needs.
Deadline: N/A
Contact: Cheryl D. Curtin, Vice President

Salem Female Charitable Society
175 Federal Street
Boston, MA 02110

Application Address:
30 Chestnut Street
Salem, MA 01970

Description: Grants for female residents of Salem.
$ Given: $19,813 for 18 grants; average range: $200–$1,700
Application Information: Write for guidelines.
Deadline: None
Contact: Jane A. Phillips, Treasurer

Shaw Fund for Mariners' Children
c/o Russell Brier & Co.
50 Congress Street
Room 800
Boston, MA 02109
Application Address:
64 Concord Avenue
Norwood, MA 02062

Description: Grants for mariners, their wives, widows, or children residing in Massachusetts who have financial emergencies.
$ Given: $114,138 for grants awarded to individuals
Application Information: Write for guidelines and program specifics.
Deadline: None
Contact: Clare M. Tolias

The Swasey Fund for Relief of Public School Teachers of Newburyport, Inc.
31 Milk Street
Boston, MA 02109
(508) 462-2784

Application Address:
83 Summit Place
Newburyport, MA 01950

Description: Grants for teachers in Newburyport with financial needs who have taught in the public school system for 10 years; also includes grants for educational and cultural opportunities for retired teachers.
$ Given: $66,600 for 21 grants to individuals; average range: $100–$10,000
Application Information: Formal application required.
Deadline: None
Contact: Jean MacDonald, Treasurer

MINNESOTA

Duluth-Superior Area Community Foundation
316 Missabe Building
227 West First Street
Duluth, MN
55802-1913
(218) 726-0232

Description: Grants for residents of Douglas and Bayfield counties, Wisconsin, and Koochiching, Itasca, St. Louis, Lake, Cook, Carlton, and Aitkin counties, Minnesota, for emergency relief, family services, employment, hunger, shelter, youth, and disadvantaged.
$ Given: $16,878 for 15 grants to individuals; average range: $362–$3,000
Application Information: Application form required; call or write for guidelines.
Deadline: February 1, May 1, October 1
Contact: Holly C. Sampson, President, or Esther Gieschen, Program Associate

Fanny S. Gilfillan Memorial, Inc.
c/o Lawrence Harder
Route 4
Redwood Falls, MN 56283

Application Address:
Redwood County
Welfare Department
P.O. Box 27
Redwood Falls, MN 56283
(507) 637-5741

Description: Grants for residents of Redwood County with financial needs, medical bills, or dental bills.
$ Given: $52,404 for 50 grants; average range: $69–$5,000
Application Information: Formal application and interview required; write for guidelines.
Deadline: None
Contact: Lawrence Harder

Hanna R. Kristianson Trust
P.O. Box 1011
Albert Lea, MN 56007

Application Address:
Clarks Grove, MN 56016
(507) 256-4415

Description: Grants for residents of Freeborn County over 50 who can demonstrate financial need.
$ Given: $9,815 for 18 grants; average range: $21–$1,660
Application Information: Write for guidelines.
Deadline: None
Contact: Richard S. Haug, Trustee

The Saint Paul Foundation
1120 Norwest Center
St. Paul, MN 55101
(612) 224-5463

Description: Grants for employees of the 3M Company and residents of St. Paul and Minneapolis.
$ Given: $130,121 for 105 grants to individuals
Application Information: Write for guidelines and annual report.
Deadline: N/A
Contact: Paul Verret, President

MISSOURI

Ina Calkins Board
c/o Boatmen's First
National Bank of
Kansas City
14 West 10th Street
Kansas City, MO
64105
(816) 221-2800

Description: Grants for elderly residents of Kansas City who can demonstrate financial need.
$ Given: $33,137 for 52 grants to individuals
Application Information: Write for guidelines.
Deadline: January 1, April 1, July 1, October 31
Contact: David P. Ross, Secretary

Sarah Cora Gladish Endowment Fund
Forest Hills Estate,
Apartment C-11
Lexington, MO 64067
(816) 259-3643

Description: Grants for elderly or accomplished artists and musicians in Lafayette, Johnson, or Jackson counties who can demonstrate financial need.
$ Given: $1,950 for 6 grants; average range: $200–$350
Application Information: Formal application required.
Deadline: July 1
Contact: Margaret Lomax, Trustee

Herschend Family Foundation
c/o Jack R. Herschend
Silver Dollar City, Inc.
Marvel Cave Park, MO
65616
(417) 338-2611

Description: Grants for Christian residents of Missouri, to meet physical, financial, and family needs.
$ Given: $250,435 for 34 grants to individuals
Application Information: Write or call detailing financial needs.
Deadline: None
Contact: Jack R. Herschend, Director

NEW YORK

Emma J. Adams Memorial Fund, Inc.
518 Fifth Avenue
Seventh Floor
New York, NY 10036
(212) 944-0077

Description: Grants for emergency aid for individuals in New York City who have financial needs, or for institutions providing the elderly or homeless with aid for medical expenses, food, or clothing.
$ Given: $48,405 for 21 grants; average range: $100–$1,000
Application Information: Write letter detailing need; formal application and interview required.
Deadline: N/A
Contact: Edward R. Finch, Jr., President

The American Society of Journalists and Authors Charitable Trust The Llewellyn Miller Fund
1501 Broadway
Suite 1907
New York, NY 10036
(212) 997-0947

Description: Grants for established professional writers who are at least 60 or disabled.
$ Given: $8,750 for 4 grants; average range: $1,250–$2,500
Application Information: Write letter detailing financial needs; formal application and references required.
Deadline: None
Contact: Murray Teigh Bloom, Chair, Board of Trustees

The Bagby Foundation for the Musical Arts, Inc.
501 Fifth Avenue
New York, NY 10017
(212) 986-6094

Description: Grants for older individuals with financial needs or emergency situations and "who have, in the past, aided the world of music."
$ Given: $15,700 for 8 grants and 1 emergency grant of $1,800; average range: $600–$2,850
Application Information: Write for guidelines, describing financial needs.
Deadline: None
Contact: Eleanor C. Mark, Executive Director

Benedict Family Charitable Foundation, Inc.
82 Wall Street
New York, NY 10005

Description: Grants for residents of New York State who can demonstrate financial need.
$ Given: $3,579 in grants awarded to individuals
Application Information: Write for guidelines.
Deadline: N/A
Contact: Alfred Benedict, President

The James Gordon Bennett Memorial Corporation
c/o New York Daily News
220 East 42nd Street
New York, NY 10017

Description: Grants for journalists who have been employees for 10 or more years on a New York City daily newspaper and who can demonstrate financial need.
Application Information: Write for guidelines; formal application required.
Deadline: None
Contact: Denise Houseman

Beulah Cliff Rest
c/o Paul S. Longo
199 Main Street
White Plains, NY 10601
(914) 919-2193

Description: Vacation grants for females with financial needs and female invalids.
$ Given: $13,500 for 51 grants; average range: $200–$400
Application Information: Write letter describing need and requesting guidelines.
Deadline: None
Contact: Hastings Ross, Secretary

Broadcasters Foundation, Inc.
320 West 57th Street
New York, NY 10019
(212) 586-2000

Description: Grants for members of the broadcast industry and their families who can demonstrate financial need.
$ Given: $14,400 for 7 grants; average range: $1,800–$2,400
Application Information: Formal application required.
Deadline: None
Contact: N/A

Brockway Foundation for the Needy of the Village and Township of Homer, New York
c/o Key Bank
25 South Main Street
Homer, NY
13077-1314

Description: Grants for residents of Homer who can demonstrate financial need.
$ Given: $15,090 for 23 grants; average range: $180–$690
Application Information: Write for guidelines.
Deadline: None
Contact: M. Lee Swartwout, Treasurer

Carnegie Fund for Authors
1 Old Country Road, Suite 113
Carle Place, NY 11514
(516) 877-2141

Description: Emergency grants for authors who have had at least one non-"vanity" book of reasonable length commercially published and publicly accepted, and who have financial needs as a result of illness or injury to themselves or their dependents or have suffered some misfortune.
$ Given: N/A
Application Information: Write for guidelines.
Deadline: None
Contact: William L. Rothenberg, Trustee

Change Inc.
P.O. Box 705
Cooper Station
New York, NY 10276
(212) 473-3742

Description: Emergency grants for professional artists in various fields with financial needs for rent, medical expenses, utility bills, and other costs.
$ Given: Average range: $1,000–$70,000
Application Information: Write letter describing financial situation and needs, including bills, a resume, and two letters of recommendation.
Deadline: None
Contact: Denise LeBeau, Secretary

The Clark Foundation
30 Wall Street
New York, NY 10005
(212) 269-1833

Description: Grants for residents of upstate New York and New York City, for medical assistance.
$ Given: $108,327 for 19 grants; average range: $565–$15,600
Application Information: Write for guidelines.
Deadline: None
Contact: Edward W. Stack, Secretary

The Correspondents Fund
c/o Rosenman & Cohen
575 Madison Avenue
New York, NY
10022-2511

Application Address:
c/o The New York Times
229 West 43rd Street
New York, NY 10036

Description: Emergency grants for men and women who have worked in press, foreign press, television, radio, news, or film organizations in the United States.
$ Given: $8,189 for 3 grants; average range: $2,500–$3,000
Application Information: Write letter describing financial needs.
Deadline: None
Contact: James L. Greenfield, President

Josiah H. Danforth Memorial Fund
8 Fremont Street
Gloversville, NY
12078

Description: Grants for residents of Fulton County, for medical assistance.
$ Given: $18,615 for 95 grants; average range: $65–$500
Application Information: Write for guidelines; formal application required.
Deadline: None
Contact: N/A

The de Kay Foundation
c/o Manufacturers Hanover Trust Company
600 Fifth Avenue
New York, NY 10020
(212) 957-1668

Description: Grants for older individuals in New Jersey, New York, and Connecticut who can demonstrate financial need.
$ Given: $202,540 for 83 grants; average range: $1,000–$5,000
Application Information: Write for guidelines; formal application required.
Deadline: None
Contact: Lloyd Saltus, II, Vice President

District Lodge No. 3, Sons of Norway Charitable Trust
c/o Frank C. Monnick
53 Ganevoort Boulevard
Staten Island, NY 10314

Description: Grants for individuals of Norwegian origin who can demonstrate financial need.
$ Given: $13,650 for 12 grants; average range: $300–$2,500
Application Information: Write for guidelines.
Deadline: None
Contact: Frank C. Monnick

Adolph and Esther Gottlieb Foundation, Inc.
380 West Broadway
New York, NY 10012
(212) 226-0581

Description: Grants for painters and sculptors of 10 years' experience with financial needs or unexpected emergencies.
$ Given: Unspecified number of grants ranging up to $10,000
Application Information: Write for guidelines.
Deadline: None
Contact: Ellen Bryson, Grants Manager

The Havens Relief Fund Society
105 East 22nd Street
Suite 805
New York, NY 10010
(212) 475-1990

Description: Grants for residents of greater New York City who can demonstrate financial need.
$ Given: $406,429 in grants awarded to individuals
Application Information: Appointees of the foundation distribute funds to individuals of their own choosing.
Deadline: N/A
Contact: Marilyn Lamarr, Executive Director

Robert F. Hildenbrand Foundation, Inc.
111 West Sunrise Highway
Freeport, NY 11520
(516) 379-3575

Description: Grants for residents of Freeport, for assistance in paying rent bills, transportation, medicine, and food costs.
$ Given: $24,450 for 228 grants; average range: $2–$200
Application Information: Write for guidelines.
Deadline: None
Contact: N/A

Mary J. Hutchins Foundation, Inc.
110 William Street
New York, NY 10038
(212) 602-8529

Description: Grants for residents of New York City who can demonstrate financial need.
$ Given: $43,795 for 14 grants; average range: $250–$4,980
Application Information: Write for guidelines.
Deadlines: N/A
Contact: John F. Hirsch, III, Senior Vice President

Ittleson–Beaumont Fund
(Formerly Ittleson Beneficial Fund)
c/o The C.I.T. Group Holdings, Inc.
135 West 50th Street
New York, NY 10020
(212) 408-6000
Application Address:
650 CIT Drive
Livingston, NJ 07039

Description: Grants for current or former employees of C.I.T. Financial Corporation who have financial needs or hardships.
$ Given: $58,946 for 20 grants; average range: $285–$18,000
Application Information: Write letter describing financial needs.
Deadline: None
Contact: Clare Carmichael

Jockey Club Foundation
40 East 52nd Street
New York, NY 10022
(212) 371-5970

Description: Grants for individuals concerned with thoroughbred racing and breeding who can demonstrate financial need.
$ Given: $394,278 in grants to individuals
Application Information: Write for guidelines and describe needs in application request.
Deadline: None
Contact: Nancy Colletti, Secretary to the Trustees

Mary W. MacKinnon Fund
c/o Wilber National Bank
Trust Department
245 Main Street
Oneonta, NY 13820
(607) 432-1700

Description: Grants for older residents of Sidney who can demonstrate financial need. Grants are in the form of medical, nursing home, and rehabilitative care.
$ Given: $48,453 for grants to individuals
Application Information: Submit application through a doctor or hospital.
Deadline: None
Contact: N/A

Max Mainzer Memorial Foundation, Inc.
570 Seventh Avenue
Third Floor
New York, NY 10018
(212) 921-3865

Description: Grants for members of the American Jewish K.C. Fraternity or their widows who can demonstrate financial need.
$ Given: $34,445 for 15 grants; average range: $250–$4,200
Application Information: Write for guidelines and application information.
Deadline: None
Contact: N/A

Israel Matz Foundation
14 East Fourth Street
Room 403
New York, NY 10012
(212) 673-8142

Description: Grants for Jewish writers, scholars, public workers, or their children who can demonstrate financial need.
$ Given: $40,790 for 28 grants; average range: $600–$3,900
Application Information: Write letter describing need; interview optional.
Deadline: None
Contact: Milton Arfa, Chair

Musicians Foundation, Inc.
200 West 55th Street
New York, NY 10019
(212) 247-5332

Description: Emergency grants for professional musicians and their families.
$ Given: $91,095 for 39 grants; average range: $500–$2,000
Application Information: Write for guidelines.
Deadline: None
Contact: Brent Williams, Secretary-Treasurer

New York Society for the Relief of Widows and Orphans of Medical Men
c/o Davies & Davies
50 East 42nd Street
New York, NY 10017

Description: Grants for widows and orphans of physicians who can demonstrate financial need.
$ Given: $96,727 for grants to individuals
Application Information: Write for guidelines.
Deadline: November 15
Contact: Walter Wichern, Secretary

Nurses House, Inc.
350 Hudson Street
New York, NY 10014
(212) 989-9393

Description: Short-term grants for current or former registered nurses in the United States who are sick or have financial needs. Grants do not cover medical care or educational expenses.
$ Given: $45,648 for grants to individuals
Application Information: Write for guidelines and information brochure; formal application required; interview optional.
Deadline: None
Contact: Patricia B. Barry, Executive Director

Pen American Center
568 Broadway
New York, NY 10012
(212) 334-1660
Fax: (212) 334-2181

Description: Emergency grants for writers with short-term financial needs or afflicted with AIDS.
$ Given: Average range: $50–$1,000
Application Information: Write for guidelines.
Deadline: None
Contact: Joan Dalin

The Pollock–Krasner Foundation, Inc.
725 Park Avenue
New York, NY 10021
(212) 517-5400
Application Address:
P.O. Box 4957
New York, NY 10185

Description: Grants for promising visual artists working in painting, sculpture, graphic, or mixed media in the United States and overseas, to help advance their careers or assist them in cases of illness or emergency.
$ Given: $1.4 million for 143 grants; average range: $2,000–$20,000
Application Information: Formal application required; provide a cover letter detailing financial need, including biographical information and 10 slides of recent work.
Deadline: None
Contact: Charles C. Bergman, Executive Vice President

Saranac Lake Voluntary Health Association, Inc.
70 Main Street
Saranac Lake, NY 12983-1706

Description: Grants for students and elderly residents of the Saranac Lake region who need dental services.
$ Given: $42,122 for 3 grants; average range: $4,498–$31,613
Application Information: Write letter detailing applicant's health.
Deadline: N/A
Contact: N/A

J. F. Schoellkopf Silver Wedding Fund
340 Elk Street
P.O. Box 7027
Buffalo, NY 14240
(716) 842-5535

Description: Grants for residents of Buffalo who are members or spouses or children of members of the Mutual Aid Society who can demonstrate financial need.
$ Given: $16,700 for 11 grants; average range: $1,550–$1,750
Application Information: Write for guidelines.
Deadline: None
Contact: Arthur Maciejewski

J. D. Shatford Memorial Trust
c/o Chemical Bank
30 Rockefeller Plaza
New York, NY 10112
(212) 621-2148

Description: Grants for residents of Hubbards, Nova Scotia, and Canada who can demonstrate financial need.
$ Given: $154,202 for 70 grants; average: $331–$24,172
Application Information: Formal application required.
Deadline: None
Contact: Barbara Strohmeier

Society for the Relief of Women and Children
c/o Turk, Marsh, Kelly, and Hoare
575 Lexington Avenue
Twentieth Floor
New York, NY
10022-6102

Description: Grants for residents of New York City who, "after leading productive lives, are unable to take care of themselves because of circumstances beyond their control."
$ Given: $25,159 for 12 grants; average range: $1,550
Application Information: Write for guidelines; society does not accept individual applications.
Deadline: N/A
Contact: N/A

St. George's Society of New York
71 West 23rd Street
New York, NY 10010
(212) 924-1434

Description: Grants for British citizens residing in New York and the tri-state area who can demonstrate financial need. Aid is in the form of grants for hospital bills, clothing, employment assistance, and Christmas gifts.
$ Given: $101,003 for 85 grants to individuals
Application Information: Write for guidelines; interviews and site visits from the society's social worker required.
Deadline: None
Contact: David Loovis

St. Luke's Nurses Benefit Fund
c/o Alumnae Association
of St. Luke's
School of Nursing
411 West 114th
Street, Apartment 6D
New York, NY 10025
Application Address:
47 Phillips Lane
Darien, CT 06820

Description: Grants for graduates of the St. Luke's School of Nursing who can demonstrate financial need.
$ Given: $2,000 for 1 grant
Application Information: Formal application required.
Deadline: None
Contact: Martha Kirk, Trustee

Suffolk County Happy Landing Fund, Inc.
c/o Peter Opromolla
P.O. Box 383
St. James, NY 11780
(516) 366-4843

Description: Grants for police officers and their families residing in Suffolk County who can demonstrate financial need.
$ Given: $3,000 for 3 grants; average: $1,000
Application Information: Formal application and interview required; superior officer must apply on behalf of applicant.
Deadline: None
Contact: Peter Opromolla

Otto Sussman Trust
P.O. Box 1374
Trainsmeadow Station
Flushing, NY
11370-9998

Description: Grants for residents of New Jersey, New York, Oklahoma, or Pennsylvania with financial needs, medical bills, or emergencies.
$ Given: $80,323 for 36 grants; average range: $329–$4,397
Application Information: Write for guidelines and describe needs of applicant; formal application required.
Deadline: N/A
Contact: Edward S. Miller, Trustee

**United Merchants
and Manufacturers
Employees Welfare
Foundation**
1407 Broadway
Sixth Floor
New York, NY
10018-5103
(212) 930-3999

Description: Grants for current or former
employees of United Merchants and
Manufacturers, Inc. or their family
members who can demonstrate financial
need.
$ Given: $9,825 for 14 grants; average
range: $375–$825
Application Information: Write for
guidelines.
Deadline: None
Contact: Lawrence Marx, Jr., Trustee

**VonderLinden
Charitable Trust**
c/o Leonard
Rachmilowitz
26 Mill Street
Rhinebeck, NY 12572
(914) 876-302!

Description: Grants for residents of
upstate New York who have financial
needs, medical bills, and other expenses.
$ Given: $23,262 for 100 grants; average
range: $4–$538
Application Information: Write for
guidelines.
Deadline: None
Contact: N/A

**Emma Reed Webster
Aid Association, Inc.**
c/o Frances E. Peglow
R.D. No. 2
Albion, NY 14411

Description: Grants for residents of New
York State who can demonstrate financial
need.
$ Given: $54,672 for 130 grants; average:
$600
Application Information: Write for
guidelines.
Deadline: None
Contact: Frances E. Peglow

OHIO

Christian BusinessCares Foundation
P.O. Box 360691
Cleveland, OH 44136
(216) 621-0096

Description: Grants for residents of northeast Ohio who have life-threatening situations or emergencies.
$ Given: $69,212 for unspecified number of grants; average range: $100–$250
Application Information: Write for guidelines; formal application and interview required.
Deadline: None
Contact: N/A

Columbus Female Benevolent Society
228 South Drexel Avenue
Columbus, OH 43209

Description: Grants for pensioned widows residing in Franklin, or for infant or handicapped infant needs.
$ Given: $32,806 for grants to individuals
Application Information: Local residents should recommend applicant.
Deadline: N/A
Contact: N/A

Virginia Gay Fund
c/o Marjorie L. Ater
751 Grandon Avenue
Columbus, OH 43209

Description: Grants for retired female schoolteachers who have taught in Ohio for at least 20 years and who can demonstrate financial need.
$ Given: $41,347 for 20 grants; average range: $1,000–$2,000
Application Information: Formal application required.
Deadline: N/A
Contact: Marjorie L. Ater, Secretary-Treasurer

Grace A. Gossens Testamentary Trust
c/o Ralph S. Boggs
240 Huron Street
Suite 800
Toledo, OH 43604
Application Address:
416 West Wayne
Maumee, OH 43537
(419) 893-8603

Description: Grants for older women residing in rest homes in Maumee who can demonstrate financial need.
$ Given: $5,000 for 2 grants of $2,500 each
Application Information: Write letter detailing financial needs.
Deadline: None
Contact: Alice J. Servais, Trustee

Meshech Frost Testamentary Trust
c/o BancOhio
National Bank Trust
Division
155 East Broad Street
Fifth Floor
Columbus, OH 43251
Application Address:
109 South Washington
Street
Tiffin, OH 44883

Description: Grants for residents of Tiffin who can demonstrate financial need.
$ Given: $1,822 for 5 grants; average range: $169–$690
Application Information: Write letter describing needs.
Deadline: None
Contact: Kenneth H. Myers, Secretary-Treasurer

National Machinery Foundation, Inc.
Greenfield Street
P.O. Box 747
Tiffin, OH 44883
(419) 447-5211

Description: Grants for former employees or other individuals residing in Seneca County who can demonstrate financial need.
$ Given: $69,950 for 205 grants; average range: $150–$4,000
Application Information: Write for guidelines.
Deadline: N/A
Contact: D. B. Bero, Administrator

Virginia Wright Mothers Guild, Inc.
426 Clinton Street
Columbus, OH
43202-2741

Description: Grants for older females residing in Columbus who can demonstrate financial need.
$ Given: $9,925 for grants to individuals
Application Information: Write for guidelines.
Deadline: N/A
Contact: M. Courtwright

OKLAHOMA

Dexter G. Johnson Educational and Benevolent Trust
900 First City Place
Oklahoma City, OK 73102
(405) 232-0003

Description: Grants for physically handicapped residents of Oklahoma in the form of medical equipment, hospitalization, and provision of other life necessities.
$ Given: $185,684 for 59 grants; average range: $350–$30,083
Application Information: Formal application required; include background information on age, finances, etc.
Deadline: None
Contact: Phil C. Daugherty, Trustee

Otto Sussman Trust
P.O. Box 1374
Trainsmeadow Station
Flushing, NY 11370-9998

Description: Grants for residents of Oklahoma, New York, New Jersey, and Pennsylvania with financial needs or in emergency situations, for help in paying medical bills or caretaking expenses.
$ Given: $35,865 for 14 grants; average range: $329–$4,397
Application Information: Formal application required; write for guidelines.
Deadline: None
Contact: Edward S. Miller, Trustee

The R. H. Wilkin Charitable Trust
P.O. Box 76561
Oklahoma City, OK 73147
(405) 235-7700

Description: Grants for crippled children of Oklahoma County for medical care or treatment.
$ Given: $14,855 for 28 grants
Application Information: Write for guidelines, including information on financial needs of applicant and doctor's recommendation for necessary treatment.
Deadline: None
Contact: Peggy Pittman, Co-Trustee

OREGON

Blanche Fischer Foundation
1001 SW Fifth Avenue
Suite 1550
Portland, OR 97204
(503) 323-9111

Description: Grants for physically disabled residents of Oregon who can demonstrate financial need.
$ Given: $70,187 for 148 grants; average range: $100–$1,000
Application Information: Formal application required; write for guidelines.
Deadline: None
Contact: William K. Shepherd, President

Sophia Byers McComas Foundation
c/o U.S. National Bank of Oregon
P.O. Box 3168
Portland, OR 97208
(503) 275-6564

Description: Grants for elderly residents of Oregon not receiving welfare assistance who can demonstrate financial need.
$ Given: $72,223 for grants to individuals
Application Information: Write for guidelines; community service groups may apply on behalf of applicants.
Deadline: N/A
Contact: U.S. National Bank of Oregon, Trustee

Scottish Rite Oregon Consistory Almoner Fund, Inc.
709 SW 15th Avenue
Portland, OR 97205
(503) 228-9405

Description: Grants for Masons and their families residing in Oregon who can demonstrate financial need.
$ Given: $19,437 for grants to individuals
Application Information: Write for guidelines.
Deadline: None
Contact: Walter Peters

PENNSYLVANIA

Margaret Baker Memorial Fund Trust
Mellon Bank (East), N.A.
P.O. Box 7236
Philadelphia, PA 19101-7236
Application Address: P.O. Box 663, Phoenixville, PA 19460

Description: Grants for widows or single women over 30, families, or children under 14 with financial needs residing in Phoenixville.
$ Given: $8,158 for 17 grants; average range: $108–$750
Application Information: Write for guidelines, describing applicant's financial status or other support materials.
Deadline: July, November
Contact: L. Darlington Lessig, Treasurer

Female Association of Philadelphia
c/o Provident
National Bank
1632 Chestnut Street
Philadelphia, PA
19103

Description: Grants for female residents of Philadelphia with financial needs or distress.
$ Given: $90,310 for grants to individuals
Application Information: Write for guidelines.
Deadline: None
Contact: Elizabeth Harbison, Treasurer

James T. Hambay Foundation
Dauphin Deposit
Bank & Trust Co.
P.O. Box 2961
Harrisburg, PA
17105-2961
(717) 255-2174

Description: Grants for blind or crippled children under 18 residing in the Harrisburg area, for medical expenses, day care costs, or camp expenses.
$ Given: $113,986 for 34 grants to individuals
Application Information: Write letter describing financial status and medical expenses.
Deadline: None
Contact: Joseph A. Marcri, Trust Officer

Edward W. Helfrick Senior Citizens Trust
400 Market Street
Sunbury, PA 17801

Description: Grants for older individuals residing in the 107th Legislative District of Pennsylvania who are sick or have extensive expenses due to fire damage.
$ Given: $2,000 for 4 grants of $500 each
Application Information: Write for guidelines.
Deadline: None
Contact: N/A

William B. Lake Foundation
Fidelity Bank, N.A.
Broad and Walnut
Streets
Philadelphia, PA
19109
(215) 985-7320

Description: Grants for residents of the Philadelphia area who have diseases of the respiratory tract.
$ Given: $30,000 for grants to individuals
Application Information: Write a letter describing in detail the applicant's needs.
Deadline: May 1, November 1
Contact: Maureen B. Evans, Secretary-Treasurer

Merchants Fund (formerly Merchants-Oliver Fund)
c/o Hemmenway and Reinhardt, Inc.
Four Park Avenue
Swarthmore, PA
19081-1723
Application Address:
P.O. Box 5920
Philadelphia, PA
19137
(215) 288-7131

Description: Grants for merchants and their families residing in Philadelphia who can demonstrate financial need.
$ Given: $207,057 for 48 grants to individuals
Application Information: Formal application required.
Deadline: None
Contact: Henry W. Kaufman, Secretary-Treasurer

Robert D. and Margaret W. Quin Foundation
Hazleton National Bank
101 West Broad Street
Hazleton, PA 18201

Description: Grants for students under 19 who have financial needs and live within 10 miles of Hazleton City Hall. Grants also for day care needs, music lessons, medication, and other expenses.
$ Given: $15,367 for 66 grants; average range: $35–$900
Application Information: Write for guidelines.
Deadline: None
Contact: N/A

St. Benedict's Charitable Society
1663 Bristol Pike
Bensalem, PA 19020
(215) 244-9900

Description: Grants for elderly or infirm individuals for help in paying medical or living expenses.
$ Given: $3,940 for 4 grants; average range: $100–$1,800
Application Information: Write for guidelines; new applications might not be considered—call for deadlines.
Deadline: N/A
Contact: Margaret Kuehmstedt, Treasurer

Private Foundation Funding

Otto Sussman Trust
P.O. Box 1374
Trainsmeadow Station
Flushing, NY
11370-9998

Description: Grants for residents of Pennsylvania, New York, New Jersey, and Oklahoma with financial needs, emergency situations, or medical expenses.
$ Given: $80,323 for 36 grants to individuals
Application Information: Write for guidelines; formal application required.
Deadline: N/A
Contact: Edward S. Miller, Trustee

The John Edgar Thomson Foundation
The Rittenhouse
Claridge
201 South 18th Street
Suite 318
Philadelphia, PA
19103
(215) 545-6083

Description: Grants for daughters of deceased railroad employees. Children can receive grants until they are 22.
$ Given: $241,396 for 141 grants; average: $2,416
Application Information: Formal application and interview required; write or call for guidelines.
Deadline: None
Contact: Gilda Verstein, Director

Western Association of Ladies for the Relief and Employment of the Poor
c/o Fidelity Bank, N.A.
Broad and Walnut Streets
Philadelphia, PA
19109
(215) 431-4679

Application Address:
404 Baumont Circle
West Chester, PA
19380
(215) 692-7962

Description: Grants for residents of Philadelphia County, to help with financial needs.
$ Given: $67,385 for grants; average range: $43–$1,500
Application Information: Social workers must submit application on behalf of applicants.
Deadline: None
Contact: Marlane Bohon, Executive Secretary

RHODE ISLAND

Bristol Home for Aged Women
c/o National Bank–
Rhode Island
Hospital Trust
One Hospital Trust
Plaza
Providence, RI 02903
(401) 278-8752

Description: Grants for older female residents of Bristol who can demonstrate financial need.
$ Given: $9,300 for 8 grants; average range: $100–$4,900
Application Information: Write letter for guidelines, including financial information.
Deadline: June 1
Contact: Shawn P. Buckless, Assistant Vice President

**Robert B. Cranston–
Theophilus T.
Pitman Fund**
18 Market Square
Newport, RI 02840
(401) 847-4260

Description: Grants for older residents of Newport County who have financial needs, medical, and other living expenses.
$ Given: $6,856 for grants to individuals
Application Information: Formal application and personal references required.
Deadline: None
Contact: D. C. Hambly, Jr., Administrator

Inez Sprague Trust
c/o Rhode Island
Hospital Trust
One Hospital Trust
Plaza
Providence, RI 02903
(401) 278-8700

Description: Grants for residents of Rhode Island, to help pay medical expenses.
$ Given: $6,001 for 23 grants; average range: $79–$1,500
Application Information: Write for guidelines.
Deadline: None
Contact: Rhode Island Hospital Trust, Trustee

Townsend Aid for the Aged
c/o Fleet National
Bank
100 Westminster
Street
Providence, RI 02903

Description: Grants for older residents of Newport who can demonstrate financial need.
$ Given: $74,700 for grants to individuals
Application Information: An advisory committee initiates the application process; write for details.
Deadline: N/A
Contact: Samuel C. Wheeler, President

SOUTH CAROLINA

Graham Memorial Fund
P.O. Box 533
Bennettsville, SC 29512
(803) 479-6804
Application Address:
308 West Main Street
Bennettsville, SC 29512

Description: Grants for residents of Bennettsville.
$ Given: $11,250 for 37 grants; average range: $200–$500
Application Information: Formal application required.
Deadline: June 1
Contact: Chair

Society for the Relief of Families of Deceased and Disabled Indigent Members of the Medical Profession of the State of South Carolina
19 Guerard Road
Charleston, SC 29407

Description: Grants for families of deceased or disabled doctors in South Carolina. Families do not have to be residents of South Carolina.
$ Given: $8,000 for 5 grants; average range: $1,100–$2,350
Application Information: Committee selects applicants.
Deadline: N/A
Contact: The Benevolent Committee

TENNESSEE

The Ruby McCown Foundation
1625 Rushing Wind Lane
Knoxville, TN 37922
(615) 966-9897

Description: Grants for residents of Knoxville.
$ Given: $6,250 for 3 grants; average: $500
Application Information: Write for guidelines.
Deadline: None
Contact: Glen McCown, President

The Quarter Century Fund
c/o International
Paper Company
6400 Poplar Avenue
Memphis, TN
38197-4031

Application Address:
c/o International
Paper Company
1290 Avenue of the
Americas
Ninth Floor
New York, NY 10104

Description: Grants for children or widows of deceased members of the Quarter Century Society, Inc.
$ Given: $5,605 for 6 grants; average range: $200–$1,500
Application Information: Write letter; formal application required; members of social agencies may apply on behalf of applicants.
Deadline: None
Contact: John J. Dillon, Secretary

State Industries Foundation
P.O. Box 307
Old Ferry Road
Ashland City, TN
37015
(615) 244-7040

Description: Grants for residents of Tennessee, including employees of State Industries, who can demonstrate financial need.
$ Given: $20,595 for 310 grants; average: $150
Application Information: Write for guidelines.
Deadline: None
Contact: Joseph P. Lanier, Manager

TEXAS

Dallas Cotton Exchange Trust
c/o MTrust
Corporation, N.A.
P.O. Box 2320
Dallas, TX 75221-2320

Application Address:
Dallas Cotton
Exchange
c/o Joe Ferguson
Dixon Trust Co.
3141 Hood Street
Suite 600
Dallas, TX 75219

Description: Grants for individuals and their families who were or are working in the cotton merchandising business in Dallas and who can demonstrate financial need.
$ Given: $18,250 for 6 grants; average range: $1,750–$3,300
Application Information: Formal application required.
Deadline: None
Contact: Joe Ferguson

H. C. Davis Fund
P.O. Box 2239
San Antonio, TX
78298

Description: Grants for Masons who are residents of the 39th Masonic District of Texas and are ill.
$ Given: $19,215 for grants; average range: $200–$3,075
Application Information: Write for guidelines.
Deadline: None
Contact: N/A

F. V. Hall, Jr. and Marylou Hall Children's Crisis Foundation
c/o NCNB Texas
National Bank
P.O. Box 830241
Dallas, TX 75283-0241

Description: Grants for children under 12 whose parents are undergoing financial emergencies or situations and who reside in Tom Green County.
$ Given: $80,407 for grants to individuals
Application Information: Formal application and interview required.
Deadline: None
Contact: Alice J. Gayle, Trust Officer, NCNB Bank

Hugh A. Hawthorne Foundation
5634 Briar Drive
Houston, TX 77056
(713) 840-8453

Description: Grants for residents of Ireland who can demonstrate financial need.
$ Given: $17,340 for 20 grants; average range: $68–$8,310
Application Information: Write letter for guidelines.
Deadline: None
Contact: Claudia Hawthorne, Manager

Walter Hightower Foundation
c/o Texas Commerce
Bank–El Paso
P.O. Drawer 140
El Paso, TX 79980
(915) 546-6515

Description: Grants for handicapped children under 21 in west Texas or southern New Mexico, for health-care equipment and other items.
$ Given: $109,064 for 657 grants; average range: $50–$1,000
Application Information: Formal application required.
Deadline: July 1
Contact: Terry Crenshaw, Charitable Services Officer

**The Kings
Foundation**
P.O. Box 27333
Austin, TX 78755

Description: Grants for residents of Texas who can demonstrate financial need.
$ Given: $1,200 for 9 grants; average range: $50–$250
Application Information: Write for guidelines.
Deadline: N/A
Contact: N/A

**The Mary L. Peyton
Foundation**
Bassett Tower
Suite 908
303 Texas Avenue
El Paso, TX 79901
(915) 533-9698

Description: Grants for residents of El Paso, especially children of employees of the Peyton Packing Company or those unable to work due to disabilities.
$ Given: $173,551 for 790 grants; average range: $8–$1,600
Application Information: Write letter describing financial situation.
Deadline: None
Contact: James Day, Executive Director

**Lulu Bryan Rambaud
Charitable Trust**
c/o NCNB Texas
P.O. Box 2518
Houston, TX
77252-2518

Description: Grants for older female residents of Houston and Harris County, for medical assistance.
$ Given: $3,870 for 5 grants; average range: $270–$1,200
Application Information: Write for guidelines.
Deadline: None
Contact: N/A

**Sunnyside
Foundation, Inc.**
8609 Northwest Plaza
Drive
Suite 201
Dallas, TX 75225
(214) 692-5686

Description: Grants for children in difficult financial situations residing in Texas, to aid in their "physical, moral, and spiritual needs," including camperships.
$ Given: $40,235 for 33 grants; average range: $39–$4,350
Application Information: Formal application required.
Deadline: None
Contact: Mary Rothenflue, Executive Director

VERMONT

Copley Fund
P.O. Box 696
Morrisville, VT 05661

Description: Grants for older residents of Lamoille County, for housing expenses.
$ Given: $80,781 for 133 grants
Application Information: Write for guidelines.
Deadline: December 31
Contact: Richard Sargent, Trustee

VIRGINIA

Harrison and Conrad Memorial Trust
c/o Sovran Bank
P.O. Box 26903
Richmond, VA 22204
Application Address:
Loudoun Memorial Hospital
Office of the Administrator
224 Cornwall Street, NW
Leesburg, VA 22075
(703) 777-3300

Description: Grants for children residing in Leesburg or Loudoun counties who have polio, muscular dystrophy, or other diseases and whose families are financially unable to afford medical treatment.
$ Given: $86,884 in grants to individuals
Application Information: Write for guidelines; interview required.
Deadline: April 1
Contact: Administrator of Loudoun Memorial Hospital

William A. Roberts Trust F/B/O Orphan Children of Chase City
c/o Central Fidelity Bank
Trust Department
828 Main Street
Lynchburg, VA 24504

Description: Grants for orphan children of Chase City who can demonstrate financial need.
$ Given: $23,310 for 13 grants; average range: $750–$3,600
Application Information: Write letter describing financial needs of applicant.
Deadline: None
Contact: Central Fidelity Bank, Trust Department

WASHINGTON

Carrie Welch Trust
P.O. Box 244
Walla Walla, WA 99362

Description: Grants for residents of Washington State, particularly the elderly in Walla Walla County, who can demonstrate financial need.
$ Given: $12,591 for 12 grants; average range: $90–$1,415
Application Information: Write for guidelines; current applications might not be immediately accepted.
Deadline: N/A
Contact: N/A

George T. Welch Testamentary Trust
c/o Baker–Boyer
National Bank
P.O. Box 1796
Walla Walla, WA 99362
(509) 525-2000

Description: Grants for residents of Walla Walla County, for medical and other financial aid.
$ Given: $21,983 for 29 grants; average range: $53–$1,500
Application Information: Formal application required.
Deadline: February 20, May 20, August 20, November 20
Contact: Bettie Loiacono, Trust Officer

WEST VIRGINIA

Jamey Harless Foundation, Inc.
Drawer D
Gilbert, WV 25621
(304) 664-3227

Description: Grants and loans for residents of Gilbert with financial emergencies.
$ Given: $4,722 for grants to individuals
Application Information: Write for guidelines; formal application required.
Deadline: None
Contact: Sharon Murphy, Secretary

Private Foundation Funding

WISCONSIN

Oshkosh Foundation
c/o First Wisconsin
National Bank of
Oshkosh
P.O. Box 2448
Oshkosh, WI 54903
(414) 424-4283

Description: Grants for residents of Oshkosh who have financial or medical needs.
$ Given: $84,903 for 22 grants; average range: $137–$30,560
Application Information: Write for guidelines.
Deadline: None
Contact: Sandra A. Noe, Trust Officer

Edward Rutledge Charity
P.O. Box 758
404 North Bridge
Street
Chippewa Falls, WI
54729
(715) 723-6618

Description: Grants and loans for residents of Chippewa County who can demonstrate financial need.
$ Given: $70,284 for 269 grants; average range: $5–$600
Application Information: Formal application and interview required.
Deadline: July 1
Contact: John Frampton, President

Theodore and Catherine Schulte Foundation
c/o Bank One
Wisconsin Trust, N.A.
P.O. Box 1308
Milwaukee, WI 53201

Application Address:
P.O. Box 221
Racine, WI 53408

Description: Grants for retired Catholic priests of Racine, for housing expenses.
$ Given: $23,000 for 10 grants; average range: $600–$2,800
Application Information: Write for guidelines.
Deadline: None
Contact: Trust Administrator

Margaret Wiegand Trust
c/o Bank One
Wisconsin Trust Co.,
N.A.
P.O. Box 1308
Milwaukee, WI 53201

Description: Grants for blind individuals in Waukesha County, for their care or needs.
$ Given: $6,837 for 5 grants; average range: $135–$4,031
Application Information: Write for guidelines.
Deadline: None
Contact: Judith Holland, Trust Officer

Flow-Through Funding

Flow-through funding is different from the other kinds of grant funding this book describes. **Flow-through funding is indirect funding:** the foundations listed in this chapter do not provide money directly to individuals, but instead give money to nonprofit organizations, which, in turn, pass funds along to people in need. These nonprofit organizations serve as sponsors for individuals who require financial assistance.

Individuals cannot apply directly to these foundations for funding. The foundations listed in this chapter accept applications only from nonprofit organizations. In order to receive funds from any of these foundations, you must work through a sponsoring nonprofit organization.

Why should you bother with a sponsor? The number of foundations included in this chapter should give you an idea of the vast amount of grant money made available as flow-through funding.

Many times, monies awarded to an organization are applied to the needs of more than one person; one grant award usually benefits a group of individuals. In asking your nonprofit sponsor to contact these foundations on your behalf, you are, in a sense, promoting the interests of other individuals served by the sponsor. However, don't let this discourage you from making use of the information in this chapter.

How do you go about finding a nonprofit sponsor? Check any local directory of nonprofit organizations (your local library will usually have such directories, perhaps in the community services section). Contact local citywide consortium-styled associations operating in your area of interest, such as the United Way or federations. Speak to their directors or public information officers and elicit their suggestions for possible sponsors. Also check national organization reference books, such as the *Encyclopedia of Associations*, for other potential candidates.

How to Apply. Although you cannot apply directly to any of the foundations listed in this chapter, your background work here can be extremely helpful to your sponsor organization. Use the information provided in this chapter to identify foundations that seem to address your specific situation. Following your nonprofit sponsor's directions, write to the appropriate foundations to request information, including application guidelines. Share any information you have received from potential funding sources. For more information on flow-through funding, refer to my book, *The Complete Guide to Getting a Grant.*

ALABAMA

Child Health Foundation
P.O. Box 530964
Birmingham, AL 35253
(205) 251-9966

Description: Grants for residents and organizations of Birmingham, to help fight illness and disease; preference is given to the needs of children.
$ Given: $50,249 for 4 grants
Application Information: Write letter; formal application required.
Deadline: August 31
Contact: Sergio Stagno

The Comer Foundation
P.O. Box 302
Sylacauga, AL 35150
(205) 249-2962

Description: Grants for charitable organizations and residents of Alabama, to help pay for higher education and medical expenses.
$ Given: $469,800 for 52 grants
Application Information: Write for guidelines.
Deadline: None
Contact: R. Larry Edmunds, Secretary-Treasurer

The Daniel Foundation of Alabama
200 Office Park Drive
Suite 100
Birmingham, AL 35223
(205) 879-0902

Description: Grants for charitable organizations and residents of the southeastern United States, to help pay for higher education and medical expenses; preference is given to Alabama.
$ Given: $1.3 million for 26 grants
Application Information: Write for guidelines.
Deadline: None
Contact: S. Garry Smith, Secretary-Treasurer

D. W. McMillan Foundation
329 Bellevill Avenue
Brewton, AL 36426
(205) 867-4881

Description: Grants for organizations and residents of Escambia County, to help pay for medical and general living expenses.
$ Given: $215,152 for 62 grants
Application Information: Write for guidelines.
Deadline: December 1
Contact: Ed Leigh McMillan, II, Managing Trustee

ARIZONA

Arizona Community Foundation
4350 East Camelback Road
Suite 216C
Phoenix, AZ 85018
(602) 952-9954

Description: Grants for organizations in Arizona, to support community-based health and youth agencies and handicapped and social services.
$ Given: $2.4 million for 350 grants; average range: $1,000–$10,000
Application Information: Formal application required; write for guidelines. See the important information in the chapter introduction about the need for institutional affiliation.
Deadline: February 1, June 1, October 1
Contact: Stephen D. Mittenthal, President

The Marshall Fund of Arizona
4000 North Scottsdale Road
Suite 203
Scottsdale, AZ 85251
(602) 941-5249

Description: Grants for organizations in Arizona, for human and social problems, social services, the homeless, and child welfare.
$ Given: $143,732 for 16 grants; average range: $2,500–$20,000
Application Information: Application form not required; write for guidelines. See the important information in the chapter introduction about the need for institutional affiliation.
Deadline: March 1, August 1, November 1
Contact: Maxine Marshall, President

Margaret T. Morris Foundation
P.O. Box 592
Prescott, AZ 86302
(602) 445-4010

Description: Grants for organizations in Arizona, for social programs, youth and child welfare, homeless, handicapped, disadvantaged, and mental health services.
$ Given: $1.2 million for 69 grants: average range: $1,000–$25,000
Application Information: Application form not required; write proposal or letter. See the important information in the chapter introduction about the need for institutional affiliation.
Deadline: Submit proposal May–November
Contact: Eugene P. Polk, Trustee

Steele Foundation, Inc.
702 East Osborn Road
Phoenix, AZ 85014-5215

Description: Grants for organizations and residents of Phoenix, for education, religious welfare, and medical expenses.
$ Given: $838,700 for 28 grants
Application Information: Write for guidelines.
Deadline: None
Contact: Joseph F. Anselno, Secretary

ARKANSAS

The John O. Anthony Charitable Trust
P.O. Box A
Murfreesboro, AR 71958
(501) 285-3471

Description: Grants for church organizations and residents of Arkansas, for the welfare of children; priority is given to residents of Murfreesboro.
$ Given: $71,000 for 4 grants
Application Information: Write for guidelines.
Deadline: None
Contact: John O. Anthony, Trustee

Arkansas Community Foundation, Inc.
604 East Sixth Street
Little Rock, AR 72202
(501) 372-1116

Description: Grants to residents and charitable organizations of Arkansas, for social services, health services, and scholarships. Grants are also available for cultural programs, community development, and environmental programs.
$ Given: $958,642
Application Information: Write or call; formal application required.
Deadline: January 1, April 1, July 1, September 1, October 1
Contact: Martha Ann Jones, Executive Director

Harold S. Seabrook Charitable Trust
c/o National Bank of Commerce,
Trust Department
P.O. Box 6208
Pine Bluff, AR 71601

Description: Grants for residents and organizations of Pine Bluff, for youth and child welfare, recreation, social services, and higher education.
$ Given: $89,495 for 25 grants
Application Information: Write for guidelines.
Deadline: October 1
Contact: Richard Metcalf

Alvin S. Tilles Item XX Testamentary Trust
P.O. Box 1392
Fort Smith, AR 72902

Description: Grants for residents and organizations of Arkansas, for hospitals, Jewish welfare, social services, and education.
$ Given: $56,758 for 8 grants
Application Information: Write for guidelines.
Deadline: N/A
Contact: Jennings J. Stein, Trustee

The Sam M. and Helen R. Walton Foundation
125 West Central, No. 210
Bentonville, AR 72712
(501) 273-5743

Description: Grants for residents and charitable organizations of Arkansas, for health services, education, youth programs, social services, and religious support.
$ Given: $440,633 for grants
Application Information: Write letter or proposal; formal application required.
Deadline: None
Contact: Jan Ney

CALIFORNIA

The Abelard Foundation, Inc.
2530 San Pablo Avenue
Suite B
Berkeley, CA 94702
(415) 644-1904

Application Address (East Coast):
P.O. Box 148
Lincoln, MA 01773

Description: Grants for organizations in New York, the southern and western states, and Appalachia, which support social programs, urban and rural economic equality, the disadvantaged, and those individuals with financial needs.
$ Given: $265,000 for 41 grants; average range: $6,000–$7,000
Application Information: Write or call for guidelines and/or send proposal. See the important information in the chapter introduction about the need for institutional affiliation.
Deadline: February 1, May 1, November 1
Contact: Leah Brumer, Executive Director

Sheldon and Carol Appel Family Foundation
2924 1/2 Main Street
Santa Monica, CA
90405-5316

Description: Grants for residents and organizations of California, for Jewish giving, Jewish welfare, and higher education expenses.
$ Given: $103,722 for 66 grants
Application Information: Write for guidelines.
Deadline: N/A
Contact: Barbara Davisson, Secretary-Treasurer

Argyros Foundation
950 South Coast
Drive
Suite 200
Costa Mesa, CA
92626
(714) 241-5000

Description: Grants for residents and organizations of California, for culture, education, religious giving, social services, recreation, and health services.
$ Given: $915,000 for 90 grants
Application Information: Write proposal; formal application required.
Deadline: June 1
Contact: Chuck Packard, Trustee

Arline and Thomas J. Bannan Foundation
P.O. Box M
Palm Desert, CA
92261
(619) 340-1330

Description: Grants for residents and organizations of California and Washington, for health services, youth services, higher education, religious purposes, child welfare, and social services.
$ Given: $76,590 for 45 grants
Application Information: Write letter or proposal; formal application required.
Deadline: None
Contact: Thomas J. Bannan, President

The Kathryne Beynon Foundation
350 West Colorado
Boulevard
Suite 400
Pasadena, CA
91105-1894

Description: Grants for organizations and residents of California, for health services, child welfare, Catholic Church support, and higher education.
$ Given: $215,000 for 20 grants
Application Information: Write letter; formal application form not required.
Deadline: None
Contact: Robert D. Bannon, Trustee

Burns–Dunphy Foundation
c/o Walter M. Gleason
Hearst Building
Third and Market
Streets
Suite 1200
San Francisco, CA
94103

Description: Grants for organizations and residents of California, for Roman Catholic welfare, education, and missionary services.
$ Given: $87,000 for 32 grants
Application Information: Write for guidelines.
Deadline: N/A
Contact: Walter M. Gleason, President

Carbonel Foundation
c/o The Tides
Foundation
1388 Sutter Street
Tenth Floor
San Francisco, CA
94109
(415) 771-4308

Description: Grants to support organizations serving families in crisis, human needs, and the disadvantaged.
$ Given: $150,000 for 14 grants; average range: $6,000–$10,000
Application Information: Write for guidelines. See the important information in the chapter introduction about the need for institutional affiliation.
Deadline: None
Contact: Ellen Friedman

C & H Charitable Trust
830 Loring Avenue
Crockett, CA 94525
(415) 356-6021

Description: Grants for residents and organizations of Crockett, for health and welfare, education, culture and the arts, and civic services.
$ Given: $102,345 for 28 grants
Application Information: Write for guidelines.
Deadline: N/A
Contact: Cheri Tillotson, Executive Secretary

Community Foundation of Santa Clara County
960 West Hedding, No. 220
San Jose, CA
95126-1215
(408) 241-2666

Description: Grants for residents and organizations of Santa Clara County, for education, AIDS programs, child welfare, women and minorities, employment and housing, the arts, community development and urban affairs, and the environment.
$ Given: $1.5 million for 300 grants; average range: $500–$35,000
Application Information: Write letter or call; application form not required.
Deadline: 12 weeks prior to board meetings
Contact: Peter Hero, Executive Director

Douglas Charitable Foundation
141 El Camino Drive
Beverly Hills, CA
90212

Description: Grants for residents and organizations of California, for Jewish welfare, social services, and the arts.
$ Given: $90,505 for 42 grants; average range: $100–$26,250
Application Information: Write for guidelines.
Deadline: N/A
Contact: Anne Douglas, Kirk Douglas, Karl Samuelian, John T. Trotter, and Jack Valenti, Managers

Lucius and Eva Eastman Fund, Inc.
24120 Summit Woods Drive
Los Gatos, CA 95030
Application Address:
P.O. Box 33037
Los Gatos, CA
95031-3037

Description: Grants for residents and organizations of California, for social services, women, cultural programs, and law and justice, including civil and human rights.
$ Given: $55,375 for 43 grants
Application Information: Write letter; formal application form not required.
Deadline: None
Contact: Lucius R. Eastman, Jr., President

Elks of Los Angeles Foundation Fund
607 South Western Avenue
Los Angeles, CA
90004
(818) 881-4728

Description: Grants for residents of Los Angeles, for youth, child welfare, and health services.
$ Given: $138,161 for 50 grants; average range: $1,000–$7,000
Application Information: Write letter; formal application required.
Deadline: February and March
Contact: Frank Lorenzi, President

Feintech Family Foundation
321 South Beverly Drive
Suite K
Beverly Hills, CA
90212
(213) 879-3262

Description: Grants for residents and organizations of California, for Jewish welfare and concerns.
$ Given: $114,178 for 30 grants; average range: $50–$36,125
Application Information: Write letter; formal application required.
Deadline: None
Contact: Norman Feintech, President, or Irving Feintech, Vice President

Audrey and Sydney Irmas Charitable Foundation
11835 West Olympic Boulevard, Suite 1160
Los Angeles, CA 90064
(310) 477-7979

Description: Grants for residents and organizations of Los Angeles, to help pay housing expenses. Grants are also available for charitable foundations, the arts, and Jewish welfare.
$ Given: $230,490 for 26 grants; average range: $100–$115,000
Application Information: Write letter; formal application not required.
Deadline: None
Contact: Robert Irmas, Administrator

Masud Mehran Foundation
P.O. Box 640
San Ramon, CA 94583

Description: Grants for residents and organizations of California, for child welfare, higher education, and social services.
$ Given: $124,914 for 54 grants; average range: $25–$32,000
Application Information: Write for guidelines.
Deadline: N/A
Contact: Masud Mehran, President

The Milken Family Foundation
c/o Foundations of the Milken Families
15250 Ventura Boulevard
Second Floor
Sherman Oaks, CA 91403

Description: Grants for residents and organizations of the Los Angeles area, to help pay general living expenses. Grants are also available for education, health and medical research, and community services.
$ Given: $4 million; average range: $100–$500,000
Application Information: Write letter or proposal.
Deadline: None
Contact: Jules Lesner, Executive Director

Ottenstein Family Foundation, Inc.
225 Stevens
Suite 210A
Solana Beach, CA 92075

Description: Grants for residents and organizations of California, for Jewish welfare and temple support: cultural programs, social services, health, and education; preference is given to San Diego.
$ Given: $113,850 for 31 grants; average range: $50–$65,500
Application Information: Write for guidelines.
Deadline: N/A
Contact: Leonard Glass

The Ralph M. Parsons Foundation
1055 Wilshire Boulevard
Suite 1701
Los Angeles, CA 90017
(213) 482-3185

Description: Grants for organizations in Los Angeles, to support health and social services for the disadvantaged.
$ Given: $6.6 million for grants; average range: $10,000–$75,000
Application Information: Application form not required; send letter and one copy of proposal. See the important information in the chapter introduction about the need for institutional affiliation.
Deadline: None
Contact: Christine Sisley, Executive Director

Paul and Magdalena Ecke Poinsettia Foundation
P.O. Box 607
Encinitas, CA 92024

Description: Grants for residents of California, for youth activity and child welfare, and for higher and some secondary education.
$ Given: $163,075 for 21 grants
Application Information: Write letter; formal application required.
Deadline: None
Contact: Barbara Ecke Winter, Secretary

**Rivendell Stewards'
Trust Dated
February 23, 1985**
2661 Tallant Road,
No. 620
Santa Barbara, CA
93105
(805) 969-5856

Description: Grants for Christian
residents and organizations of California,
missionary efforts and needy individuals
who work in the Christian church.
$ Given: $175,300 for grants
Application Information: Write letter.
Deadline: September 15–October 15
Contact: K. N. Hansen, Trustee

COLORADO

**Adolph Coors
Foundation**
350-C Clayton Street
Denver, CO 80206
(303) 388-1636

Description: Grants for organizations in
Colorado, to support social, health, and
youth services for the disadvantaged.
$ Given: $4.6 million for 130 grants;
average range: $5,000–$20,000
Application Information: Formal
application not required; send letter and
one copy of proposal. See the important
information in the chapter introduction
about the need for institutional affiliation.
Deadline: November 1, February 1, May 1,
August 1
Contact: Linda S. Tafoya, Executive
Director

**Lulu Frankel
Foundation**
2800 South University
Boulevard, No. 147
Denver, CO 80210

Description: Grants for hospitals and
Jewish residents of Colorado who can
demonstrate financial need.
$ Given: $59,753 for 33 grants; average
range: $25–$15,000
Application Information: Write for
guidelines.
Deadline: None
Contact: Beth Weisberg, Secretary

The Aksel Nielsen Foundation
Three Melody Lane
Parker, CO
80134-8631

Description: Grants for residents and organizations of Colorado, for cultural programs, museums, and general living expenses.
$ Given: $70,000 for 14 grants; average range: $500–$12,000
Application Information: Write letter; formal application required.
Deadline: None
Contact: Virginia N. Muse, President

The Piton Foundation
Kittredge Building
511 16th Street
Suite 700
Denver, CO 80202
(303) 825-6246

Description: Grants for residents and organizations of the Denver metropolitan area who can demonstrate financial need; preference is given to families with children.
$ Given: $25,000 for 40 grants; average range: $300–$3,000
Application Information: Write letter; formal application required.
Deadline: January 15, April 15, July 15, October 15
Contact: Phyllis Buchele

Harry W. Rabb Foundation
6242 South Elmira Circle
Englewood, CO 80111
(303) 773-3918

Description: Grants for hospitals, Jewish welfare funds, and needy senior citizens of Denver.
$ Given: $115,740 for 38 grants; average range: $1,000–$21,000
Application Information: Write for guidelines.
Deadline: N/A
Contact: Richard A. Zarlengo, Secretary-Treasurer

The Bal F. and Hilda N. Swan Foundation
c/o First Interstate Bank of Denver, N.A.
P.O. Box 5825
Terminal Annex
Denver, CO 80217
(303) 293-5275

Description: Grants for residents and organizations of Colorado, for handicapped services, medical research, child welfare, cultural programs, social services, and higher education.
$ Given: $291,250 for 29 grants; average range: $500–$36,800
Application Information: Write letter; formal application required.
Deadline: None
Contact: Julie Ham

CONNECTICUT

Louis H. Aborn Foundation, Inc.
46 Wilshire Road
Greenwich, CT 06830
(203) 661-4046

Description: Grants for residents and organizations of Connecticut, for public health, education, and child welfare.
$ Given: $151,000 for 4 grants; average range: $1,000–$90,000
Application Information: Write letter; formal application required.
Deadline: N/A
Contact: Louis H. Aborn, President

Fisher Foundation, Inc.
36 Brookside Boulevard
West Hartford, CT 06107
(203) 523-7247

Description: Grants for residents and organizations of the greater Hartford area, for Jewish welfare, health services, education, senior citizens, the disadvantaged, employment, and housing.
$ Given: $435,543 for 69 grants; average range: $100–$69,000
Application Information: Write letter; formal application not required.
Deadline: February 1, May 1, October 1
Contact: Martha Newman, Executive Director

**Charles and
Mabel P. Jost
Foundation, Inc.**
c/o Nestor, Sarka
& Co.
1140 Fairfield Avenue
Bridgeport, CT 06605
(203) 336-0166

Description: Grants for residents and hospitals of Connecticut, for handicapped services, health services, and higher education.
$ Given: $215,000 for 23 grants; average range: $500–$25,000
Application Information: Write letter; formal application required.
Deadline: None
Contact: Alexander R. Nestor, Chair

DELAWARE

**Stephen and Mary
Birch Foundation,
Inc.**
501 Silverside Road
Suite 13
Wilmington, DE
19809

Description: Grants for residents and organizations of Delaware, for the blind, health services, youth services, cultural programs, social services, and civic services.
$ Given: $1.7 million for 8 grants; average range: $500–$1.5 million
Application Information: Write letter; formal application not required.
Deadline: None.
Contact: Elfriede Looze

Crystal Trust
1088 DuPont Building
Wilmington, DE
19898
(302) 774-8421

Description: Grants for organizations in Delaware, especially Wilmington, to support social, family, and youth services for the disadvantaged.
$ Given: $2.6 million for 41 grants; average range: $10,000–$100,000
Application Information: Application form not required; send one copy of proposal. See the important information in the chapter introduction about the need for institutional affiliation.
Deadline: October 1
Contact: Burt C. Pratt, Director

DISTRICT OF COLUMBIA

Melvin and Estelle Gelman Foundation
2120 L Street, NW
Suite 800
Washington, DC
20037

Description: Grants for residents and organizations of the District of Columbia, for Jewish welfare, cultural programs, the arts, and medical research.
$ Given: $368,556 for 187 grants; average: $10–$4,000
Application Information: Write for guidelines. See the important information in the chapter introduction about the need for institutional affiliation.
Deadline: N/A
Contact: Estelle S. Gelman, President and Treasurer

Aaron and Cecile Goldman Foundation
1725 K Street, NW
Suite 907
Washington, DC
20006
(202) 833-8714

Description: Grants for residents and organizations of the District of Columbia, for Jewish welfare, cultural activities, and education.
$ Given: $96,150 for 94 grants; average range: $100–$13,000
Application Information: Write letter; formal application not required.
Deadline: None
Contact: Aaron Goldman, Trustee

Walter G. Ross Foundation
c/o ASB Capital Management Inc.
655 15th Street, NW
Suite 800
Washington, DC
20005

Description: Grants to support family services and child welfare and development for the disadvantaged in the Washington, DC area and Florida.
$ Given: $372,000 for 19 grants; average range: $2,500–$100,000
Application Information: Application form not required; send letter and one proposal. See the important information in the chapter introduction about the need for institutional affiliation.
Deadline: September 15
Contact: Ian W. Jones, Secretary

FLORIDA

Hope Foundation
2335 Tamiami Trail,
North
Suite 510
Naples, FL 33940
(813) 262-2131

Description: Grants for social services and general charitable causes.
$ Given: $49,983 for 38 grants; average range: $100–$10,000
Application Information: Write for guidelines. See the important information in the chapter introduction about the need for institutional affiliation.
Deadline: None
Contact: Philip M. Francoeur, Trustee

Jacksonville Community Foundation
112 West Adams
Street, No. 1414
Jacksonville, FL 32202
(904) 356-4483

Description: Grants for general charitable giving, including emergency funds, loans, and seed money, primarily in northeastern Florida.
$ Given: $1.8 million for 223 grants; average range: $100–$20,000
Application Information: Write for guidelines. See the important information in the chapter introduction about the need for institutional affiliation.
Deadline: December 1, March 1, June 1, September 1
Contact: L. Andrew Bell, III, President

The Lee Foundation
P.O. Box 2113
Orlando, FL 32802

Description: Grants for civic affairs and charitable giving, primarily in Orlando.
$ Given: $177,059 for 31 grants; average range: $25–$102,400
Application Information: Write letter.
Deadline: None
Contact: Richard Lee, Trustee

The Ryder System Charitable Foundation, Inc.
c/o Ryder System, Inc.
3600 NW 82nd Avenue
Miami, FL 33166
(305) 593-3642

Description: Grants given primarily in areas of company operations—southern Florida; Atlanta, Georgia; Detroit, Michigan; St. Louis, Missouri; Cincinnati, Ohio; and Dallas, Texas—to support health and human services for the disadvantaged.
$ Given: $2.3 million for 306 grants; average range: $1,000–$30,000
Application Information: Application form not required; send letter and one proposal. See the important information in the chapter introduction about the need for institutional affiliation.
Deadline: First half of calendar year
Contact: Office of Corporate Programs

Hugh and Mary Wilson Foundation, Inc.
7188 Beneva Road South
Sarasota, FL 34238
(813) 921-2856

Description: Grants for social and family services, women, and child welfare as well as general charitable giving, in the Manatee–Sarasota, Florida, and Lewisburg–Danville, Pennsylvania areas.
$ Given: $231,918 for 18 grants; average range: $1,000–$50,000
Application Information: Write or call.
Deadline: July 31
Contact: John R. Wood, President

GEORGIA

Francis L. Abreu Charitable Trust
c/o Trust Co. Bank
P.O. Box 4655
Atlanta, GA 30302-4655
(404) 588-7356

Description: Grants for social services, especially for women and youth, primarily in Atlanta.
$ Given: $63,000 for 28 grants; average range: $250–$25,000
Application Information: Write letter/proposal.
Deadline: March 15, September 15
Contact: Brenda Rambeau, Trust Officer, Trust Co. Bank

Colonial Foundation, Inc.
P.O. Box 576
Savannah, GA 31420
(912) 236-1331

Description: Grants for various causes, including social services, primarily in Georgia.
$ Given: $292,690 for 64 grants; average range: $100–$150,000
Application Information: Write for guidelines.
Deadline: None
Contact: Francis A. Brown, Treasurer

John H. Harland Company Foundation
P.O. Box 105250
Atlanta, GA 30348
(404) 981-9460

Description: Grants for social services, youth, and general purpose support.
$ Given: $152,605 for 61 grants; average range: $100–$33,000
Application Information: Write letter.
Deadline: None
Contact: Robert R. Woodson, Secretary

Joe E. Johnston Foundation
P.O. Box 4655
Atlanta, GA 30302
Application Address:
Two South Main Street
Woodstock, GA 30188

Description: Grants for family services primarily in Georgia.
$ Given: $3,500 for 2 grants; average range: $500–$3,000
Application Information: Write letter. See the important information in the chapter introduction about the need for institutional affiliation.
Deadline: None
Contact: A. Smith Johnston

Helen S. Lanier Foundation, Inc.
c/o Trust Co. Bank
P.O. Box 4655
Atlanta, GA 30302

Description: Grants for general charitable needs primarily in Atlanta, Georgia, and Florida.
$ Given: $56,400 for 30 grants; average range: $100–$10,000
Application Information: Write letter.
Deadline: None
Contact: Helen S. Lanier, Chair

J. C. Lewis Foundation, Inc.
9505 Abercorn Street
P.O. Box 13666
Savannah, GA 31406
(912) 925-0234

Description: Grants for social services and general charitable causes primarily in Savannah.
$ Given: $47,010 for 73 grants; average range $10–$15,630
Application Information: Write letter. See the important information in the chapter introduction about the need for institutional affiliation.
Deadline: None
Contact: J. C. Lewis, Jr., President

Harriet McDaniel Marshall Trust in Memory of Sanders McDaniel
c/o Trust Co. Bank
P.O. Box 4418,
MC 041
Atlanta, GA 30302
(404) 588-8246

Description: Grants for organizations of metropolitan Atlanta, for assisting the disadvantaged.
$ Given: $195,968 in grants awarded; average range: $3,000–$5,000
Application Information: Formal application required; send letter and one proposal. See the important information in the chapter introduction about the need for institutional affiliation.
Deadline: March 1, June 1, September 1, December 1
Contact: Victor A. Gregory, Secretary

Oglethorpe Fund
c/o Citizens & Southern Trust Co.
P.O. Box 9626
Savannah, GA
31412-9626

Description: Grants for general charitable needs in Chatham County.
$ Given: Grants awarded: $3,381
Application Information: Write letter.
Deadline: None
Contact: Anita Waring Lane, Trustee

J. W. and Ethel I. Woodruff Foundation
P.O. Box 750
Columbus, GA
31902-0750
(404) 322-6005

Description: Grants for general charitable causes and social services primarily in Georgia.
$ Given: $39,850 for 32 grants; average range: $300–$5,800
Application Information: Write letter. See the important information in the chapter introduction about the need for institutional affiliation.
Deadline: None
Contact: J. Barnett Woodruff, Vice Chair

HAWAII

Hawaiian Electric Industries Charitable Foundation
P.O. Box 730
Honolulu, HI 96808
(808) 532-5860

Description: Grants and support services for the disadvantaged and the community given to organizations primarily in Hawaii.
$ Given: $951,720 for 84 grants; average range: $300–$300,000
Application Information: Application form not required; send letter with project data and one proposal. See the important information in the chapter introduction about the need for institutional affiliation.
Deadline: December 1, June 1
Contact: Scott Shirai, Director of Community Relations

IDAHO

Margaret W. Reed Foundation
P.O. Box A
Coeur d'Alene, ID 83814
(208) 664-2161

Description: Grants for charitable giving primarily in the northwestern United States, with emphasis on Idaho and Washington.
$ Given: $34,500 for 15 grants; average range: $1,000–$11,000
Application Information: Write letter. See the important information in the chapter introduction about the need for institutional affiliation.
Deadline: None
Contact: Scott W. Reed, Trustee

ILLINOIS

ACP Foundation
30 Bridlewood Road
Northbrook, IL
60062-4702
(708) 272-3034

Description: Grants for social services and general charitable causes, among others.
$ Given: $116,255 for grants
Application Information: Write letter.
Deadline: None
Contact: A. C. Buehler, Jr., President

Alton Foundation
P.O. Box 1078
Alton, IL 62002
(618) 462-3953

Description: Grants for social services, women, youth, family services, and minorities, among others, in Madison County and adjoining counties.
$ Given: $228,842 for grants
Application Information: Write letter first; one copy of proposal; formal application required.
Deadline: None
Contact: R. S. Minsker, Secretary

Norman and Joan Chapman Foundation
Two Woodley Road
Winnetka, IL 60093

Description: Grants for Jewish organizations and general charitable giving.
$ Given: $100,000 for 16 grants; average range: $50–$25,475
Application Information: Write letter. See the important information in the chapter introduction about the need for institutional affiliation.
Deadline: None
Contact: Norman Chapman, President

Cole Taylor Charitable Foundation
350 East Dundee Road
Suite 305
Wheeling, IL 60090
(708) 459-1111

Description: Grants for social services and Jewish welfare, primarily in Chicago.
$ Given: $189,725 for 74 grants; average range: $50–$90,000
Application Information: Write letter. See the important information in the chapter introduction about the need for institutional affiliation.
Deadline: None
Contact: Sidney J. Taylor, President

Crane Fund for Widows and Children
222 West Adams Street
Room 849
Chicago, IL 60606

Description: Grants for social services and individuals with financial needs primarily in Illinois.
$ Given: $402,335 for 3 grants; average range: $1,500–$11,760
Application Information: Write letter first.
Deadline: None
Contact: Trustees

Doris and Victor Day Foundation, Inc.
1705 Second Avenue
Suite 424
Rock Island, IL 61201
(309) 788-2300

Description: Grants for social services, child welfare, and general purposes in the quad cities area of Rock County, Illinois, and Scott County, Iowa.
$ Given: $630,267 for 98 grants; average range: $1,000–$25,000
Application Information: Write or call first; submit one copy of proposal.
Deadline: May 1
Contact: Alan Egly, Executive Director

Geifman Family Foundation, Inc.
2239 29th Street
Rock Island, IL
61201-5025
(309) 788-9531

Description: Grants for Jewish giving and welfare primarily in Illinois, with emphasis on Rock Island.
$ Given: $109,360 for 73 grants; average range: $50–$25,000
Application Information: Write letter.
Deadline: None
Contact: Morris M. Geifman, President

Hochberg Family Foundation
7233 West Dempster Street
Niles, IL 60648

Description: Grants for Jewish welfare services and giving primarily in Chicago.
$ Given: $235,386 for 101 grants; average range: $5–$156,375
Application Information: Write letter. See the important information in the chapter introduction about the need for institutional affiliation.
Deadline: None
Contact: Larry Hochberg, Director

**Katten, Muchin &
Zavis Foundation,
Inc.**
525 West Monroe
Street
Suite 1600
Chicago, IL 60606
(312) 902-5200

Description: Grants for Jewish welfare
primarily in the Chicago area.
$ Given: $466,460 for 102 grants; average
range: $50–$327,840
Application Information: Write letter. See
the important information in the chapter
introduction about the need for
institutional affiliation.
Deadline: None
Contact: Norman Steinberg

**Meyers Charitable
Family Fund**
2141 South Jefferson
Street
Chicago, IL
60616-1856
(312) 421-4030

Description: Grants for general charitable
giving primarily in the greater Chicago
area.
$ Given: $105,890 for 49 grants; average
range: $100–$110,868
Application Information: Write letter.
Deadline: None
Contact: David R. Meyers, President

**Robert and Patricia
Moore Foundation**
803 Chestnut Street
Wilmette, IL 60091

Description: Grants for general charitable
giving primarily in Chicago and Wisconsin.
$ Given: $108,835 for 39 grants; average
range: $30–$50,000
Application Information: Write for
guidelines.
Deadline: N/A
Contact: Robert B. Moore, President

**Prince Charitable
Trusts**
10 South Wacker
Drive
Suite 2575
Chicago, IL 60606
(312) 454-9130

Description: Grants and social services
support for the disadvantaged in
Washington, DC; Chicago, Illinois; and
Rhode Island.
$ Given: $4.2 million for grants; average
range: $5,000–$25,000
Application Information: Application
form not required; send letter or one
proposal. See the important information
in the chapter introduction about the
need for institutional affiliation.
Deadline: N/A
Contact: Tracey Shafroth, Program
Director, or Jill Darrow, Program Officer

Albert and Joyce Rubenstein Family Foundation
200 Adams Street
Chicago, IL
60606-6963
(312) 663-9500

Description: Grants for Jewish giving and welfare primarily in Illinois.
$ Given: $26,360 for 77 grants; average range: $10–$2,500
Application Information: Send proposal.
Deadline: None
Contact: Joyce Rubenstein, Director

INDIANA

The Bowsher– Booher Foundation
First Interstate Bank of Northern Indiana, N.A.
112 West Jefferson Boulevard
South Bend, IN 46601
(219) 237-3313

Description: Grants for social services to residents of South Bend and St. Joseph counties.
$ Given: $113,685 for 15 grants; average range: $2,000–$28,000
Application Information: Write letter first; seven copies of proposal required.
Deadline: April 1 for May; October 1 for November
Contact: Robert R. Cleppe

The Indianapolis Foundation
615 North Alabama Street
Room 119
Indianapolis, IN 46204
(317) 634-7497

Description: Grants for family, social, and health services in Indianapolis and Marion counties.
$ Given: $3.2 million for 87 grants; average range: $4,000–$50,000
Application Information: Application form not required; write or call for guidelines. See the important information in the chapter introduction about the need for institutional affiliation.
Deadline: End of January, March, May, July, September, November
Contact: Kenneth I. Chapman, Executive Director

**Frank L. and
Laura L. Smock
Foundation**
c/o Lincoln National
Bank & Trust Co.
P.O. Box 2363
Fort Wayne, IN 46801
(219) 461-6451

Description: Grants for the health and welfare of ailing, needy, crippled, blind, or elderly men and women.
$ Given: $166,180 for 40 grants to individuals; average range: $3–$30,480
Application Information: Write letter.
Deadline: None
Contact: Alice Kopfer, Vice President, Lincoln National Bank & Trust Co.

IOWA

**William C. Brown
Company Charitable
Foundation**
c/o Mark C. Falb
2460 Kerper
Boulevard
Dubuque, IA
52001-2293
(319) 588-1451

Description: Grants for social services in the Dubuque community.
$ Given: $102,299 for 74 grants; average range: $10–$21,500
Application Information: Write letter. See the important information in the chapter introduction about the need for institutional affiliation.
Deadline: None
Contact: Mark C. Falb, Trustee

Engman Foundation
P.O. Box 864
Des Moines, IA 50304

Description: Grants for welfare, social services, and Jewish organizations primarily in Iowa.
$ Given: $127,529 for 67 grants; average range: $25–$33,000
Application Information: Write letter. See the important information in the chapter introduction about the need for institutional affiliation.
Deadline: None
Contact: Lawrence B. Engman, Director

The John K. and Luise V. Hanson Foundation
P.O. Box 450
Forest City, IA 50436
(515) 582-2825

Description: Grants for matching funds for community and general charitable causes serving individuals with financial needs primarily in northcentral Iowa.
$ Given: $290,334 for 34 grants; average range: $1,000–$2,000
Application Information: Write for guidelines. See the important information in the chapter introduction about the need for institutional affiliation.
Deadline: None
Contact: Linda Johnson

Peter H. and E. Lucille Gaass Kuyper Foundation
c/o Rolscreen Co.
Pella, IA 50219
(515) 628-1000

Description: Grants for general charitable causes serving individuals with financial needs in the Pella area.
$ Given: $758,667 for 103 grants; average range: $100–$200,000
Application Information: Write for guidelines.
Deadline: None
Contact: Joan Farver, President

The Greater Cedar Rapids Foundation
122 Second Street, SE
Suite 409
Cedar Rapids, IA 52401
(319) 366-2862

Description: Grants for social services and community development in Linn County.
$ Given: $148,067 for 19 grants; average range: $1,250–$50,000
Application Information: Write letter. See the important information in the chapter introduction about the need for institutional affiliation.
Deadline: May
Contact: Malcolm L. Peel, Executive Director

Mid-Iowa Health Foundation
550 39th Street
Suite 104
Des Moines, IA 50312
(515) 277-6411

Description: Grants for the disadvantaged, elderly, homeless, and general purpose in Polk County and seven surrounding counties.
$ Given: $502,079 for 46 grants; average range: $500–$25,000
Application Information: Write or call; application required.
Deadlines: February 1, May 1, August 1, November 1
Contact: Kathryn Bradley

Hobart A. and Alta V. Ross Family Foundation
P.O. Box AK
Spirit Lake, IA 51360
Application Address:
RR 9492-24,
Spirit Lake, IA 51360

Description: Grants for family services, child welfare, and others primarily in Dickinson County and neighboring counties.
$ Given: $120,950 for 15 grants
Application Information: Write letter.
Deadline: None
Contact: Keith A. Ross, President

John Ruan Foundation Trust
33200 Ruan Center
Des Moines, IA 50304
(515) 245-2555

Description: Grants in several areas, including general charitable causes, primarily in Des Moines.
$ Given: $191,717 for 115 grants; average range: $49–$100,000
Application Information: Write letter.
Deadline: None
Contact: John Ruan, Trustee

W. A. Sheaffer Memorial Foundation, Inc.
817 Avenue G
Fort Madison, IA
52627-2912

Description: Grants for social services and community organizations primarily in Iowa.
$ Given: $64,500 for 7 grants; average range: $500–$28,000
Application Information: Write for guidelines. See the important information in the chapter introduction about the need for institutional affiliation.
Deadline: N/A
Contact: Walter A. Sheaffer, President

KANSAS

DeVore Foundation, Inc.
P.O. Box 118
Wichita, KS 67201
Application Address:
1199 East Central
Wichita, KS 67201
(316) 267-3211

Description: Grants for social services and community foundations primarily in Wichita.
$ Given: $45,856 for 49 grants; average range: $50–$11,450
Application Information: Send letter or proposal. See the important information in the chapter introduction about the need for institutional affiliation.
Deadline: None
Contact: Richard A. DeVore, President

Stella A. and Ray E. Dillon Foundation, Inc.
One Compound Drive
Hutchinson, KS 67502
(316) 665-5421

Description: Grants for social services and community development primarily in Reno County.
$ Given: $104,000 for 19 grants; average range: $500–$30,400
Application Information: Send proposal. See the important information in the chapter introduction about the need for institutional affiliation.
Deadline: None
Contact: Ray E. Dillon, III, Treasurer

Gerson Family Foundation
6100 Broadmoor
Mission, KS
66202-3229

Description: Grants for general charitable giving primarily in Missouri.
$ Given: $128,958 for 19 grants; average range: $50–$91,000
Application Information: Write letter.
Deadline: None
Contact: Peter Gerson, Vice President

Ethel and Raymond F. Rice Foundation
700 Massachusetts Street
Lawrence, KS 66044
(913) 843-0420

Description: Grants for youth and social services agencies in Douglas County and Lawrence.
$ Given: $270,300 for 90 grants; average range: $500–$26,000
Application Information: Write proposal. See the important information in the chapter introduction on institutional affiliation.
Deadline: November 15
Contact: Robert B. Oyler, President, or George M. Clem, Treasurer

Security Benefit Life Insurance Company Charitable Trust
700 SW Harrison Street
Topeka, KS 66636
(913) 295-3000

Description: Grants and employee matching funds for women, youth, disadvantaged, and homeless who are residents of Topeka.
$ Given: $74,175 for 86 grants; average range: $25–$34,000
Application Information: Write letter.
Deadline: None
Contact: Howard R. Fricke, Trustee

Topeka Community Foundation
5100 SW 10th
P.O. Box 4525
Topeka, KS 66604
(913) 272-4804

Description: Grants for social and family services in Topeka and Shawnee counties.
$ Given: $159,585 for 38 grants; average range: $500–$5,000
Application Information: Application form required. See the important information in the chapter introduction about the need for institutional affiliation.
Deadline: February 15
Contact: Karen Welch, Executive Director

KENTUCKY

The Cralle Foundation
c/o First Trust Center
Suite 503
200 South Fifth Street
Louisville, KY 40202
(502) 581-1148

Description: Grants for general purpose support, including homeless, youth, and health services, primarily in Kentucky with emphasis on Louisville.
$ Given: $785,833 for 18 grants; average range: $3,500–$300,000
Application Information: Application required.
Deadline: None
Contact: James T. Crain, Jr., Executive Director

Foundation for the Tri-State Community
P.O. Box 2096
Ashland, KY 41105
(606) 324-3888

Description: Grants for general charitable purposes to residents of Ashland, Kentucky; Ironton, Ohio; and Huntington, West Virginia.
$ Given: $177,363 for grants
Application Information: Write letter, call, or submit proposal.
Deadline: September 15 for grants from unrestricted funds
Contact: Linda L. Ball, Executive Director

Annie Gardner Foundation
South Sixth and College
Mayfield, KY 42066
(502) 247-5803

Description: Grants primarily for the disadvantaged in Graves County, for rent, medical care, clothing, and other necessities.
$ Given: $389,896 for 3,214 grants
Application Information: Application available from foundation. See the important information in the chapter introduction about the need for institutional affiliation.
Deadline: July 1
Contact: Nancy H. Sparks, Education Director, or Thomas McCue

Hayswood Foundation
One McDonald Parkway
Suite 2-C
Maysville, KY 41056

Description: Grants for social services and welfare in Maysville.
$ Given: $16,149 for 3 grants; average range: $586–$12,000
Application Information: Write letter. See the important information in the chapter introduction about the need for institutional affiliation.
Deadline: None
Contact: John C. Schumacher, Director

Julia and Isadore Klein Family Foundation, Inc.
P.O. Box 1101
Louisville, KY 40201
(502) 589-3351

Application Address:
510 West Broadway
Louisville, KY 40202
(502) 562-5413

Description: Grants for general charitable causes primarily in Louisville.
$ Given: $129,926 for 102 grants; average range: $5–$40,000
Application Information: Write letter. See the important information in the chapter introduction about the need for institutional affiliation.
Deadline: None
Contact: Bertram W. Klein, Secretary

Rudd Foundation, Inc.
4344 Poplar Level Road
Louisville, KY 40232
(502) 456-4050

Description: Grants for general charitable support primarily for Jewish welfare funds.
$ Given: $122,075 for 5 grants; average range: $125–$120,000
Application Information: Write letter.
Deadline: None
Contact: Mason C. Rudd, President

MAINE

The Maine Community Foundation, Inc.
210 Main Street
P.O. Box 148
Ellsworth, ME 04605
(207) 667-9735

Description: Grants for organizations in Maine, for projects affecting the disadvantaged.
$ Given: $559,688 for 234 grants; average range: $500–$5,000
Application Information: Application form required; send letter and one copy of proposal. See the important information in the chapter introduction about the need for institutional affiliation.
Deadline: February 1, April 1, August 1, October 1
Contact: Rebecca Buyers-Baso, Program Director

MARYLAND

Charles S. Abell Foundation, Inc.
8401 Connecticut Avenue
Chevy Chase, MD 20815
(301) 652-2224

Description: Grants for church-related food and shelter centers, job training, abused women and children, the mentally handicapped, and especially homeless or disadvantaged individuals primarily in Washington, District of Columbia, and five nearby Maryland counties.
$ Given: $221,672 for 16 grants; average range: $1,020–$50,000
Application Information: No application form required; send one copy of proposal.
Deadline: None
Contact: W. Shepherdson Abell, Secretary-Treasurer

MASSACHUSETTS

Association for the Relief of Aged Women of New Bedford
27 South Sixth Street
New Bedford, MA
02740

Description: Grants for elderly female residents of New Bedford who can demonstrate financial need.
$ Given: $225,165 for 21 grants to individuals; average range: $85–$31,862
Application Information: Write for guidelines.
Deadline: N/A
Contact: Mrs. Thorton Klaren, President

The Boston Foundation, Inc.
One Boston Place
Twenty-fourth Floor
Boston, MA
02108-4402
(617) 723-7415

Description: Grants for organizations serving the disadvantaged, welfare, homeless, or women in the Boston metropolitan area.
$ Given: $15.1 million for 989 grants; average range: $20,000–$50,000
Application Information: Send letter and one copy of proposal. See the important information in the chapter introduction about the need for institutional affiliation.
Deadline: March, June, August, December
Contact: Anna Faith Jones, President

The Hoche–Scofield Foundation
c/o Shawmut Bank, N.A.
446 Main Street
Boston, MA 01608
(508) 793-4205

Description: Grants for organizations and social services serving women or the disadvantaged in the city and county of Worcester.
$ Given: $608,413 for 81 grants; average range: $1,000–$10,000
Application Information: Application form required; call or send letter. See the important information in the chapter introduction about the need for institutional affiliation.
Deadline: February 15, May 15, August 15, November 15
Contact: Stephen G. Fritch, Vice President, Shawmut Bank, N.A.

Greater Worcester Community Foundation, Inc.
44 Front Street
Suite 530
Worcester, MA 01608
(508) 755-0980

Description: Grants for residents of greater Worcester or employees of Rotman's Furniture, "for the health, educational, social welfare, cultural and civic needs of the residents of Greater Worcester," including grants for employment, homeless, and housing.
$ Given: $134,922 for grants; average range: $100–$100,000
Application Information: Submit eight copies of foundation summary sheet plus two copies of proposal; application form required.
Deadline: June 1 (women and children); December 1 (discretionary awards)
Contact: Kay M. Marquet, Executive Director

MICHIGAN

The Barstow Foundation
c/o Chemical Bank
333 East Main Street
Midland, MI 48640
(517) 631-9200

Description: Grants for organizations in Michigan, primarily for the disadvantaged of the community.
$ Given: $212,500 for 15 grants; average range: $1,000–$50,000
Application Information: Application form not required; send two copies of proposal. See the important information in the chapter introduction about the need for institutional affiliation.
Deadline: October 31
Contact: Bruce M. Groom, Senior Vice President, Chemical Bank

Steelcase Foundation
P.O. Box 1967
Grand Rapids, MI
49507
(616) 246-4695

Description: Grants for organizations serving the disadvantaged, disabled, or elderly in areas of company operations, including Grand Rapids, Michigan; Orange County, California; Ashville, North Carolina; Athens, Alabama; and Toronto, Canada.
$ Given: $4 million for 120 grants; average range: $2,000–$25,000
Application Information: Application form required; write letter. See the important information in the chapter introduction about the need for institutional affiliation.
Deadline: None
Contact: Kate Pew Wolters, Executive Director

MISSISSIPPI

William Robert Baird Charitable Trust
c/o Citizens National Bank
512 22nd Avenue
Box 911
Meridian, MS 39302
(601) 693-1331

Description: Grants to support the disadvantaged and general welfare in Louisiana and Mississippi.
$ Given: $102,800 for 12 grants; average range: $2,500–$28,000
Application Information: Application form not required; write letter and proposal. See the important information in the chapter introduction about the need for institutional affiliation.
Deadline: None
Contact: Fred O. Poitevent, Jr., Vice President and Trust Officer, Citizens National Bank

MISSOURI

Hallmark Corporate Foundation
P.O. Box 419580
Department 323
Kansas City, MO
64141-6580
(816) 274-8515

Description: Grants for employment, delinquent youth, social services, handicapped, housing, and hunger, limited to Kansas City and cities in which Hallmark facilities are located.
$ Given: $4.2 million for 800 grants; average range: $200–$10,000
Application Information: Send proposal; application form not required.
Deadline: None
Contact: Jeanne Bates, Vice President

Ewing Marion Kauffman Foundation
9300 Ward Parkway
P.O. Box 8480
Kansas City, MO
64114
(816) 966-4000

Description: Grants for the disadvantaged, at-risk youth and families in need, and general health services in Kansas and Missouri.
$ Given: $391,922 for grants
Application Information: Application form not required; send brief proposal. See the important information in the chapter introduction about the need for institutional affiliation.
Deadline: None
Contact: Carl Mitchell, Treasurer

MONTANA

Sample Foundation, Inc.
14 North 24th Street
P.O. Box 279
Billings, MT 59103
(406) 256-5667

Description: Grants for social services for the disadvantaged or the community in Montana and Collier County, Florida.
$ Given: $204,240 for 41 grants; average range: $500–$50,000
Application Information: Send letter of interest. See the important information in the chapter introduction about the need for institutional affiliation.
Deadline: N/A
Contact: Miriam T. Sample, Vice President

NEBRASKA

The Beatrice Foundation
c/o ConAgra, Inc.
One ConAgra Drive
Omaha, NE 68102
(402) 595-4158

Description: Grants for community priorities programs with special attention to disadvantaged populations in the Chicago, Illinois metropolitan area.
$ Given: $2 million for 191 grants; average range: $5,000–$15,000
Application Information: Application form required; send letter. See the important information in the chapter introduction about the need for institutional affiliation.
Deadline: February 1, May 1, August 1, November 1
Contact: Patricia Schweiger, Manager of Community Affairs

NEW HAMPSHIRE

Mascoma Savings Bank Foundation
c/o Mascoma Savings Bank
67 North Park Street
Lebanon, NH
03766-1317
(603) 448-3650

Application Address:
P.O. Box 435
Lebanon, NH
03766-0435

Description: Grants for services for welfare or the disadvantaged primarily in Lebanon, West Lebanon, Enfield, Canaan, Hanover, Meriden, Plainfield, and Lyme.
$ Given: $49,560 for 24 grants; average range: $300–$15,000
Application Information: Application form not required; send letter for initial approach. See the important information in the chapter introduction about the need for institutional affiliation.
Deadline: April 1, October 1
Contact: Jean Kennedy, Chair

NEW JERSEY

Mary Owen Borden Memorial Foundation
160 Hodge Road
Princeton, NJ 08540
(609) 924-3637

Description: Grants limited primarily to Monmouth and Mercer counties for programs focusing on the special needs of youth, including family planning for teenagers; assistance to unwed teenage mothers; day care centers for young disadvantaged parents; and assistance to families in which instability prevails.
$ Given: $394,502 for 52 grants; average: $7,586
Application Information: Application form required; write for guidelines. See the important information in the chapter introduction about the need for institutional affiliation.
Deadline: January 1, April 1, September 1
Contact: John C. Borden, Jr., Executive Director

Innovating Worthy Projects Foundation
426 Shore Road
Suite E
Somers Point, NJ 08244
(609) 926-1111

Description: Grants for the education, service, or care of handicapped children, the aged, and the disadvantaged.
$ Given: $266,241 for 35 grants; average range: $50–$30,000
Application Information: Application form required; call for initial approach. See the important information in the chapter introduction about the need for institutional affiliation.
Deadline: None
Contact: Irving W. Packer, Chair

Anne Earle Talcott Fund
c/o First Fidelity Bank, N.A.
Philanthropic Services Group
765 Broad Street
Newark, NJ 07102
(201) 430-4533

Description: Grants for human service activities for disadvantaged families and the mentally ill in New Jersey.
$ Given: $67,500 for 9 grants; average range: $1,000–$25,000
Application Information: Application form not required; send one copy of proposal. See the important information in the chapter introduction about the need for institutional affiliation.
Deadline: February 1, August 1
Contact: James S. Hohn, Assistant Vice President, First Fidelity Bank, N.A., New Jersey

NEW YORK

Altman Foundation
220 East 42nd Street
Suite 411
New York, NY 10017
(212) 682-0970

Description: Grants for social welfare programs providing long-term solutions to the needs of the disadvantaged in New York, with emphasis on the boroughs of New York City.
$ Given: $4.7 million for 146 grants; average range: $10,000–$100,000
Application Information: Application form not required; write for guidelines. See the important information in the chapter introduction about the need for institutional affiliation.
Deadline: None
Contact: John S. Burke, President

Louis Calder Foundation
230 Park Avenue
Room 1530
New York, NY 10169
(212) 687-1680

Description: Grants for programs designed to enhance the potential and increase the self-sufficiency of disadvantaged children, youth, and their families in New York City.
$ Given: $5 million for 181 grants; average range: $15,000–$50,000
Application Information: Application form not required; send a one- to three-page letter. See the important information in the chapter introduction about the need for institutional affiliation.
Deadline: March 31
Contact: Trustees

Stella and Charles Guttman Foundation, Inc.
595 Madison Avenue
Suite 1604
New York, NY 10022
(212) 371-7082

Description: Grants for organizations providing social and educational services for the disadvantaged in the New York City metropolitan area.
$ Given: $1.3 million for 106 grants; average range: $5,000–$20,000
Application Information: Application form not required; write for guidelines. See the important information in the chapter introduction about the need for institutional affiliation.
Deadline: None
Contact: Elizabeth Olofson, Executive Director

Daisy Marquis Jones Foundation
620 Granite Building
130 East Main Street
Rochester, NY
14604-1620
(716) 263-3331

Description: Grants to support improvement in the quality of health care for residents of Monroe and Yates counties with special emphasis on the disadvantaged.
$ Given: $1.3 million for 113 grants; average range: $5,000–$10,000
Application Information: Application form required; write for guidelines. See the important information in the chapter introduction about the need for institutional affiliation.
Deadline: None
Contact: Pearl W. Rubin, President

The Pinkerton Foundation
725 Park Avenue
New York, NY 10021
(212) 772-6110

Description: Grants for economically disadvantaged children, youth, and families at risk in New York City.
$ Given: $1.2 million for 39 grants; average range: $2,000–$330,000
Application Information: Application form not required; write for guidelines. See the important information in the chapter introduction about the need for institutional affiliation.
Deadline: February 1, September 1
Contact: Joan Colello, Executive Director

NORTH CAROLINA

Kate B. Reynolds Charitable Trust
2422 Reynolds Road
Winston-Salem, NC 27106
(919) 723-1456

Description: Grants for health and social services in rural areas of North Carolina serving individuals with financial needs. Some grants limited to Winston-Salem and Forsyth County but healthcare giving is statewide.
$ Given: $12.8 million for 307 grants; average range: $15,000–$35,000
Application Information: Application form required; call or write for guidelines. See the important information in the chapter introduction about the need for institutional affiliation.
Deadline: January 15, May 15, August 15
Contact: Edwin W. Monroe, Executive Director; Ray Cope, Deputy Executive Director; or W. Vance Frye, Associate Director

NORTH DAKOTA

North Dakota Community Foundation
P.O. Box 387
Bismarck, ND
58502-0387
(701) 222-8349

Description: Grants largely for aid to the elderly and disadvantaged of North Dakota.
$ Given: $230,015 for 178 grants; average: $1,000
Application Information: Application form required; write for guidelines. See the important information in the chapter introduction about the need for institutional affiliation.
Deadline: August 31
Contact: Richard H. Timmins, President

OHIO

Borden Foundation, Inc.
180 East Broad Street
Thirty-Fourth Floor
Columbus, OH 43215
(614) 225-4340

Description: Grants for programs benefiting disadvantaged children and community services in areas of company operations.
$ Given: $2.1 million for 225 grants; average range: $1,000–$5,000
Application Information: Application form not required; write for guidelines. See the important information in the chapter introduction about the need for institutional affiliation.
Deadline: March 1, July 1, October 1
Contact: Judy Barker, President

The Nordson Corporation Foundation
28601 Clemens Road
Westlake, OH
44145-1148
(216) 892-1580 or
(216) 988-9411

Description: Grants for community programs, projects, human services, community development, disadvantaged, health services, homeless, hunger, and social services in the northern Ohio and Atlanta, Georgia areas.
$ Given: $311,165 for 51 grants; average range: $550–$25,000
Application Information: Application form not required; write letter or proposal. See the important information in the chapter introduction about the need for institutional affiliation.
Deadline: None
Contact: James C. Doughman, Director of Public Affairs

Albert G. and Olive H. Schlink Foundation
401 Citizens National Bank Building
Norwalk, OH 44857

Description: Grants for organizations providing aid to the disadvantaged and the aged in Ohio.
$ Given: $274,735 for 16 grants; average range: $2,500–$65,000
Application Information: Application form not required; write for guidelines. See the important information in the chapter introduction about the need for institutional affiliation.
Deadline: None
Contact: Robert A. Wiedemann, President

PENNSYLVANIA

Bethlehem Area Foundation
430 East Broad Street
Bethlehem, PA 18018
(215) 867-7588

Description: Grants for community, health, and social services, including for the disadvantaged, in the Bethlehem area.
$ Given; $217,537 for 44 grants; average range: $1,000–$6,000
Application Information: Write or call for guidelines; application form not required; send proposal. See the important information in the chapter introduction about the need for institutional affiliation.
Deadline: June 1–August 1
Contact: Eleanor A. Boylston, Executive Director

Dolfinger–McMahon Foundation
c/o Duane, Morris & Heckscher
One Liberty Place
Philadelphia, PA 19103-7396
(215) 979-1768

Description: Grants for social health services or for emergency situations in the Philadelphia area.
$ Given: $499,827 for 89 grants; average range: $1,000–$20,000
Application Information: Write for guidelines; application form not required. See the important information in the chapter introduction about the need for institutional affiliation.
Deadline: April 1, October 1
Contact: Joyce E. Robbins, Executive Secretary

RHODE ISLAND

Citizens Charitable Foundation
c/o Citizens Bank
One Citizens Plaza
Providence, RI 02903
(401) 456-7285

Description: Grants for community development, disadvantaged, or other social services limited to agencies in Rhode Island.
$ Given: $399,250 for 54 grants; average range: $500–$2,500
Application Information: Write for guidelines; send proposal. See the important information in the chapter introduction about the need for institutional affiliation.
Deadline: None, but preferably in June
Contact: D. Faye Sanders, Chair

The Rhode Island Foundation/ The Rhode Island Community Foundation
70 Elm Street
Providence, RI 02903
(401) 274-4564

Description: Grants to improve the living conditions of residents of Rhode Island, including the elderly, and health and social service agencies.
$ Given: $4.8 million for grants; average range: $20–$272,318
Application Information: Write for guidelines; application form not required.
Deadline: None
Contact: Douglas M. Jansson, Executive Director

TENNESSEE

H. W. Durham Foundation
5050 Poplar Avenue
Suite 1522
Memphis, TN 38157
(901) 683-3583

Description: Grants for programs for the elderly, disadvantaged, and health and social services limited to organizations in Memphis.
$ Given: $403,602 for 19 grants; average range: $1,500–$64,101
Application Information: Write letter; application form not required; send five copies of proposal. See the important information in the chapter introduction about the need for institutional affiliation.
Deadline: January 1, April 1, August 1
Contact: Jenks McCrory, Program Director

TEXAS

The Effie and Wofford Cain Foundation
6116 North Central Expressway
Suite 909-LB65
Dallas, TX 75206
(214) 361-4201

Description: Grants for organizations in Texas, for health services, the handicapped, the disadvantaged, and community services.
$ Given: $2 million for 54 grants; average range: $2,000–$500,000
Application Information: Write or call for required application form. See the important information in the chapter introduction about the need for institutional affiliation.
Deadline: August 31
Contact: Harvey L. Walker, Executive Director

The Clark Foundation
6116 North Central Expressway
Suite 906
Dallas, TX 75206
(214) 361-7498

Description: Grants for organizations in Texas, primarily in the Dallas–Fort Worth area, for social services, including programs for the disadvantaged.
$ Given: $100,000 for 9 grants; average range: $10,000–$15,000
Application Information: Write for guidelines; formal application not required, submit proposal. See the important information in the chapter introduction about the need for institutional affiliation.
Deadline: N/A
Contact: Robert H. Middleton, Trustee

VERMONT

The Ben and Jerry's Foundation
c/o Cindy L. Houston
79 Weaver Street
P.O. Box 67
Winooski, VT 05404
(802) 655-6215

Description: Grants for programs serving disadvantaged groups, homelessness, and social change
$ Given: $1.3 million for 23 grants; average range: $27,561–$176,814
Application Information: Write or call for guidelines and application form; three-page proposal required. See the important information in the chapter introduction about the need for institutional affiliation.
Deadline: None
Contact: Robert M. Briem, Associate Director

The Windham Foundation, Inc.
P.O. Box 70
Grafton, VT 05146
(802) 843-2211

Description: Grants for programs for the disadvantaged, youth, and handicapped, as well as for social services, in Vermont, especially Windham County.
$ Given: $212,375 for 127 grants; average range: $100–$5,000
Application Information: Write for guidelines; formal application required. See the important information in the chapter introduction about the need for institutional affiliation.
Deadline: January, April, June, September
Contact: Stephen A. Morse, President

VIRGINIA

Mustard Seed Foundation, Inc.
1001 North 19th Street
Suite 1900
Arlington, VA 22209
(703) 524-5620

Description: Grants and loans "to Christians to relieve human suffering."
$ Given: $150,000 for grants
Application Information: Write for guidelines; formal application and proposal required; a board member must recommend applicant.
Deadline: None
Contact: Craig E. Nauta, Executive Vice President

The Edgar A. Thurman Charitable Foundation for Children
c/o Crestar Bank, N.A.
Tax Services
P.O. Box 27385
Richmond, VA 23261

Description: Grants for children and the disadvantaged with financial needs, youth agencies, and social services in Virginia, especially the Roanoke area.
$ Given: $246,600 for 36 grants; average range: $2,000–$12,000
Application Information: Write for guidelines; formal application required. See the important information in the chapter introduction about the need for institutional affiliation.
Deadline: June 30
Contact: Cam Murchison

WASHINGTON

Comstock Foundation
819 Washington Trust Financial Center
West 717 Sprague Avenue
Spokane, WA 99204
(509) 747-1527

Description: Grants for social service agencies, the disadvantaged, handicapped, and health organizations in Washington State, primarily the Spokane and Inland Empire areas.
$ Given: $804,421 for 54 grants; average range: $300–$35,000
Application Information: Write for guidelines; formal application and proposal required. See the important information in the chapter introduction about the need for institutional affiliation.
Deadline: None
Contact: Horton Herman, Trustee

Glaser Foundation, Inc.
P.O. Box 6548
Bellevue, WA
98008-0548

Description: Grants for health and social service agencies serving individuals with financial needs and children in the Puget Sound area.
$ Given: $270,562 for 50 grants; average range: $3,000–$5,000
Application Information: Write for guidelines; application form and two copies of proposal required. See the important information in the chapter introduction about the need for institutional affiliation.
Deadline: None
Contact: Joanne Van Sickle

WEST VIRGINIA

Clay Foundation, Inc.
1426 Kanawha
Boulevard, East
Charleston, WV 25301
(304) 344-8656

Description: Grants for programs serving the elderly, disadvantaged youth, and their families in West Virginia, especially the Kanawha Valley area.
$ Given: $1.5 million for 26 grants; average range: $10,000–$50,000
Application Information: Write letter; send three copies of proposal. See the important information in the chapter introduction about the need for institutional affiliation.
Deadline: None
Contact: Charles M. Avampato, President

WISCONSIN

Curative Workshop of Oshkosh Wisconsin, Inc.
P.O. Box 1082
Oshkosh, WI
54902-1082
Application Address:
1323 Maricopa
Oshkosh, WI 54904
(414) 231-3088

Description: Grants for social services serving the handicapped or physically injured and individuals with financial needs in Oshkosh.
$ Given: $13,696 for 18 grants; average range: $100–$5,000
Application Information: Write for guidelines. See the important information in the chapter introduction about the need for institutional affiliation.
Deadline: None
Contact: Elizabeth Murken, President

The Gardner Foundation
111 East Wisconsin Avenue
Suite 1359
Milwaukee, WI 53202
(414) 272-0383

Description: Grants for social services, homeless, employment, community development, and health services primarily in the greater Milwaukee area.
$ Given: $103,667 for 52 grants; average range: $1,000–$5,000
Application Information: Application form required; write for guidelines. See the important information in the chapter introduction about the need for institutional affiliation.
Deadline: March, August, November
Contact: Theodore Friedlander, Jr., President

Lindsay Foundation, Inc.
31982 West Treasure Isle Drive
Hartland, WI 53029

Description: Grants for organizations in Wisconsin, for social and health services, and services for the handicapped, disadvantaged, and elderly.
$ Given: $80,000 for 17 grants; average: $5,000
Application Information: Write for guidelines. See the important information in the chapter introduction about the need for institutional affiliation.
Deadline: N/A
Contact: Lorna L. Mayer, President

WYOMING

Tom and Helen Tonkin Foundation
c/o Norwest Bank Wyoming, Casper, N.A.
P.O. Box 2799
Casper, WY 82602
(307) 266-1100

Description: Grants for local youth ages 6–21, particularly those handicapped by illness or injury, or with financial needs, from Wyoming, with emphasis on the Casper area.
$ Given: $103,932 for 25 grants; average range: $1,000–$10,000
Application Information: Application form not required; write letter and proposal. See the important information in the chapter introduction about the need for institutional affiliation.
Deadline: None
Contact: Elona Anderson

Federal Grants

The federal government appropriates hundreds of millions of dollars each year for employment-related grants and job services, mostly through the Department of Labor. The bulk of this money is administered by state employment security offices. There are also special programs and grants for women (through the Women's Bureau—also Department of Labor), for farmers (through the Farmers Home Administration, Department of Agriculture), and for businesspersons (through the Small Business Administration).

ALABAMA

EMPLOYMENT SERVICE

United States Employment Service
Employment and Training Administration, Department of Labor
Washington, DC 20210
(202) 535-0157
Description: Provides placement services for job seekers and employers. These include services to special applicant groups, such as veterans, the handicapped, youth, minority, and older workers; a computerized interstate job listing; and other labor market information.
$ Given: FY 93 est. $821.6 million
Application Information: Contact the Employment Security Department for your state.
Deadline: N/A
Contact: John G. Allen, Director
Department of Industrial Relations
Industrial Relations Building
649 Monroe Street
Montgomery, AL 36130
(205) 261-5386

UNEMPLOYMENT INSURANCE

Unemployment Insurance Service
Employment and Training Administration, Department of Labor
Washington, DC 20210
(202) 523-7831
Description: Provides unemployment insurance for workers whose employers have contributed to state unemployment funds, federal civilian employees, ex-service persons, those who have become unemployed as a result of product imports, and those whose unemployment comes under the purview of a presidentially declared disaster.
$ Given: $25.5 billion for FY 93
Application Information: Contact the Employment Security Department for your state.
Deadline: N/A

Contact: John G. Allen, Director
Department of Industrial Relations
Industrial Relations Building
649 Monroe Street
Montgomery, AL 36130
(205) 261-5386

EMPLOYMENT AND TRAINING ASSISTANCE—DISLOCATED WORKERS

Employment and Training Administration, Department of Labor
200 Constitution Avenue, NW
Washington, DC 20210
(202) 535-0577
Description: Federal grants given to state and local programs to assist workers through training and employment services. These are workers who have been terminated or laid off, or who have received notice of such, and are not likely to return to their previous occupation or industry, or who are long-term unemployed. Targeted individuals include those affected by mass layoffs and natural disasters.
$ Given: Total nationwide of $571.1 million for FY 93
Application Information: Inquire at Employment Security Office listed below.
Deadline: N/A
Contact: John G. Allen, Director
Department of Industrial Relations
Industrial Relations Building
649 Monroe Street
Montgomery, AL 36130
(205) 261-5386

WOMEN'S SPECIAL EMPLOYMENT ASSISTANCE

Office of Administrative Management
Women's Bureau
Room S3305
Office of the Secretary, Department of Labor
Washington, DC 20210
(202) 523-6606
Description: Provides advisory services and counseling, and disseminates technical information to help the employment

opportunities of women—especially in the realm of nontraditional women's jobs and jobs in new technologies.

$ Given: N/A

Application Information: Write to Women's Bureau in your region listed below.

Deadline: N/A

Contact: Delores L. Crockett, Regional Administrator
Region IV, Women's Bureau
Department of Labor
1371 Peachtree Street, NE
Room 323
Atlanta, GA 30367
(404) 347-4461

EMERGENCY LOANS

Farmers Home Administration
Department of Agriculture
14th Street Independence Avenue, SW
Washington, DC 20250
(202) 690-1533

Description: Provides loans to family farmers (either owner or tenant), ranchers, and aquaculture operators to cover losses resulting from natural or other major disasters. Recipients must be unable to obtain credit from other sources.

$ Given: $81.4 million est. FY 92. Average size for FY 92 was est. $42,300.

Application Information: Consult local telephone directory under United States Government, Department of Agriculture, for Farmers Home Administration Office.

Deadline: N/A

Contact: Farmers Home Administration
Aronov Building
Room 717
474 South Court Street
Montgomery, AL 36104
(205) 223-7077

ECONOMIC INJURY DISASTER LOANS

Office of Disaster Assistance
Small Business Administration
409 3rd Street, SW
Washington, DC 20416
(202) 205-6734

Description: Provides loans to small businesses suffering economic damage under presidential, Small Business Administration, and/or Department of Agriculture declared disaster. Must be a small business or agricultural concern, be located within declared disaster area, and be unable to obtain credit elsewhere.

$ Given: $60 million for FY 92. During FY 91, 1,076 loans were made.

Application Information: Refer to local Disaster Area Office of the Small Business Administration.

Deadline: N/A

Contact: Small Business Administration, Region IV
1375 Peachtree Street, NE
Fifth Floor
Atlanta, GA 30367-8102
(404) 347-2797

ALASKA

EMPLOYMENT SERVICE

United States Employment Service
Employment and Training Administration, Department of Labor
Washington, DC 20210
(202) 535-0157

Description: Provides placement services for job seekers and employers. These include services to special applicant groups, such as veterans, the handicapped, youth, minority, and older workers; a computerized interstate job listing; and other labor market information.

$ Given: FY 93 est. $821.6 million

Application Information: Contact the Employment Security Department for your state.

Deadline: N/A

Contact: J. M. Sittion, Director
Employment Security Division
Department of Labor
1111 West 8th Street
P.O. Box 3-7000
Juneau, AK 99802-1218
(907) 465-2712

UNEMPLOYMENT INSURANCE

Unemployment Insurance Service
Employment and Training Administration, Department of Labor
Washington, DC 20210
(202) 523-7831
Description: Provides unemployment insurance for workers whose employers have contributed to state unemployment funds, federal civilian employees, ex-service persons, those who have become unemployed as a result of product imports, and those whose unemployment comes under the purview of a presidentially declared disaster.
$ Given: $25.5 billion for FY 93
Application Information: Contact the Employment Security Department for your state.
Deadline: N/A
Contact: J. M. Sittion, Director
Employment Security Division
Department of Labor
1111 West 8th Street
P.O. Box 3-7000
Juneau, AK 99802-1218
(907) 465-2712

EMPLOYMENT AND TRAINING ASSISTANCE—DISLOCATED WORKERS

Employment and Training Administration, Department of Labor
200 Constitution Avenue, NW
Washington, DC 20210
(202) 535-0577
Description: Federal grants given to state and local programs to assist workers through training and employment services. These are workers who have been terminated or laid off, or who have received notice of such, and are not likely to return to their previous occupation or industry, or who are long-term unemployed. Targeted

individuals include those affected by mass layoffs and natural disasters.

$ Given: Total nationwide of $571.1 million for FY 93

Application Information: Inquire at Employment Security Office listed below.

Deadline: N/A

Contact: J. M. Sittion, Director
Employment Security Division
Department of Labor
1111 West 8th Street
P.O. Box 3-7000
Juneau, AK 99802-1218
(907) 465-2712

WOMEN'S SPECIAL EMPLOYMENT ASSISTANCE

Office of Administrative Management
Women's Bureau
Room S3305
Office of the Secretary, Department of Labor
Washington, DC 20210
(202) 523-6606

Description: Provides advisory services and counseling, and disseminates technical information to help the employment opportunities of women—especially in the realm of nontraditional women's jobs and jobs in new technologies.

$ Given: N/A

Application Information: Write to Women's Bureau in your region listed below.

Deadline: N/A

Contact: Regional Administrator
Region X, Women's Bureau
Department of Labor
1111 Third Avenue
Room 885
Seattle, WA 98101-3211
(206) 553-1534

EMERGENCY LOANS

Farmers Home Administration
Department of Agriculture
14th Street Independence Avenue, SW
Washington, DC 20250
(202) 690-1533
Description: Provides loans to family farmers (either owner or tenant), ranchers, and aquaculture operators to cover losses resulting from natural or other major disasters. Recipients must be unable to obtain credit from other sources.
$ Given: $81.4 million est. FY 92. Average size for FY 92 was est. $42,300.
Application Information: Consult local telephone directory under United States Government, Department of Agriculture, for Farmers Home Administration Office.
Deadline: N/A
Contact: Farmers Home Administration
          634 South Bailey
          Suite 103
          Palmer, AK 99645
          (907) 745-2176

ECONOMIC INJURY DISASTER LOANS

Office of Disaster Assistance
Small Business Administration
409 3rd Street, SW
Washington, DC 20416
(202) 205-6734
Description: Provides loans to small businesses suffering economic damage under presidential, Small Business Administration, and/or Department of Agriculture declared disaster. Must be a small business or agricultural concern, be located within declared disaster area, and be unable to obtain credit elsewhere.
$ Given: $60 million for FY 92. During FY 91, 1,076 loans were made.
Application Information: Refer to local Disaster Area Office of the Small Business Administration.
Deadline: N/A

Contact: Small Business Administration, Region X
2615 4th Avenue
Room 440
Seattle, WA 98121
(206) 442-5676

ARIZONA

EMPLOYMENT SERVICE

United States Employment Service
Employment and Training Administration, Department of Labor
Washington, DC 20210
(202) 535-0157
Description: Provides placement services for job seekers and employers. These include services to special applicant groups, such as veterans, the handicapped, youth, minority, and older workers; a computerized interstate job listing; and other labor market information.
$ Given: FY 93 est. $821.6 million
Application Information: Contact the Employment Security Department for your state.
Deadline: N/A
Contact: Linda Moore-Cannon, Director
Department of Economic Security
1717 West Jefferson Street
P.O. Box 6123
Phoenix, AZ 85007
(602) 542-5678

UNEMPLOYMENT INSURANCE

Unemployment Insurance Service
Employment and Training Administration, Department of Labor
Washington, DC 20210
(202) 523-7831
Description: Provides unemployment insurance for workers whose employers have contributed to state unemployment funds, federal civilian employees, ex-service persons, those who have become unemployed as a result of product imports, and those whose unemployment comes under the purview of a presidentially declared disaster.

$ Given: $25.5 billion for FY 93
Application Information: Contact the Employment Security Department for your state.
Deadline: N/A
Contact: Linda Moore-Cannon, Director
              Department of Economic Security
              1717 West Jefferson Street
              P.O. Box 6123
              Phoenix, AZ 85007
              (602) 542-5678

EMPLOYMENT AND TRAINING ASSISTANCE—DISLOCATED WORKERS

Employment and Training Administration, Department of Labor
200 Constitution Avenue, NW
Washington, DC 20210
(202) 535-0577
Description: Federal grants given to state and local programs to assist workers through training and employment services. These are workers who have been terminated or laid off, or who have received notice of such, and are not likely to return to their previous occupation or industry, or who are long-term unemployed. Targeted individuals include those affected by mass layoffs and natural disasters.
$ Given: Total nationwide of $571.1 million for FY 93
Application Information: Inquire at Employment Security Office listed below.
Deadline: N/A
Contact: Linda Moore-Cannon, Director
              Department of Economic Security
              1717 West Jefferson Street
              P.O. Box 6123
              Phoenix, AZ 85007
              (602) 542-5678

WOMEN'S SPECIAL EMPLOYMENT ASSISTANCE

Office of Administrative Management
Women's Bureau
Room S3305
Office of the Secretary, Department of Labor
Washington, DC 20210
(202) 523-6606
Description: Provides advisory services and counseling, and disseminates technical information to help the employment opportunities of women—especially in the realm of nontraditional women's jobs and jobs in new technologies.
$ Given: N/A
Application Information: Write to Women's Bureau in your region listed below.
Deadline: N/A
Contact: Madeline Mixer, Regional Administrator
Region IX, Women's Bureau
Department of Labor
71 Stevenson Street
Room 927
San Francisco, CA 94105
(415) 774-6679

EMERGENCY LOANS

Farmers Home Administration
Department of Agriculture
14th Street Independence Avenue, SW
Washington, DC 20250
(202) 690-1533
Description: Provides loans to family farmers (either owner or tenant), ranchers, and aquaculture operators to cover losses resulting from natural or other major disasters. Recipients must be unable to obtain credit from other sources.
$ Given: $81.4 million est. FY 92. Average size for FY 92 was est. $42,300.
Application Information: Consult local telephone directory under United States Government, Department of Agriculture, for Farmers Home Administration Office.
Deadline: N/A

Contact: Farmers Home Administration
201 East Indianola
Suite 275
Phoenix, AZ 85012
(602) 640-5086

ECONOMIC INJURY DISASTER LOANS

Office of Disaster Assistance
Small Business Administration
409 3rd Street, SW
Washington, DC 20416
(202) 205-6734
Description: Provides loans to small businesses suffering economic damage under presidential, Small Business Administration, and/or Department of Agriculture declared disaster. Must be a small business or agricultural concern, be located within declared disaster area, and be unable to obtain credit elsewhere.
$ Given: $60 million for FY 92. During FY 91, 1,076 loans were made.
Application Information: Refer to local Disaster Area Office of the Small Business Administration.
Deadline: N/A
Contact: Small Business Administration, Region IX
71 Stevenson Street
Twentieth Floor
San Francisco, CA 94105-2939
(415) 744-6402

ARKANSAS

EMPLOYMENT SERVICE

United States Employment Service
Employment and Training Administration, Department of Labor
Washington, DC 20210
(202) 535-0157
Description: Provides placement services for job seekers and employers. These include services to special applicant groups, such as veterans, the handicapped, youth, minority, and older workers; a computerized interstate job listing; and other labor market information.

$ Given: FY 93 est. $821.6 million
Application Information: Contact the Employment Security Department for your state.
Deadline: N/A
Contact: William D. Gaddy, Administrator
Arkansas Employment Security Division
P.O. Box 2981
Capitol Mall
Little Rock, AR 72203-2981
(501) 682-2121

UNEMPLOYMENT INSURANCE

Unemployment Insurance Service
Employment and Training Administration, Department of Labor
Washington, DC 20210
(202) 523-7831
Description: Provides unemployment insurance for workers whose employers have contributed to state unemployment funds, federal civilian employees, ex-service persons, those who have become unemployed as a result of product imports, and those whose unemployment comes under the purview of a presidentially declared disaster.
$ Given: $25.5 billion for FY 93
Application Information: Contact the Employment Security Department for your state.
Deadline: N/A
Contact: William D. Gaddy, Administrator
Arkansas Employment Security Division
P.O. Box 2981
Capitol Mall
Little Rock, AR 72203-2981
(501) 682-2121

EMPLOYMENT AND TRAINING ASSISTANCE—DISLOCATED WORKERS

Employment and Training Administration, Department of Labor
200 Constitution Avenue, NW
Washington, DC 20210
(202) 535-0577
Description: Federal grants given to state and local programs to assist workers through training and employment services. These are workers who have been terminated or laid off, or who have received

notice of such, and are not likely to return to their previous occupation or industry, or who are long-term unemployed. Targeted individuals include those affected by mass layoffs and natural disasters.

$ Given: Total nationwide of $571.1 million for FY 93

Application Information: Inquire at Employment Security Office listed below.

Deadline: N/A

Contact: William D. Gaddy, Administrator
Arkansas Employment Security Division
P.O. Box 2981
Capitol Mall
Little Rock, AR 72203-2981
(501) 682-2121

WOMEN'S SPECIAL EMPLOYMENT ASSISTANCE

Office of Administrative Management
Women's Bureau
Room S3305
Office of the Secretary, Department of Labor
Washington, DC 20210
(202) 523-6606

Description: Provides advisory services and counseling, and disseminates technical information to help the employment opportunities of women—especially in the realm of nontraditional women's jobs and jobs in new technologies.

$ Given: N/A

Application Information: Write to Women's Bureau in your region listed below.

Deadline: N/A

Contact: Evelyn Smith, Regional Administrator
Region VI, Women's Bureau
Department of Labor
Federal Building
Suite 731
525 Griffin Street
Dallas, TX 75202
(214) 767-6985

EMERGENCY LOANS
Farmers Home Administration
Department of Agriculture
14th Street Independence Avenue, SW
Washington, DC 20250
(202) 690-1533
Description: Provides loans to family farmers (either owner or tenant), ranchers, and aquaculture operators to cover losses resulting from natural or other major disasters. Recipients must be unable to obtain credit from other sources.
$ Given: $81.4 million est. FY 92. Average size for FY 92 was est. $42,300.
Application Information: Consult local telephone directory under United States Government, Department of Agriculture, for Farmers Home Administration Office.
Deadline: N/A
Contact: Farmers Home Administration
700 West Capitol
P.O. Box 72203
Little Rock, AR 72203
(501) 324-6281

ECONOMIC INJURY DISASTER LOANS
Office of Disaster Assistance
Small Business Administration
409 3rd Street, SW
Washington, DC 20416
(202) 205-6734
Description: Provides loans to small businesses suffering economic damage under presidential, Small Business Administration, and/or Department of Agriculture declared disaster. Must be a small business or agricultural concern, be located within declared disaster area, and be unable to obtain credit elsewhere.
$ Given: $60 million for FY 92. During FY 91, 1,076 loans were made.
Application Information: Refer to local Disaster Area Office of the Small Business Administration.
Deadline: N/A
Contact: Federal Information Center
(800) 366-2998 in Little Rock

UNEMPLOYMENT INSURANCE

Unemployment Insurance Service
Employment and Training Administration, Department of Labor
Washington, DC 20210
(202) 523-7831
Description: Provides unemployment insurance for workers whose employers have contributed to state unemployment funds, federal civilian employees, ex-service persons, those who have become unemployed as a result of product imports, and those whose unemployment comes under the purview of a presidentially declared disaster.
$ Given: $25.5 billion for FY 93
Application Information: Contact the Employment Security Department for your state.
Deadline: N/A
Contact: James A. Davenport, Commissioner
Department of Employment Security
Volunteer Plaza Building
Twelfth Floor
500 James Robertson Parkway
Nashville, TN 37245-0001
(615) 741-2131

CALIFORNIA

EMPLOYMENT SERVICE

United States Employment Service
Employment and Training Administration, Department of Labor
Washington, DC 20210
(202) 535-0157
Description: Provides placement services for job seekers and employers. These include services to special applicant groups, such as veterans, the handicapped, youth, minority, and older workers; a computerized interstate job listing; and other labor market information.
$ Given: FY 93 est. $821.6 million
Application Information: Contact the Employment Security Department for your state.
Deadline: N/A

Contact: Alice J. Gonzales, Director
Employment Development Department
800 Capitol Mall
P.O. Box 942880
Sacramento, CA 94280-0001
(916) 445-9212

UNEMPLOYMENT INSURANCE

Unemployment Insurance Service
Employment and Training Administration, Department of Labor
Washington, DC 20210
(202) 523-7831
Description: Provides unemployment insurance for workers whose employers have contributed to state unemployment funds, federal civilian employees, ex-service persons, those who have become unemployed as a result of product imports, and those whose unemployment comes under the purview of a presidentially declared disaster.
$ Given: $25.5 billion for FY 93
Application Information: Contact the Employment Security Department for your state.
Deadline: N/A
Contact: Alice J. Gonzales, Director
Employment Development Department
800 Capitol Mall
P.O. Box 942880
Sacramento, CA 94280-0001
(916) 445-9212

EMPLOYMENT AND TRAINING ASSISTANCE—DISLOCATED WORKERS

Employment and Training Administration, Department of Labor
200 Constitution Avenue, NW
Washington, DC 20210
(202) 535-0577
Description: Federal grants given to state and local programs to assist workers through training and employment services. These are workers who have been terminated or laid off, or who have received notice of such, and are not likely to return to their previous occupation or industry, or who are long-term unemployed. Targeted individuals include those affected by mass layoffs and natural disasters.

$ Given: Total nationwide of $571.1 million for FY 93
Application Information: Inquire at Employment Security Office
listed below.
Deadline: N/A
Contact: Alice J. Gonzales, Director
Employment Development Department
800 Capitol Mall
P.O. Box 942880
Sacramento, CA 94280-0001
(916) 445-9212

WOMEN'S SPECIAL EMPLOYMENT ASSISTANCE

Office of Administrative Management
Women's Bureau
Room S3305
Office of the Secretary, Department of Labor
Washington, DC 20210
(202) 523-6606
Description: Provides advisory services and counseling, and
disseminates technical information to help the employment
opportunities of women—especially in the realm of nontraditional
women's jobs and jobs in new technologies.
$ Given: N/A
Application Information: Write to Women's Bureau in your region
listed below.
Deadline: N/A
Contact: Madeline Mixer, Regional Administrator
Region IX, Women's Bureau
Department of Labor
71 Stevenson Street
Room 927
San Francisco, CA 94105
(415) 774-6679

EMERGENCY LOANS

Farmers Home Administration
Department of Agriculture
14th Street Independence Avenue, SW
Washington, DC 20250
(202) 690-1533
Description: Provides loans to family farmers (either owner or
tenant), ranchers, and aquaculture operators to cover losses

resulting from natural or other major disasters. Recipients must be unable to obtain credit from other sources.
$ Given: $81.4 million est. FY 92. Average size for FY 92 was est. $42,300.
Application Information: Consult local telephone directory under United States Government, Department of Agriculture, for Farmers Home Administration Office.
Deadline: N/A
Contact: Farmers Home Administration
194 West Main Street
Suite F
Woodland, CA 95695-2915
(916) 666-3382

ECONOMIC INJURY DISASTER LOANS

Office of Disaster Assistance
Small Business Administration
409 3rd Street, SW
Washington, DC 20416
(202) 205-6734
Description: Provides loans to small businesses suffering economic damage under presidential, Small Business Administration, and/or Department of Agriculture declared disaster. Must be a small business or agricultural concern, be located within declared disaster area, and be unable to obtain credit elsewhere.
$ Given: $60 million for FY 92. During FY 91, 1,076 loans were made.
Application Information: Refer to local Disaster Area Office of the Small Business Administration.
Deadline: N/A
Contact: Small Business Administration, Region IX
71 Stevenson Street
Twentieth Floor
San Francisco, CA 94105-2939
(415) 744-6402

COLORADO

EMPLOYMENT SERVICE

United States Employment Service
Employment and Training Administration, Department of Labor
Washington, DC 20210
(202) 535-0157
Description: Provides placement services for job seekers and employers. These include services to special applicant groups, such as veterans, the handicapped, youth, minority, and older workers; a computerized interstate job listing; and other labor market information.
$ Given: FY 93 est. $821.6 million
Application Information: Contact the Employment Security Department for your state.
Deadline: N/A
Contact: Luis Sepulveda
  Department of Labor and Employment Training
  1961 Stout Street
  Room 1668
  Denver, CO 80294
  (303) 844-4401

EMERGENCY LOANS

Farmers Home Administration
Department of Agriculture
14th Street Independence Avenue, SW
Washington, DC 20250
(202) 690-1533
Description: Provides loans to family farmers (either owner or tenant), ranchers, and aquaculture operators to cover losses resulting from natural or other major disasters. Recipients must be unable to obtain credit from other sources.
$ Given: $81.4 million est. FY 92. Average size for FY 92 was est. $42,300.
Application Information: Consult local telephone directory under United States Government, Department of Agriculture, for Farmers Home Administration Office.
Deadline: N/A

Contact: Home Farmers Administration
655 Parfet Street
Room E-100
Lakewood, CO 80215
(303) 236-2801

ECONOMIC INJURY DISASTER LOANS

Office of Disaster Assistance
Small Business Administration
409 3rd Street, SW
Washington, DC 20416
(202) 205-6734
Description: Provides loans to small businesses suffering economic damage under presidential, Small Business Administration, and/or Department of Agriculture declared disaster. Must be a small business or agricultural concern, be located within declared disaster area, and be unable to obtain credit elsewhere.
$ Given: $60 million for FY 92. During FY 91, 1,076 loans were made.
Application Information: Refer to local Disaster Area Office of the Small Business Administration.
Deadline: N/A
Contact: Small Business Administration, Region VIII
999 18th Street
Suite 701
Denver, CO 80202
(303) 294-7001

CONNECTICUT

EMPLOYMENT SERVICE

United States Employment Service
Employment and Training Administration, Department of Labor
Washington, DC 20210
(202) 535-0157
Description: Provides placement services for job seekers and employers. These include services to special applicant groups, such as veterans, the handicapped, youth, minority, and older workers; a computerized interstate job listing; and other labor market information.

$ Given: FY 93 est. $821.6 million
Application Information: Contact the Employment Security
Department for your state.
Deadline: N/A
Contact: John C. Souchuns, Executive Director
Connecticut Labor Department
Employment Security Division
200 Folly Brook Boulevard
Wethersfield, CT 06109
(203) 566-4280

UNEMPLOYMENT INSURANCE
Unemployment Insurance Service
Employment and Training Administration, Department of Labor
Washington, DC 20210
(202) 523-7831
Description: Provides unemployment insurance for workers whose
employers have contributed to state unemployment funds, federal
civilian employees, ex-service persons, those who have become
unemployed as a result of product imports, and those whose
unemployment comes under the purview of a presidentially declared
disaster.
$ Given: $25.5 billion for FY 93
Application Information: Contact the Employment Security
Department for your state.
Deadline: N/A
Contact: John C. Souchuns, Executive Director
Connecticut Labor Department
Employment Security Division
200 Folly Brook Boulevard
Wethersfield, CT 06109
(203) 566-4280

EMPLOYMENT AND TRAINING ASSISTANCE—DISLOCATED WORKERS
Employment and Training Administration, Department of Labor
200 Constitution Avenue, NW
Washington, DC 20210
(202) 535-0577
Description: Federal grants given to state and local programs to
assist workers through training and employment services. These are
workers who have been terminated or laid off, or who have received

notice of such, and are not likely to return to their previous occupation or industry, or who are long-term unemployed. Targeted individuals include those affected by mass layoffs and natural disasters.

$ Given: Total nationwide of $571.1 million for FY 93

Application Information: Inquire at Employment Security Office listed below.

Deadline: N/A

Contact: John C. Souchuns, Executive Director
Connecticut Labor Department
Employment Security Division
200 Folly Brook Boulevard
Wethersfield, CT 06109
(203) 566-4280

WOMEN'S SPECIAL EMPLOYMENT ASSISTANCE

Office of Administrative Management
Women's Bureau
Room S3305
Office of the Secretary, Department of Labor
Washington, DC 20210
(202) 523-6606

Description: Provides advisory services and counseling, and disseminates technical information to help the employment opportunities of women—especially in the realm of nontraditional women's jobs and jobs in new technologies.

$ Given: N/A

Application Information: Write to Women's Bureau in your region listed below.

Deadline: N/A

Contact: Martha Izzi, Regional Administrator
Region I, Women's Bureau
Department of Labor
One Congress Street
Boston, MA 02214
(617) 565-1988

EMERGENCY LOANS

Farmers Home Administration
Department of Agriculture
14th Street Independence Avenue, SW
Washington, DC 20250
(202) 690-1533
Description: Provides loans to family farmers (either owner or tenant), ranchers, and aquaculture operators to cover losses resulting from natural or other major disasters. Recipients must be unable to obtain credit from other sources.
$ Given: $81.4 million est. FY 92. Average size for FY 92 was est. $42,300.
Application Information: Consult local telephone directory under United States Government, Department of Agriculture, for Farmers Home Administration Office.
Deadline: N/A
Contact:　Farmers Home Administration
　　　　　451 West Street
　　　　　Amherst, MA 01002
　　　　　(413) 253-4300

ECONOMIC INJURY DISASTER LOANS

Office of Disaster Assistance
Small Business Administration
409 3rd Street, SW
Washington, DC 20416
(202) 205-6734
Description: Provides loans to small businesses suffering economic damage under presidential, Small Business Administration, and/or Department of Agriculture declared disaster. Must be a small business or agricultural concern, be located within declared disaster area, and be unable to obtain credit elsewhere.
$ Given: $60 million for FY 92. During FY 91, 1,076 loans were made.
Application Information: Refer to local Disaster Area Office of the Small Business Administration.
Deadline: N/A
Contact:　Small Business Administration, Region I
　　　　　155 Federal Street
　　　　　Ninth Floor
　　　　　Boston, MA 02110

DELAWARE

EMPLOYMENT SERVICE

United States Employment Service
Employment and Training Administration, Department of Labor
Washington, DC 20210
(202) 535-0157
Description: Provides placement services for job seekers and employers. These include services to special applicant groups, such as veterans, the handicapped, youth, minority, and older workers; a computerized interstate job listing; and other labor market information.
$ Given: FY 93 est. $821.6 million
Application Information: Contact the Employment Security Department for your state.
Deadline: N/A
Contact: Jan E. Robinson
                Secretary of Labor
                Department of Labor
                State Office Building
                820 North French Street
                Wilmington, DE 19801
                (302) 577-2710

UNEMPLOYMENT INSURANCE

Unemployment Insurance Service
Employment and Training Administration, Department of Labor
Washington, DC 20210
(202) 523-7831
Description: Provides unemployment insurance for workers whose employers have contributed to state unemployment funds, federal civilian employees, ex-service persons, those who have become unemployed as a result of product imports, and those whose unemployment comes under the purview of a presidentially declared disaster.
$ Given: $25.5 billion for FY 93
Application Information: Contact the Employment Security Department for your state.
Deadline: N/A

Contact: Jan E. Robinson
Secretary of Labor
Department of Labor
State Office Building
820 North French Street
Wilmington, DE 19801
(302) 577-2710

EMPLOYMENT AND TRAINING ASSISTANCE—DISLOCATED WORKERS

Employment and Training Administration, Department of Labor
200 Constitution Avenue, NW
Washington, DC 20210
(202) 535-0577
Description: Federal grants given to state and local programs to assist workers through training and employment services. These are workers who have been terminated or laid off, or who have received notice of such, and are not likely to return to their previous occupation or industry, or who are long-term unemployed. Targeted individuals include those affected by mass layoffs and natural disasters.
$ Given: Total nationwide of $571.1 million for FY 93
Application Information: Inquire at Employment Security Office listed below.
Deadline: N/A
Contact: Jan E. Robinson
Secretary of Labor
Department of Labor
State Office Building
820 North French Street
Wilmington, DE 19801
(302) 577-2710

WOMEN'S SPECIAL EMPLOYMENT ASSISTANCE

Office of Administrative Management
Women's Bureau
Room S3305
Office of the Secretary, Department of Labor
Washington, DC 20210
(202) 523-6606
Description: Provides advisory services and counseling, and disseminates technical information to help the employment

opportunities of women—especially in the realm of nontraditional women's jobs and jobs in new technologies.

$ Given: N/A

Application Information: Write to Women's Bureau in your region listed below.

Deadline: N/A

Contact: Regional Administrator
Region III, Women's Bureau
Department of Labor
Gateway Building
Room 13280
3535 Market Street
Philadelphia, PA 19104
(215) 596-1184

EMERGENCY LOANS

Farmers Home Administration
Department of Agriculture
14th Street Independence Avenue, SW
Washington, DC 20250
(202) 690-1533

Description: Provides loans to family farmers (either owner or tenant), ranchers, and aquaculture operators to cover losses resulting from natural or other major disasters. Recipients must be unable to obtain credit from other sources.

$ Given: $81.4 million est. FY 92. Average size for FY 92 was est. $42,300.

Application Information: Consult local telephone directory under United States Government, Department of Agriculture, for Farmers Home Administration Office.

Deadline: N/A

Contact: Farmers Home Administration
4611 South Dupont Highway
P.O. Box 400
Camden, DE 19934-9998
(302) 697-4300

ECONOMIC INJURY DISASTER LOANS

Office of Disaster Assistance
Small Business Administration
409 3rd Street, SW
Washington, DC 20416
(202) 205-6734
Description: Provides loans to small businesses suffering economic damage under presidential, Small Business Administration, and/or Department of Agriculture declared disaster. Must be a small business or agricultural concern, be located within declared disaster area, and be unable to obtain credit elsewhere.
$ Given: $60 million for FY 92. During FY 91, 1,076 loans were made.
Application Information: Refer to local Disaster Area Office of the Small Business Administration.
Deadline: N/A
Contact: Small Business Administration, Region III
475 Allendale Road
Suite 201
King of Prussia, PA 19406
(215) 962-3700

DISTRICT OF COLUMBIA

EMPLOYMENT SERVICE

United States Employment Service
Employment and Training Administration, Department of Labor
Washington, DC 20210
(202) 535-0157
Description: Provides placement services for job seekers and employers. These include services to special applicant groups, such as veterans, the handicapped, youth, minority, and older workers; a computerized interstate job listing; and other labor market information.
$ Given: FY 93 est. $821.6 million
Application Information: Contact the Employment Security Department for your state.
Deadline: N/A

Contact: Maria Borrero, Director
Department of Employment Services
Department of Labor
500 C Street, NW
Room 600
Washington, DC 20001
(202) 639-1000

UNEMPLOYMENT INSURANCE

Unemployment Insurance Service
Employment and Training Administration, Department of Labor
Washington, DC 20210
(202) 523-7831
Description: Provides unemployment insurance for workers whose employers have contributed to state unemployment funds, federal civilian employees, ex-service persons, those who have become unemployed as a result of product imports, and those whose unemployment comes under the purview of a presidentially declared disaster.
$ Given: $25.5 billion for FY 93
Application Information: Contact the Employment Security Department for your state.
Deadline: N/A
Contact: Maria Borrero, Director
Department of Employment Services
Department of Labor
500 C Street, NW
Room 600
Washington, DC 20001
(202) 639-1000

EMPLOYMENT AND TRAINING ASSISTANCE—DISLOCATED WORKERS

Employment and Training Administration, Department of Labor
200 Constitution Avenue, NW
Washington, DC 20210
(202) 535-0577
Description: Federal grants given to state and local programs to assist workers through training and employment services. These are workers who have been terminated or laid off, or who have received notice of such, and are not likely to return to their previous occupation or industry, or who are long-term unemployed. Targeted

individuals include those affected by mass layoffs and natural disasters.

$ Given: Total nationwide of $571.1 million for FY 93

Application Information: Inquire at Employment Security Office listed below.

Deadline: N/A

Contact: Maria Borrero, Director
Department of Employment Services
Department of Labor
500 C Street, NW
Room 600
Washington, DC 20001
(202) 639-1000

WOMEN'S SPECIAL EMPLOYMENT ASSISTANCE

Office of Administrative Management
Women's Bureau
Room S3305
Office of the Secretary, Department of Labor
Washington, DC 20210
(202) 523-6606

Description: Provides advisory services and counseling, and disseminates technical information to help the employment opportunities of women—especially in the realm of nontraditional women's jobs and jobs in new technologies.

$ Given: N/A

Application Information: Write to Women's Bureau in your region listed below.

Deadline: N/A

Contact: Regional Administrator
Region III, Women's Bureau
Department of Labor
Gateway Building
Room 13280
3535 Market Street
Philadelphia, PA 19104
(215) 596-1184

EMERGENCY LOANS

Farmers Home Administration
Department of Agriculture
14th Street Independence Avenue, SW
Washington, DC 20250
(202) 690-1533
Description: Provides loans to family farmers (either owner or tenant), ranchers, and aquaculture operators to cover losses resulting from natural or other major disasters. Recipients must be unable to obtain credit from other sources.
$ Given: $81.4 million est. FY 92. Average size for FY 92 was est. $42,300.
Application Information: Consult local telephone directory under United States Government, Department of Agriculture, for Farmers Home Administration Office.
Deadline: N/A
Contact: Farmers Home Administration
               4611 South Dupont Highway
               P.O. Box 400
               Camden, DE 19934-9998
               (302) 697-4300

ECONOMIC INJURY DISASTER LOANS

Office of Disaster Assistance
Small Business Administration
409 3rd Street, SW
Washington, DC 20416
(202) 205-6734
Description: Provides loans to small businesses suffering economic damage under presidential, Small Business Administration, and/or Department of Agriculture declared disaster. Must be a small business or agricultural concern, be located within declared disaster area, and be unable to obtain credit elsewhere.
$ Given: $60 million for FY 92. During FY 91, 1,076 loans were made.
Application Information: Refer to local Disaster Area Office of the Small Business Administration.
Deadline: N/A

Contact: Small Business Administration, Region III
475 Allendale Road
Suite 201
King of Prussia, PA 19406
(215) 962-3700

FLORIDA

EMPLOYMENT SERVICE

United States Employment Service
Employment and Training Administration, Department of Labor
Washington, DC 20210
(202) 535-0157
Description: Provides placement services for job seekers and employers. These include services to special applicant groups, such as veterans, the handicapped, youth, minority, and older workers; a computerized interstate job listing; and other labor market information.
$ Given: FY 93 est. $821.6 million
Application Information: Contact the Employment Security Department for your state.
Deadline: N/A
Contact: Frank Scruggs, Secretary
Department of Labor and Employment Security
2012 Capitol Circle SE
Hartman Building
Suite 303
Tallahassee, FL 32399-2152
(904) 488-4398

UNEMPLOYMENT INSURANCE

Unemployment Insurance Service
Employment and Training Administration, Department of Labor
Washington, DC 20210
(202) 523-7831
Description: Provides unemployment insurance for workers whose employers have contributed to state unemployment funds, federal civilian employees, ex-service persons, those who have become unemployed as a result of product imports, and those whose unemployment comes under the purview of a presidentially declared disaster.

$ Given: $25.5 billion for FY 93
Application Information: Contact the Employment Security
Department for your state.
Deadline: N/A
Contact: Frank Scruggs, Secretary
Department of Labor and Employment Security
2012 Capitol Circle SE
Hartman Building
Suite 303
Tallahassee, FL 32399-2152
(904) 488-4398

EMPLOYMENT AND TRAINING ASSISTANCE—DISLOCATED WORKERS

Employment and Training Administration, Department of Labor
200 Constitution Avenue, NW
Washington, DC 20210
(202) 535-0577
Description: Federal grants given to state and local programs to
assist workers through training and employment services. These are
workers who have been terminated or laid off, or who have received
notice of such, and are not likely to return to their previous
occupation or industry, or who are long-term unemployed. Targeted
individuals include those affected by mass layoffs and natural
disasters.
$ Given: Total nationwide of $571.1 million for FY 93
Application Information: Inquire at Employment Security Office
listed below.
Deadline: N/A
Contact: Frank Scruggs, Secretary
Department of Labor and Employment Security
2012 Capitol Circle SE
Hartman Building
Suite 303
Tallahassee, FL 32399-2152
(904) 488-4398

WOMEN'S SPECIAL EMPLOYMENT ASSISTANCE

Office of Administrative Management
Women's Bureau
Room S3305
Office of the Secretary, Department of Labor
Washington, DC 20210
(202) 523-6606
Description: Provides advisory services and counseling, and disseminates technical information to help the employment opportunities of women—especially in the realm of nontraditional women's jobs and jobs in new technologies.
$ Given: N/A
Application Information: Write to Women's Bureau in your region listed below.
Deadline: N/A
Contact: Delores L. Crockett, Regional Administrator
                Region IV, Women's Bureau
                Department of Labor
                1371 Peachtree Street, NE
                Room 323
                Atlanta, GA 30367
                (404) 347-4461

EMERGENCY LOANS

Farmers Home Administration
Department of Agriculture
14th Street Independence Avenue, SW
Washington, DC 20250
(202) 690-1533
Description: Provides loans to family farmers (either owner or tenant), ranchers, and aquaculture operators to cover losses resulting from natural or other major disasters. Recipients must be unable to obtain credit from other sources.
$ Given: $81.4 million est. FY 92. Average size for FY 92 was est. $42,300.
Application Information: Consult local telephone directory under United States Government, Department of Agriculture, for Farmers Home Administration Office.
Deadline: N/A

Contact: Farmers Home Administration
Federal Building
4440 NW 25th Place
P.O. Box 147010
Gainesville, FL 32614-7010
(904) 338-3400

ECONOMIC INJURY DISASTER LOANS

Office of Disaster Assistance
Small Business Administration
409 3rd Street, SW
Washington, DC 20416
(202) 205-6734

Description: Provides loans to small businesses suffering economic damage under presidential, Small Business Administration, and/or Department of Agriculture declared disaster. Must be a small business or agricultural concern, be located within declared disaster area, and be unable to obtain credit elsewhere.

$ Given: $60 million for FY 92. During FY 91, 1,076 loans were made.

Application Information: Refer to local Disaster Area Office of the Small Business Administration.

Deadline: N/A

Contact: Small Business Administration, Region IV
1375 Peachtree Street, NE
Fifth Floor
Atlanta, GA 30367-8102
(404) 347-2797

GEORGIA

EMPLOYMENT SERVICE

United States Employment Service
Employment and Training Administration, Department of Labor
Washington, DC 20210
(202) 535-0157

Description: Provides placement services for job seekers and employers. These include services to special applicant groups, such as veterans, the handicapped, youth, minority, and older workers; a computerized interstate job listing; and other labor market information.

$ Given: FY 93 est. $821.6 million

Application Information: Contact the Employment Security Department for your state.

Deadline: N/A

Contact: Al Scott, Commissioner
Department of Labor
Employment Security Agency
Sussex Place
148 International Boulevard, NE
Atlanta, GA 30303
(404) 656-3011

UNEMPLOYMENT INSURANCE

Unemployment Insurance Service
Employment and Training Administration, Department of Labor
Washington, DC 20210
(202) 523-7831

Description: Provides unemployment insurance for workers whose employers have contributed to state unemployment funds, federal civilian employees, ex-service persons, those who have become unemployed as a result of product imports, and those whose unemployment comes under the purview of a presidentially declared disaster.

$ Given: $25.5 billion for FY 93

Application Information: Contact the Employment Security Department for your state.

Deadline: N/A

Contact: Al Scott, Commissioner
Department of Labor
Employment Security Agency
Sussex Place
148 International Boulevard, NE
Atlanta, GA 30303
(404) 656-3011

EMPLOYMENT AND TRAINING ASSISTANCE—DISLOCATED WORKERS

Employment and Training Administration, Department of Labor
200 Constitution Avenue, NW
Washington, DC 20210
(202) 535-0577

Description: Federal grants given to state and local programs to assist workers through training and employment services. These are workers who have been terminated or laid off, or who have received notice of such, and are not likely to return to their previous occupation or industry, or who are long-term unemployed. Targeted individuals include those affected by mass layoffs and natural disasters.

$ Given: Total nationwide of $571.1 million for FY 93

Application Information: Inquire at Employment Security Office listed below.

Deadline: N/A

Contact: Al Scott, Commissioner
Department of Labor
Employment Security Agency
Sussex Place
148 International Boulevard, NE
Atlanta, GA 30303
(404) 656-3011

WOMEN'S SPECIAL EMPLOYMENT ASSISTANCE

Office of Administrative Management
Women's Bureau
Room S3305
Office of the Secretary, Department of Labor
Washington, DC 20210
(202) 523-6606

Description: Provides advisory services and counseling, and disseminates technical information to help the employment opportunities of women—especially in the realm of nontraditional women's jobs and jobs in new technologies.

$ Given: N/A

Application Information: Write to Women's Bureau in your region listed below.

Deadline: N/A

Contact: Delores L. Crockett, Regional Administrator
Region IV, Women's Bureau
Department of Labor
1371 Peachtree Street, NE
Room 323
Atlanta, GA 30367
(404) 347-4461

EMERGENCY LOANS

Farmers Home Administration
Department of Agriculture
14th Street Independence Avenue, SW
Washington, DC 20250
(202) 690-1533
Description: Provides loans to family farmers (either owner or tenant), ranchers, and aquaculture operators to cover losses resulting from natural or other major disasters. Recipients must be unable to obtain credit from other sources.
$ Given: $81.4 million est. FY 92. Average size for FY 92 was est. $42,300.
Application Information: Consult local telephone directory under United States Government, Department of Agriculture, for Farmers Home Administration Office.
Deadline: N/A
Contact: Farmers Home Administration
355 East Hancock Avenue
Stephens Federal Building
Athens, GA 30610
(404) 546-2162

ECONOMIC INJURY DISASTER LOANS

Office of Disaster Assistance
Small Business Administration
409 3rd Street, SW
Washington, DC 20416
(202) 205-6734
Description: Provides loans to small businesses suffering economic damage under presidential, Small Business Administration, and/or Department of Agriculture declared disaster. Must be a small business or agricultural concern, be located within declared disaster area, and be unable to obtain credit elsewhere.

$ Given: $60 million for FY 92. During FY 91, 1,076 loans were made.
Application Information: Refer to local Disaster Area Office of the Small Business Administration.
Deadline: N/A
Contact: Small Business Administration, Region IV
1375 Peachtree Street, NE
Fifth Floor
Atlanta, GA 30367-8102
(404) 347-2797

GUAM

EMPLOYMENT SERVICE
United States Employment Service
Employment and Training Administration, Department of Labor
Washington, DC 20210
(202) 535-0157
Description: Provides placement services for job seekers and employers. These include services to special applicant groups, such as veterans, the handicapped, youth, minority, and older workers; a computerized interstate job listing; and other labor market information.
$ Given: FY 93 est. $821.6 million
Application Information: Contact the Employment Security Department for your state.
Deadline: N/A
Contact: Edward Guerrero, Director
Department of Labor
P.O. Box 2950 GMF
Agana, GU 96910
(671) 477-9821

UNEMPLOYMENT INSURANCE
Unemployment Insurance Service
Employment and Training Administration, Department of Labor
Washington, DC 20210
(202) 523-7831
Description: Provides unemployment insurance for workers whose employers have contributed to state unemployment funds, federal civilian employees, ex-service persons, those who have become unemployed as a result of product imports, and those whose

unemployment comes under the purview of a presidentially declared disaster.

$ Given: $25.5 billion for FY 93

Application Information: Contact the Employment Security Department for your state.

Deadline: N/A

Contact: Edward Guerrero, Director
Department of Labor
P.O. Box 2950 GMF
Agana, GU 96910
(671) 477-9821

EMPLOYMENT AND TRAINING ASSISTANCE—DISLOCATED WORKERS

Employment and Training Administration, Department of Labor
200 Constitution Avenue, NW
Washington, DC 20210
(202) 535-0577

Description: Federal grants given to state and local programs to assist workers through training and employment services. These are workers who have been terminated or laid off, or who have received notice of such, and are not likely to return to their previous occupation or industry, or who are long-term unemployed. Targeted individuals include those affected by mass layoffs and natural disasters.

$ Given: Total nationwide of $571.1 million for FY 93

Application Information: Inquire at Employment Security Office listed below.

Deadline: N/A

Contact: Edward Guerrero, Director
Department of Labor
P.O. Box 2950 GMF
Agana, GU 96910
(671) 477-9821

WOMEN'S SPECIAL EMPLOYMENT ASSISTANCE

Office of Administrative Management
Women's Bureau
Room S3305
Office of the Secretary, Department of Labor
Washington, DC 20210
(202) 523-6606

Description: Provides advisory services and counseling, and disseminates technical information to help the employment opportunities of women—especially in the realm of nontraditional women's jobs and jobs in new technologies.
$ Given: N/A
Application Information: Write to Women's Bureau in your region listed below.
Deadline: N/A
Contact: Women's Bureau
   Room S3305
   Office of the Secretary, Department of Labor
   Washington, DC 20210
   (202) 523-6606

EMERGENCY LOANS

Farmers Home Administration
Department of Agriculture
14th Street Independence Avenue, SW
Washington, DC 20250
(202) 690-1533
Description: Provides loans to family farmers (either owner or tenant), ranchers, and aquaculture operators to cover losses resulting from natural or other major disasters. Recipients must be unable to obtain credit from other sources.
$ Given: $81.4 million est. FY 92. Average size for FY 92 was est. $42,300.
Application Information: Consult local telephone directory under United States Government, Department of Agriculture, for Farmers Home Administration Office.
Deadline: N/A
Contact: Farmers Home Administration
   Department of Agriculture
   14th Street Independence Avenue, SW
   Washington, DC 20250
   (202) 690-1533

ECONOMIC INJURY DISASTER LOANS

Office of Disaster Assistance
Small Business Administration
409 3rd Street, SW
Washington, DC 20416
(202) 205-6734

Description: Provides loans to small businesses suffering economic damage under presidential, Small Business Administration, and/or Department of Agriculture declared disaster. Must be a small business or agricultural concern, be located within declared disaster area, and be unable to obtain credit elsewhere.

$ Given: $60 million for FY 92. During FY 91, 1,076 loans were made.

Application Information: Refer to local Disaster Area Office of the Small Business Administration.

Deadline: N/A

Contact: Small Business Administration, Region IX
71 Stevenson Street
Twentieth Floor
San Francisco, CA 94105-2939
(415) 744-6402

HAWAII

EMPLOYMENT SERVICE

United States Employment Service
Employment and Training Administration, Department of Labor
Washington, DC 20210
(202) 535-0157

Description: Provides placement services for job seekers and employers. These include services to special applicant groups, such as veterans, the handicapped, youth, minority, and older workers; a computerized interstate job listing; and other labor market information.

$ Given: FY 93 est. $821.6 million

Application Information: Contact the Employment Security Department for your state.

Deadline: N/A

Contact: Mario R. Ramil, Director
Department of Labor and Industrial Relations
830 Punchbowl Street
Room 204
Honolulu, HI 96813
(808) 548-3150

UNEMPLOYMENT INSURANCE

Unemployment Insurance Service
Employment and Training Administration, Department of Labor
Washington, DC 20210
(202) 523-7831
Description: Provides unemployment insurance for workers whose
employers have contributed to state unemployment funds, federal
civilian employees, ex-service persons, those who have become
unemployed as a result of product imports, and those whose
unemployment comes under the purview of a presidentially declared
disaster.
$ Given: $25.5 billion for FY 93
Application Information: Contact the Employment Security
Department for your state.
Deadline: N/A
Contact: Mario R. Ramil, Director
Department of Labor and Industrial Relations
830 Punchbowl Street
Room 204
Honolulu, HI 96813
(808) 548-3150

EMPLOYMENT AND TRAINING ASSISTANCE—DISLOCATED WORKERS

Employment and Training Administration, Department of Labor
200 Constitution Avenue, NW
Washington, DC 20210
(202) 535-0577
Description: Federal grants given to state and local programs to
assist workers through training and employment services. These are
workers who have been terminated or laid off, or who have received
notice of such, and are not likely to return to their previous
occupation or industry, or who are long-term unemployed. Targeted
individuals include those affected by mass layoffs and natural
disasters.
$ Given: Total nationwide of $571.1 million for FY 93
Application Information: Inquire at Employment Security Office
listed below.
Deadline: N/A

Contact: Mario R. Ramil, Director
Department of Labor and Industrial Relations
830 Punchbowl Street
Room 204
Honolulu, HI 96813
(808) 548-3150

WOMEN'S SPECIAL EMPLOYMENT ASSISTANCE
Office of Administrative Management
Women's Bureau
Room S3305
Office of the Secretary, Department of Labor
Washington, DC 20210
(202) 523-6606
Description: Provides advisory services and counseling, and disseminates technical information to help the employment opportunities of women—especially in the realm of nontraditional women's jobs and jobs in new technologies.
$ Given: N/A
Application Information: Write to Women's Bureau in your region listed below.
Deadline: N/A
Contact: Madeline Mixer, Regional Administrator
Region IX, Women's Bureau
Department of Labor
71 Stevenson Street
Room 927
San Francisco, CA 94105
(415) 774-6679

EMERGENCY LOANS
Farmers Home Administration
Department of Agriculture
14th Street Independence Avenue, SW
Washington, DC 20250
(202) 690-1533
Description: Provides loans to family farmers (either owner or tenant), ranchers, and aquaculture operators to cover losses resulting from natural or other major disasters. Recipients must be unable to obtain credit from other sources.
$ Given: $81.4 million est. FY 92. Average size for FY 92 was est. $42,300.

161

Application Information: Consult local telephone directory under United States Government, Department of Agriculture, for Farmers Home Administration Office.

Deadline: N/A

Contact: Farmers Home Administration
Federal Building
Room 311
154 Waianuenue Avenue
Hilo, HI 96720
(808) 933-3000

ECONOMIC INJURY DISASTER LOANS

Office of Disaster Assistance
Small Business Administration
409 3rd Street, SW
Washington, DC 20416
(202) 205-6734

Description: Provides loans to small businesses suffering economic damage under presidential, Small Business Administration, and/or Department of Agriculture declared disaster. Must be a small business or agricultural concern, be located within declared disaster area, and be unable to obtain credit elsewhere.

$ Given: $60 million for FY 92. During FY 91, 1,076 loans were made.

Application Information: Refer to local Disaster Area Office of the Small Business Administration.

Deadline: N/A

Contact: Small Business Administration, Region IX
71 Stevenson Street
Twentieth Floor
San Francisco, CA 94105-2939
(415) 744-6402

IDAHO

EMPLOYMENT SERVICE

United States Employment Service
Employment and Training Administration, Department of Labor
Washington, DC 20210
(202) 535-0157

Description: Provides placement services for job seekers and employers. These include services to special applicant groups, such as veterans, the handicapped, youth, minority, and older workers; a computerized interstate job listing; and other labor market information.

$ Given: FY 93 est. $821.6 million

Application Information: Contact the Employment Security Department for your state.

Deadline: N/A

Contact: Julie Kilgrow, Director
Department of Employment
P.O. Box 35
317 Main Street
Boise, ID 83735-0001
(208) 334-6110

UNEMPLOYMENT INSURANCE

Unemployment Insurance Service
Employment and Training Administration, Department of Labor
Washington, DC 20210
(202) 523-7831

Description: Provides unemployment insurance for workers whose employers have contributed to state unemployment funds, federal civilian employees, ex-service persons, those who have become unemployed as a result of product imports, and those whose unemployment comes under the purview of a presidentially declared disaster.

$ Given: $25.5 billion for FY 93

Application Information: Contact the Employment Security Department for your state.

Deadline: N/A

Contact: Julie Kilgrow, Director
Department of Employment
P.O. Box 35
317 Main Street
Boise, ID 83735-0001
(208) 334-6110

EMPLOYMENT AND TRAINING ASSISTANCE—DISLOCATED WORKERS

Employment and Training Administration, Department of Labor
200 Constitution Avenue, NW
Washington, DC 20210
(202) 535-0577

Description: Federal grants given to state and local programs to assist workers through training and employment services. These are workers who have been terminated or laid off, or who have received notice of such, and are not likely to return to their previous occupation or industry, or who are long-term unemployed. Targeted individuals include those affected by mass layoffs and natural disasters.

$ Given: Total nationwide of $571.1 million for FY 93

Application Information: Inquire at Employment Security Office listed below.

Deadline: N/A

Contact: Julie Kilgrow, Director
Department of Employment
P.O. Box 35
317 Main Street
Boise, ID 83735-0001
(208) 334-6110

WOMEN'S SPECIAL EMPLOYMENT ASSISTANCE

Office of Administrative Management
Women's Bureau
Room S3305
Office of the Secretary, Department of Labor
Washington, DC 20210
(202) 523-6606

Description: Provides advisory services and counseling, and disseminates technical information to help the employment opportunities of women—especially in the realm of nontraditional women's jobs and jobs in new technologies.

$ Given: N/A

Application Information: Write to Women's Bureau in your region listed below.

Deadline: N/A

Contact: Regional Administrator
Region X, Women's Bureau
Department of Labor
1111 Third Avenue
Room 885
Seattle, WA 98101-3211
(206) 553-1534

EMERGENCY LOANS

Farmers Home Administration
Department of Agriculture
14th Street Independence Avenue, SW
Washington, DC 20250
(202) 690-1533
Description: Provides loans to family farmers (either owner or tenant), ranchers, and aquaculture operators to cover losses resulting from natural or other major disasters. Recipients must be unable to obtain credit from other sources.
$ Given: $81.4 million est. FY 92. Average size for FY 92 was est. $42,300.
Application Information: Consult local telephone directory under United States Government, Department of Agriculture, for Farmers Home Administration Office.
Deadline: N/A
Contact: Farmers Home Administration
3232 Elder Street
Boise, ID 83705
(208) 334-1303

ECONOMIC INJURY DISASTER LOANS

Office of Disaster Assistance
Small Business Administration
409 3rd Street, SW
Washington, DC 20416
(202) 205-6734
Description: Provides loans to small businesses suffering economic damage under presidential, Small Business Administration, and/or Department of Agriculture declared disaster. Must be a small business or agricultural concern, be located within declared disaster area, and be unable to obtain credit elsewhere.
$ Given: $60 million for FY 92. During FY 91, 1,076 loans were made.

Application Information: Refer to local Disaster Area Office of the Small Business Administration.
Deadline: N/A
Contact: Small Business Administration, Region X
2615 4th Avenue
Room 440
Seattle, WA 98121
(206) 442-5676

ILLINOIS

EMPLOYMENT SERVICE

United States Employment Service
Employment and Training Administration, Department of Labor
Washington, DC 20210
(202) 535-0157
Description: Provides placement services for job seekers and employers. These include services to special applicant groups, such as veterans, the handicapped, youth, minority, and older workers; a computerized interstate job listing; and other labor market information.
$ Given: FY 93 est. $821.6 million
Application Information: Contact the Employment Security Department for your state.
Deadline: N/A
Contact: Sally A. Jackson, Director
Bureau of Employment Security
Department of Employment Security
401 South State Street
Suite 615 South
Chicago, IL 60605
(312) 793-5700

UNEMPLOYMENT INSURANCE

Unemployment Insurance Service
Employment and Training Administration, Department of Labor
Washington, DC 20210
(202) 523-7831
Description: Provides unemployment insurance for workers whose employers have contributed to state unemployment funds, federal civilian employees, ex-service persons, those who have become

unemployed as a result of product imports, and those whose unemployment comes under the purview of a presidentially declared disaster.

$ Given: $25.5 billion for FY 93

Application Information: Contact the Employment Security Department for your state.

Deadline: N/A

Contact: Sally A. Jackson, Director
Bureau of Employment Security
Department of Employment Security
401 South State Street
Suite 615 South
Chicago, IL 60605
(312) 793-5700

EMPLOYMENT AND TRAINING ASSISTANCE—DISLOCATED WORKERS

Employment and Training Administration, Department of Labor
200 Constitution Avenue, NW
Washington, DC 20210
(202) 535-0577

Description: Federal grants given to state and local programs to assist workers through training and employment services. These are workers who have been terminated or laid off, or who have received notice of such, and are not likely to return to their previous occupation or industry, or who are long-term unemployed. Targeted individuals include those affected by mass layoffs and natural disasters.

$ Given: Total nationwide of $571.1 million for FY 93

Application Information: Inquire at Employment Security Office listed below.

Deadline: N/A

Contact: Sally A. Jackson, Director
Bureau of Employment Security
Department of Employment Security
401 South State Street
Suite 615 South
Chicago, IL 60605
(312) 793-5700

WOMEN'S SPECIAL EMPLOYMENT ASSISTANCE

Office of Administrative Management
Women's Bureau
Room S3305
Office of the Secretary, Department of Labor
Washington, DC 20210
(202) 523-6606

Description: Provides advisory services and counseling, and disseminates technical information to help the employment opportunities of women—especially in the realm of nontraditional women's jobs and jobs in new technologies.

$ Given: N/A

Application Information: Write to Women's Bureau in your region listed below.

Deadline: N/A

Contact: Sandra K. Frank, Regional Administrator
Region V, Women's Bureau
Department of Labor
230 South Dearborn Street
Room 1022
Chicago, IL 60604
(312) 353-6985

EMERGENCY LOANS

Farmers Home Administration
Department of Agriculture
14th Street Independence Avenue, SW
Washington, DC 20250
(202) 690-1533

Description: Provides loans to family farmers (either owner or tenant), ranchers, and aquaculture operators to cover losses resulting from natural or other major disasters. Recipients must be unable to obtain credit from other sources.

$ Given: $81.4 million est. FY 92. Average size for FY 92 was est. $42,300

Application Information: Consult local telephone directory under United States Government, Department of Agriculture, for Farmers Home Administration Office.

Deadline: N/A

Contact: Farmers Home Administration
Illini Plaza
Suite 103
1817 South Neil Street
Champaign, IL 61820
(217) 398-5235

ECONOMIC INJURY DISASTER LOANS
Office of Disaster Assistance
Small Business Administration
409 3rd Street, SW
Washington, DC 20416
(202) 205-6734
Description: Provides loans to small businesses suffering economic damage under presidential, Small Business Administration, and/or Department of Agriculture declared disaster. Must be a small business or agricultural concern, be located within declared disaster area, and be unable to obtain credit elsewhere.
$ Given: $60 million for FY 92. During FY 91, 1,076 loans were made.
Application Information: Refer to local Disaster Area Office of the Small Business Administration.
Deadline: N/A
Contact: Small Business Administration, Region V
Federal Building
300 South Riverside Plaza
Room 1975
Chicago, IL 60606-6611
(312) 353-0359

INDIANA

EMPLOYMENT SERVICE
United States Employment Service
Employment and Training Administration, Department of Labor
Washington, DC 20210
(202) 535-0157
Description: Provides placement services for job seekers and employers. These include services to special applicant groups, such as veterans, the handicapped, youth, minority, and older workers; a computerized interstate job listing; and other labor market information.

$ Given: FY 93 est. $821.6 million
Application Information: Contact the Employment Security
Department for your state.
Deadline: N/A
Contact: Jack A. Cruse, Executive Director
             Employment Security Division
             10 North Senate Avenue
             Indianapolis, IN 46204
             (317) 232-3270

UNEMPLOYMENT INSURANCE

Unemployment Insurance Service
Employment and Training Administration, Department of Labor
Washington, DC 20210
(202) 523-7831
Description: Provides unemployment insurance for workers whose
employers have contributed to state unemployment funds, federal
civilian employees, ex-service persons, those who have become
unemployed as a result of product imports, and those whose
unemployment comes under the purview of a presidentially declared
disaster.
$ Given: $25.5 billion for FY 93
Application Information: Contact the Employment Security
Department for your state.
Deadline: N/A
Contact: Jack A. Cruse, Executive Director
             Employment Security Division
             10 North Senate Avenue
             Indianapolis, IN 46204
             (317) 232-3270

EMPLOYMENT AND TRAINING ASSISTANCE—DISLOCATED WORKERS

Employment and Training Administration, Department of Labor
200 Constitution Avenue, NW
Washington, DC 20210
(202) 535-0577
Description: Federal grants given to state and local programs to
assist workers through training and employment services. These are
workers who have been terminated or laid off, or who have received
notice of such, and are not likely to return to their previous
occupation or industry, or who are long-term unemployed. Targeted

individuals include those affected by mass layoffs and natural disasters.

$ Given: Total nationwide of $571.1 million for FY 93

Application Information: Inquire at Employment Security Office listed below.

Deadline: N/A

Contact: Jack A. Cruse, Executive Director
Employment Security Division
10 North Senate Avenue
Indianapolis, IN 46204
(317) 232-3270

WOMEN'S SPECIAL EMPLOYMENT ASSISTANCE

Office of Administrative Management
Women's Bureau
Room S3305
Office of the Secretary, Department of Labor
Washington, DC 20210
(202) 523-6606

Description: Provides advisory services and counseling, and disseminates technical information to help the employment opportunities of women—especially in the realm of nontraditional women's jobs and jobs in new technologies.

$ Given: N/A

Application Information: Write to Women's Bureau in your region listed below.

Deadline: N/A

Contact: Sandra K. Frank, Regional Administrator
Region V, Women's Bureau
Department of Labor
230 South Dearborn Street
Room 1022
Chicago, IL 60604
(312) 353-6985

EMERGENCY LOANS

Farmers Home Administration
Department of Agriculture
14th Street Independence Avenue, SW
Washington, DC 20250
(202) 690-1533

Description: Provides loans to family farmers (either owner or tenant), ranchers, and aquaculture operators to cover losses resulting from natural or other major disasters. Recipients must be unable to obtain credit from other sources.
$ Given: $81.4 million est. FY 92. Average size for FY 92 was est. $42,300.
Application Information: Consult local telephone directory under United States Government, Department of Agriculture, for Farmers Home Administration Office.
Deadline: N/A
Contact: Farmers Home Administration
5975 Lakeside Boulevard
Indianapolis, IN 46278
(317) 290-3100

ECONOMIC INJURY DISASTER LOANS
Office of Disaster Assistance
Small Business Administration
409 3rd Street, SW
Washington, DC 20416
(202) 205-6734
Description: Provides loans to small businesses suffering economic damage under presidential, Small Business Administration, and/or Department of Agriculture declared disaster. Must be a small business or agricultural concern, be located within declared disaster area, and be unable to obtain credit elsewhere.
$ Given: $60 million for FY 92. During FY 91, 1,076 loans were made.
Application Information: Refer to local Disaster Area Office of the Small Business Administration.
Deadline: N/A
Contact: Small Business Administration, Region V
Federal Building
300 South Riverside Plaza
Room 1975
Chicago, IL 60606-6611
(312) 353-0359

IOWA

EMPLOYMENT SERVICE

United States Employment Service
Employment and Training Administration, Department of Labor
Washington, DC 20210
(202) 535-0157
Description: Provides placement services for job seekers and employers. These include services to special applicant groups, such as veterans, the handicapped, youth, minority, and older workers; a computerized interstate job listing; and other labor market information.
$ Given: FY 93 est. $821.6 million
Application Information: Contact the Employment Security Department for your state.
Deadline: N/A
Contact: Cynthia P. Eisenhower, Director
              Job Service of Iowa
              Iowa Department of Employment Services
              1000 East Grand Avenue
              Des Moines, IA 50319
              (515) 281-5365

UNEMPLOYMENT INSURANCE

Unemployment Insurance Service
Employment and Training Administration, Department of Labor
Washington, DC 20210
(202) 523-7831
Description: Provides unemployment insurance for workers whose employers have contributed to state unemployment funds, federal civilian employees, ex-service persons, those who have become unemployed as a result of product imports, and those whose unemployment comes under the purview of a presidentially declared disaster.
$ Given: $25.5 billion for FY 93
Application Information: Contact the Employment Security Department for your state.
Deadline: N/A

Contact: Cynthia P. Eisenhower, Director
Job Service of Iowa
Iowa Department of Employment Services
1000 East Grand Avenue
Des Moines, IA 50319
(515) 281-5365

EMPLOYMENT AND TRAINING ASSISTANCE—DISLOCATED WORKERS

Employment and Training Administration, Department of Labor
200 Constitution Avenue, NW
Washington, DC 20210
(202) 535-0577
Description: Federal grants given to state and local programs to assist workers through training and employment services. These are workers who have been terminated or laid off, or who have received notice of such, and are not likely to return to their previous occupation or industry, or who are long-term unemployed. Targeted individuals include those affected by mass layoffs and natural disasters.
$ Given: Total nationwide of $571.1 million by FY 93
Application Information: Inquire at Employment Security Office listed below.
Deadline: N/A
Contact: Cynthia P. Eisenhower, Director
Job Service of Iowa
Iowa Department of Employment Services
1000 East Grand Avenue
Des Moines, IA 50319
(515) 281-5365

WOMEN'S SPECIAL EMPLOYMENT ASSISTANCE

Office of Administrative Management
Women's Bureau
Room S3305
Office of the Secretary, Department of Labor
Washington, DC 20210
(202) 523-6606
Description: Provides advisory services and counseling, and disseminates technical information to help the employment opportunities of women—especially in the realm of nontraditional women's jobs and jobs in new technologies.

$ Given: N/A
Application Information: Write to Women's Bureau in your region listed below.
Deadline: N/A
Contact: Rose A. Kemp, Regional Administrator
Region VII, Women's Bureau
Department of Labor
Federal Building
Room 2511
911 Walnut Street
Kansas City, MO 64106
(816) 426-6108

EMERGENCY LOANS

Farmers Home Administration
Department of Agriculture
14th Street Independence Avenue, SW
Washington, DC 20250
(202) 690-1533
Description: Provides loans to family farmers (either owner or tenant), ranchers, and aquaculture operators to cover losses resulting from natural or other major disasters. Recipients must be unable to obtain credit from other sources.
$ Given: $81.4 million est. FY 92. Average size for FY 92 was est. $42,300.
Application Information: Consult local telephone directory under United States Government, Department of Agriculture, for Farmers Home Administration Office.
Deadline: N/A
Contact: Farmers Home Administration
Federal Building
Room 873
210 Walnut Street
Des Moines, IA 50309
(515) 284-4663

ECONOMIC INJURY DISASTER LOANS

Office of Disaster Assistance
Small Business Administration
409 3rd Street, SW
Washington, DC 20416
(202) 205-6734

Description: Provides loans to small businesses suffering economic damage under presidential, Small Business Administration, and/or Department of Agriculture declared disaster. Must be a small business or agricultural concern, be located within declared disaster area, and be unable to obtain credit elsewhere.
$ Given: $60 million for FY 92. During FY 91, 1,076 loans were made.
Application Information: Refer to local Disaster Area Office of the Small Business Administration.
Deadline: N/A
Contact: Small Business Administration, Region VII
911 Walnut Street
Thirteenth Floor
Kansas City, MO 64106
(816) 426-3609

KANSAS

EMPLOYMENT SERVICE

United States Employment Service
Employment and Training Administration, Department of Labor
Washington, DC 20210
(202) 535-0157
Description: Provides placement services for job seekers and employers. These include services to special applicant groups, such as veterans, the handicapped, youth, minority, and older workers; a computerized interstate job listing; and other labor market information.
$ Given: FY 93 est. $821.6 million
Application Information: Contact the Employment Security Department for your state.
Deadline: N/A
Contact: Michael L. Johnston, Secretary
Department of Human Resources
401 SW Topeka Avenue
Topeka, KS 66603
(913) 296-7474

UNEMPLOYMENT INSURANCE

Unemployment Insurance Service
Employment and Training Administration, Department of Labor
Washington, DC 20210
(202) 523-7831

Description: Provides unemployment insurance for workers whose employers have contributed to state unemployment funds, federal civilian employees, ex-service persons, those who have become unemployed as a result of product imports, and those whose unemployment comes under the purview of a presidentially declared disaster.

$ Given: $25.5 billion for FY 93

Application Information: Contact the Employment Security Department for your state.

Deadline: N/A

Contact: Michael L. Johnston, Secretary
Department of Human Resources
401 SW Topeka Avenue
Topeka, KS 66603
(913) 296-7474

EMPLOYMENT AND TRAINING ASSISTANCE—DISLOCATED WORKERS

Employment and Training Administration, Department of Labor
200 Constitution Avenue, NW
Washington, DC 20210
(202) 535-0577

Description: Federal grants given to state and local programs to assist workers through training and employment services. These are workers who have been terminated or laid off, or who have received notice of such, and are not likely to return to their previous occupation or industry, or who are long-term unemployed. Targeted individuals include those affected by mass layoffs and natural disasters.

$ Given: Total nationwide of $571.1 million for FY 93

Application Information: Inquire at Employment Security Office listed below.

Deadline: N/A

Contact: Michael L. Johnston, Secretary
Department of Human Resources
401 SW Topeka Avenue
Topeka, KS 66603
(913) 296-7474

WOMEN'S SPECIAL EMPLOYMENT ASSISTANCE

Office of Administrative Management
Women's Bureau
Room S3305
Office of the Secretary, Department of Labor
Washington, DC 20210
(202) 523-6606

Description: Provides advisory services and counseling, and disseminates technical information to help the employment opportunities of women—especially in the realm of nontraditional women's jobs and jobs in new technologies.

$ Given: N/A

Application Information: Write to Women's Bureau in your region listed below.

Deadline: N/A

Contact: Rose A. Kemp, Regional Administrator
Region VII, Women's Bureau
Department of Labor
Federal Building
Room 2511
911 Walnut Street
Kansas City, MO 64106
(816) 426-6108

EMERGENCY LOANS

Farmers Home Administration
Department of Agriculture
14th Street Independence Avenue, SW
Washington, DC 20250
(202) 690-1533

Description: Provides loans to family farmers (either owner or tenant), ranchers, and aquaculture operators to cover losses resulting from natural or other major disasters. Recipients must be unable to obtain credit from other sources.

$ Given: $81.4 million est. FY 92. Average size for FY 92 was est. $42,300.

Application Information: Consult local telephone directory under United States Government, Department of Agriculture, for Farmers Home Administration Office.

Deadline: N/A

Contact: Farmers Home Administration
1201 SW Summit Executive Court
P.O. Box 4653
Topeka, KS 66604
(913) 271-7300

ECONOMIC INJURY DISASTER LOANS

Office of Disaster Assistance
Small Business Administration
409 3rd Street, SW
Washington, DC 20416
(202) 205-6734

Description: Provides loans to small businesses suffering economic damage under presidential, Small Business Administration, and/or Department of Agriculture declared disaster. Must be a small business or agricultural concern, be located within declared disaster area, and be unable to obtain credit elsewhere.

$ Given: $60 million for FY 92. During FY 91, 1,076 loans were made.

Application Information: Refer to local Disaster Area Office of the Small Business Administration.

Deadline: N/A

Contact: Small Business Administration, Region VII
911 Walnut Street
Thirteenth Floor
Kansas City, MO 64106
(816) 426-3609

KENTUCKY

EMPLOYMENT SERVICE

United States Employment Service
Employment and Training Administration, Department of Labor
Washington, DC 20210
(202) 535-0157

Description: Provides placement services for job seekers and employers. These include services to special applicant groups, such as veterans, the handicapped, youth, minority, and older workers; a computerized interstate job listing; and other labor market information.
$ Given: FY 93 est. $821.6 million
Application Information: Contact the Employment Security Department for your state.
Deadline: N/A
Contact: Harry J. Cowherd, Commissioner
Department of Employment Service
Department of Human Resources
Cabinet for Human Resources
275 East Main Street
Second Floor West
Frankfort, KY 40621
(502) 564-5331

UNEMPLOYMENT INSURANCE
Unemployment Insurance Service
Employment and Training Administration, Department of Labor
Washington, DC 20210
(202) 523-7831
Description: Provides unemployment insurance for workers whose employers have contributed to state unemployment funds, federal civilian employees, ex-service persons, those who have become unemployed as a result of product imports, and those whose unemployment comes under the purview of a presidentially declared disaster.
$ Given: $25.5 billion for FY 93
Application Information: Contact the Employment Security Department for your state.
Deadline: N/A
Contact: Harry J. Cowherd, Commissioner
Department of Employment Service
Department of Human Resources
Cabinet for Human Resources
275 East Main Street
Second Floor West
Frankfort, KY 40621
(502) 564-5331

EMPLOYMENT AND TRAINING ASSISTANCE—DISLOCATED WORKERS

Employment and Training Administration, Department of Labor
200 Constitution Avenue, NW
Washington, DC 20210
(202) 535-0577
Description: Federal grants given to state and local programs to assist workers through training and employment services. These are workers who have been terminated or laid off, or who have received notice of such, and are not likely to return to their previous occupation or industry, or who are long-term unemployed. Targeted individuals include those affected by mass layoffs and natural disasters.
$ Given: Total nationwide of $571.1 million for FY 93
Application Information: Inquire at Employment Security Office listed below.
Deadline: N/A
Contact: Harry J. Cowherd, Commissioner
Department of Employment Service
Department of Human Resources
Cabinet for Human Resources
275 East Main Street
Second Floor West
Frankfort, KY 40621
(502) 564-5331

WOMEN'S SPECIAL EMPLOYMENT ASSISTANCE

Office of Administrative Management
Women's Bureau
Room S3305
Office of the Secretary, Department of Labor
Washington, DC 20210
(202) 523-6606
Description: Provides advisory services and counseling, and disseminates technical information to help the employment opportunities of women—especially in the realm of nontraditional women's jobs and jobs in new technologies.
$ Given: N/A
Application Information: Write to Women's Bureau in your region listed below.
Deadline: N/A

Contact: Delores L. Crockett, Regional Administrator
Region IV, Women's Bureau
Department of Labor
1371 Peachtree Street, NE
Room 323
Atlanta, GA 30367
(404) 347-4461

EMERGENCY LOANS

Farmers Home Administration
Department of Agriculture
14th Street Independence Avenue, SW
Washington, DC 20250
(202) 690-1533
Description: Provides loans to family farmers (either owner or tenant), ranchers, and aquaculture operators to cover losses resulting from natural or other major disasters. Recipients must be unable to obtain credit from other sources.
$ Given: $81.4 million est. FY 92. Average size for FY 92 was est. $42,300.
Application Information: Consult local telephone directory under United States Government, Department of Agriculture, for Farmers Home Administration Office.
Deadline: N/A
Contact: Farmers Home Administration
333771 Corporate Plaza
Suite 200
Lexington, KY 40503
(606) 224-7300

ECONOMIC INJURY DISASTER LOANS

Office of Disaster Assistance
Small Business Administration
409 3rd Street, SW
Washington, DC 20416
(202) 205-6734
Description: Provides loans to small businesses suffering economic damage under presidential, Small Business Administration, and/or Department of Agriculture declared disaster. Must be a small business or agricultural concern, be located within declared disaster area, and be unable to obtain credit elsewhere.

$ Given: $60 million for FY 92. During FY 91, 1,076 loans were made.
Application Information: Refer to local Disaster Area Office of the Small Business Administration.
Deadline: N/A
Contact: Small Business Administration, Region IV
1375 Peachtree Street, NE
Fifth Floor
Atlanta, GA 30367-8102
(404) 347-2797

LOUISIANA

EMPLOYMENT SERVICE

United States Employment Service
Employment and Training Administration, Department of Labor
Washington, DC 20210
(202) 535-0157
Description: Provides placement services for job seekers and employers. These include services to special applicant groups, such as veterans, the handicapped, youth, minority, and older workers; a computerized interstate job listing; and other labor market information.
$ Given: FY 93 est. $821.6 million
Application Information: Contact the Employment Security Department for your state.
Deadline: N/A
Contact: Alfreda Tilman Bester, Acting Secretary
Louisiana Department of Employment and Training
Employment Security Building
1001 North 23rd Street
P.O. Box 94094
Capitol Station
Baton Rouge, LA 70804-9094
(504) 342-3013

UNEMPLOYMENT INSURANCE

Unemployment Insurance Service
Employment and Training Administration, Department of Labor
Washington, DC 20210
(202) 523-7831

Description: Provides unemployment insurance for workers whose employers have contributed to state unemployment funds, federal civilian employees, ex-service persons, those who have become unemployed as a result of product imports, and those whose unemployment comes under the purview of a presidentially declared disaster.

$ Given: $25.5 billion for FY 93

Application Information: Contact the Employment Security Department for your state.

Deadline: N/A

Contact: Alfreda Tilman Bester, Acting Secretary
Louisiana Department of Employment and Training
Employment Security Building
1001 North 23rd Street
P.O. Box 94094
Capitol Station
Baton Rouge, LA 70804-9094
(504) 342-3013

EMPLOYMENT AND TRAINING ASSISTANCE—DISLOCATED WORKERS

Employment and Training Administration, Department of Labor
200 Constitution Avenue, NW
Washington, DC 20210
(202) 535-0577

Description: Federal grants given to state and local programs to assist workers through training and employment services. These are workers who have been terminated or laid off, or who have received notice of such, and are not likely to return to their previous occupation or industry, or who are long-term unemployed. Targeted individuals include those affected by mass layoffs and natural disasters.

$ Given: Total nationwide of $571.1 million for FY 93

Application Information: Inquire at Employment Security Office listed below.

Deadline: N/A

Contact: Alfreda Tilman Bester, Acting Secretary
Louisiana Department of Employment and Training
Employment Security Building
1001 North 23rd Street
P.O. Box 94094
Capitol Station
Baton Rouge, LA 70804-9094
(504) 342-3013

WOMEN'S SPECIAL EMPLOYMENT ASSISTANCE
Office of Administrative Management
Women's Bureau
Room S3305
Office of the Secretary, Department of Labor
Washington, DC 20210
(202) 523-6606
Description: Provides advisory services and counseling, and disseminates technical information to help the employment opportunities of women—especially in the realm of nontraditional women's jobs and jobs in new technologies.
$ Given: N/A
Application Information: Write to Women's Bureau in your region listed below.
Deadline: N/A
Contact: Evelyn Smith, Regional Administrator
Region VI, Women's Bureau
Department of Labor
Federal Building
Suite 731
525 Griffin Street
Dallas, TX 75202
(214) 767-6985

EMERGENCY LOANS
Farmers Home Administration
Department of Agriculture
14th Street Independence Avenue, SW
Washington, DC 20250
(202) 690-1533
Description: Provides loans to family farmers (either owner or tenant), ranchers, and aquaculture operators to cover losses

resulting from natural or other major disasters. Recipients must be unable to obtain credit from other sources.

$ Given: $81.4 million est. FY 92. Average size for FY 92 was est. $42,300.

Application Information: Consult local telephone directory under United States Government, Department of Agriculture, for Farmers Home Administration Office.

Deadline: N/A

Contact: Farmers Home Administration
3727 Government Street
Alexandria, LA 71302
(318) 473-7920

ECONOMIC INJURY DISASTER LOANS
Office of Disaster Assistance
Small Business Administration
409 3rd Street, SW
Washington, DC 20416
(202) 205-6734

Description: Provides loans to small businesses suffering economic damage under presidential, Small Business Administration, and/or Department of Agriculture declared disaster. Must be a small business or agricultural concern, be located within declared disaster area, and be unable to obtain credit elsewhere.

$ Given: $60 million for FY 92. During FY 91, 1,076 loans were made.

Application Information: Refer to local Disaster Area Office of the Small Business Administration.

Deadline: N/A

Contact: Small Business Administration, Region VI
8625 King George Drive
Building C
Dallas, TX 75235-3391
(214) 767-7643

MAINE

EMPLOYMENT SERVICE
United States Employment Service
Employment and Training Administration, Department of Labor
Washington, DC 20210
(202) 535-0157

Description: Provides placement services for job seekers and employers. These include services to special applicant groups, such as veterans, the handicapped, youth, minority, and older workers; a computerized interstate job listing; and other labor market information.
$ Given: FY 93 est. $821.6 million
Application Information: Contact the Employment Security Department for your state.
Deadline: N/A
Contact: Charles Morrison, Commissioner of Labor
Department of Labor
Bureau of Employment Security
20 Union Street
P.O. Box 309
Augusta, ME 04330-0309
(207) 289-3788

UNEMPLOYMENT INSURANCE

Unemployment Insurance Service
Employment and Training Administration, Department of Labor
Washington, DC 20210
(202) 523-7831
Description: Provides unemployment insurance for workers whose employers have contributed to state unemployment funds, federal civilian employees, ex-service persons, those who have become unemployed as a result of product imports, and those whose unemployment comes under the purview of a presidentially declared disaster.
$ Given: $25.5 billion for FY 93
Application Information: Contact the Employment Security Department for your state.
Deadline: N/A
Contact: Charles Morrison, Commissioner of Labor
Department of Labor
Bureau of Employment Security
20 Union Street
P.O. Box 309
Augusta, ME 04330-0309
(207) 289-3788

EMPLOYMENT AND TRAINING ASSISTANCE—DISLOCATED WORKERS

Employment and Training Administration, Department of Labor
200 Constitution Avenue, NW
Washington, DC 20210
(202) 535-0577

Description: Federal grants given to state and local programs to assist workers through training and employment services. These are workers who have been terminated or laid off, or who have received notice of such, and are not likely to return to their previous occupation or industry, or who are long-term unemployed. Targeted individuals include those affected by mass layoffs and natural disasters.

$ Given: Total nationwide of $571.1 million for FY 93

Application Information: Inquire at Employment Security Office listed below.

Deadline: N/A

Contact: Charles Morrison, Commissioner of Labor
Department of Labor
Bureau of Employment Security
20 Union Street
P.O. Box 309
Augusta, ME 04330-0309
(207) 289-3788

WOMEN'S SPECIAL EMPLOYMENT ASSISTANCE

Office of Administrative Management
Women's Bureau
Room S3305
Office of the Secretary, Department of Labor
Washington, DC 20210
(202) 523-6606

Description: Provides advisory services and counseling, and disseminates technical information to help the employment opportunities of women—especially in the realm of nontraditional women's jobs and jobs in new technologies.

$ Given: N/A

Application Information: Write to Women's Bureau in your region listed below.

Deadline: N/A

Contact: Martha Izzi, Regional Administrator
Region I, Women's Bureau
Department of Labor
One Congress Street
Boston, MA 02214
(617) 565-1988

EMERGENCY LOANS

Farmers Home Administration
Department of Agriculture
14th Street Independence Avenue, SW
Washington, DC 20250
(202) 690-1533
Description: Provides loans to family farmers (either owner or tenant), ranchers, and aquaculture operators to cover losses resulting from natural or other major disasters. Recipients must be unable to obtain credit from other sources.
$ Given: $81.4 million est. FY 92. Average size for FY 92 was est. $42,300.
Application Information: Consult local telephone directory under United States Government, Department of Agriculture, for Farmers Home Administration Office.
Deadline: N/A
Contact: Farmers Home Administration
444 Stillwater Avenue
Suite 2
P.O. Box 405
Bangor, ME 04402-0405
(207) 990-9106

ECONOMIC INJURY DISASTER LOANS

Office of Disaster Assistance
Small Business Administration
409 3rd Street, SW
Washington, DC 20416
(202) 205-6734
Description: Provides loans to small businesses suffering economic damage under presidential, Small Business Administration, and/or Department of Agriculture declared disaster. Must be a small business or agricultural concern, be located within declared disaster area, and be unable to obtain credit elsewhere.

$ Given: $60 million for FY 92. During FY 91, 1,076 loans were made.
Application Information: Refer to local Disaster Area Office of the Small Business Administration.
Deadline: N/A
Contact: Small Business Administration, Region I
155 Federal Street
Ninth Floor
Boston, MA 02110
(617) 451-2023

MARYLAND

EMPLOYMENT SERVICE

United States Employment Service
Employment and Training Administration, Department of Labor
Washington, DC 20210
(202) 535-0157
Description: Provides placement services for job seekers and employers. These include services to special applicant groups, such as veterans, the handicapped, youth, minority, and older workers; a computerized interstate job listing; and other labor market information.
$ Given: FY 93 est. $821.6 million
Application Information: Contact the Employment Security Department for your state.
Deadline: N/A
Contact: Charles O. Middlebrooks, Assistant Secretary
Division of Employment and Training
Department of Economic and Employment Development
State Office Building
1100 North Eutaw Street
Room 616
Baltimore, MD 21201
(301) 333-5070

UNEMPLOYMENT INSURANCE

Unemployment Insurance Service
Employment and Training Administration, Department of Labor
Washington, DC 20210
(202) 523-7831

Description: Provides unemployment insurance for workers whose employers have contributed to state unemployment funds, federal civilian employees, ex-service persons, those who have become unemployed as a result of product imports, and those whose unemployment comes under the purview of a presidentially declared disaster.

$ Given: $25.5 billion for FY 93

Application Information: Contact the Employment Security Department for your state.

Deadline: N/A

Contact: Charles O. Middlebrooks, Assistant Secretary
Division of Employment and Training
Department of Economic and Employment Development
State Office Building
1100 North Eutaw Street
Room 616
Baltimore, MD 21201
(301) 333-5070

EMPLOYMENT AND TRAINING ASSISTANCE—DISLOCATED WORKERS

Employment and Training Administration, Department of Labor
200 Constitution Avenue, NW
Washington, DC 20210
(202) 535-0577

Description: Federal grants given to state and local programs to assist workers through training and employment services. These are workers who have been terminated or laid off, or who have received notice of such, and are not likely to return to their previous occupation or industry, or who are long-term unemployed. Targeted individuals include those affected by mass layoffs and natural disasters.

$ Given: Total nationwide of $571.1 million for FY 93

Application Information: Inquire at Employment Security Office listed below.

Deadline: N/A

Contact: Charles O. Middlebrooks, Assistant Secretary
Division of Employment and Training
Department of Economic and Employment Development
State Office Building
1100 North Eutaw Street
Room 616
Baltimore, MD 21201
(301) 333-5070

WOMEN'S SPECIAL EMPLOYMENT ASSISTANCE

Office of Administrative Management
Women's Bureau
Room S3305
Office of the Secretary, Department of Labor
Washington, DC 20210
(202) 523-6606
Description: Provides advisory services and counseling, and disseminates technical information to help the employment opportunities of women—especially in the realm of nontraditional women's jobs and jobs in new technologies.
$ Given: N/A
Application Information: Write to Women's Bureau in your region listed below.
Deadline: N/A
Contact: Regional Administrator
Region III, Women's Bureau
Department of Labor
Gateway Building
Room 13280
3535 Market Street
Philadelphia, PA 19104
(215) 596-1184

EMERGENCY LOANS

Farmers Home Administration
Department of Agriculture
14th Street Independence Avenue, SW
Washington, DC 20250
(202) 690-1533
Description: Provides loans to family farmers (either owner or tenant), ranchers, and aquaculture operators to cover losses

resulting from natural or other major disasters. Recipients must be unable to obtain credit from other sources.

$ Given: $81.4 million est. FY 92. Average size for FY 92 was est. $42,300.

Application Information: Consult local telephone directory under United States Government, Department of Agriculture, for Farmers Home Administration Office.

Deadline: N/A

Contact: Farmers Home Administration
4611 South Dupont Highway
P.O. Box 400
Camden, DE 19934-9998
(302) 697-4300

ECONOMIC INJURY DISASTER LOANS

Office of Disaster Assistance
Small Business Administration
409 3rd Street, SW
Washington, DC 20416
(202) 205-6734

Description: Provides loans to small businesses suffering economic damage under presidential, Small Business Administration, and/or Department of Agriculture declared disaster. Must be a small business or agricultural concern, be located within declared disaster area, and be unable to obtain credit elsewhere.

$ Given: $60 million for FY 92. During FY 91, 1,076 loans were made.

Application Information: Refer to local Disaster Area Office of the Small Business Administration.

Deadline: N/A

Contact: Small Business Administration, Region III
475 Allendale Road
Suite 201
King of Prussia, PA 19406
(215) 962-3700

MASSACHUSETTS

EMPLOYMENT SERVICE

United States Employment Service
Employment and Training Administration, Department of Labor
Washington, DC 20210
(202) 535-0157
Description: Provides placement services for job seekers and employers. These include services to special applicant groups, such as veterans, the handicapped, youth, minority, and older workers; a computerized interstate job listing; and other labor market information.
$ Given: FY 93 est. $821.6 million
Application Information: Contact the Employment Security Department for your state.
Deadline: N/A
Contact: Nils L. Nordberg, Commissioner
Department of Employment and Training
Charles F. Hurley Building
Third Floor
Government Center
Boston, MA 02114
(617) 727-6600

UNEMPLOYMENT INSURANCE

Unemployment Insurance Service
Employment and Training Administration, Department of Labor
Washington, DC 20210
(202) 523-7831
Description: Provides unemployment insurance for workers whose employers have contributed to state unemployment funds, federal civilian employees, ex-service persons, those who have become unemployed as a result of product imports, and those whose unemployment comes under the purview of a presidentially declared disaster.
$ Given: $25.5 billion for FY 93
Application Information: Contact the Employment Security Department for your state.
Deadline: N/A

Contact: Nils L. Nordberg, Commissioner
Department of Employment and Training
Charles F. Hurley Building
Third Floor
Government Center
Boston, MA 02114
(617) 727-6600

EMPLOYMENT AND TRAINING ASSISTANCE—DISLOCATED WORKERS

Employment and Training Administration, Department of Labor
200 Constitution Avenue, NW
Washington, DC 20210
(202) 535-0577
Description: Federal grants given to state and local programs to assist workers through training and employment services. These are workers who have been terminated or laid off, or who have received notice of such, and are not likely to return to their previous occupation or industry, or who are long-term unemployed. Targeted individuals include those affected by mass layoffs and natural disasters.
$ Given: Total nationwide of $571.1 million for FY 93
Application Information: Inquire at Employment Security Office listed below.
Deadline: N/A
Contact: Nils L. Nordberg, Commissioner
Department of Employment and Training
Charles F. Hurley Building
Third Floor
Government Center
Boston, MA 02114
(617) 727-6600

WOMEN'S SPECIAL EMPLOYMENT ASSISTANCE

Office of Administrative Management
Women's Bureau
Room S3305
Office of the Secretary, Department of Labor
Washington, DC 20210
(202) 523-6606
Description: Provides advisory services and counseling, and disseminates technical information to help the employment

opportunities of women—especially in the realm of nontraditional women's jobs and jobs in new technologies.

$ Given: N/A

Application Information: Write to Women's Bureau in your region listed below.

Deadline: N/A

Contact: Martha Izzi, Regional Administrator
Region I, Women's Bureau
Department of Labor
One Congress Street
Boston, MA 02214
(617) 565-1988

EMERGENCY LOANS

Farmers Home Administration
Department of Agriculture
14th Street Independence Avenue, SW
Washington, DC 20250
(202) 690-1533

Description: Provides loans to family farmers (either owner or tenant), ranchers, and aquaculture operators to cover losses resulting from natural or other major disasters. Recipients must be unable to obtain credit from other sources.

$ Given: $81.4 million est. FY 92. Average size for FY 92 was est. $42,300.

Application Information: Consult local telephone directory under United States Government, Department of Agriculture, for Farmers Home Administration Office.

Deadline: N/A

Contact: Farmers Home Administration
451 West Street
Amherst, MA 01002
(413) 253-4300

ECONOMIC INJURY DISASTER LOANS

Office of Disaster Assistance
Small Business Administration
409 3rd Street, SW
Washington, DC 20416
(202) 205-6734

Description: Provides loans to small businesses suffering economic damage under presidential, Small Business Administration, and/or

Department of Agriculture declared disaster. Must be a small business or agricultural concern, be located within declared disaster area, and be unable to obtain credit elsewhere.
$ Given: $60 million for FY 92. During FY 91, 1,076 loans were made.
Application Information: Refer to local Disaster Area Office of the Small Business Administration.
Deadline: N/A
Contact: Small Business Administration, Region I
155 Federal Street
Ninth Floor
Boston, MA 02110
(617) 451-2023

MICHIGAN

EMPLOYMENT SERVICE
United States Employment Service
Employment and Training Administration, Department of Labor
Washington, DC 20210
(202) 535-0157
Description: Provides placement services for job seekers and employers. These include services to special applicant groups, such as veterans, the handicapped, youth, minority, and older workers; a computerized interstate job listing; and other labor market information.
$ Given: FY 93 est. $821.6 million
Application Information: Contact the Employment Security Department for your state.
Deadline: N/A
Contact: Jack C. Barthwell, III, Director
Department of Labor
Michigan Employment Security Commission
7310 Woodward Avenue
Detroit, MI 48202
(313) 876-5500

UNEMPLOYMENT INSURANCE
Unemployment Insurance Service
Employment and Training Administration, Department of Labor
Washington, DC 20210
(202) 523-7831

Description: Provides unemployment insurance for workers whose employers have contributed to state unemployment funds, federal civilian employees, ex-service persons, those who have become unemployed as a result of product imports, and those whose unemployment comes under the purview of a presidentially declared disaster.

$ Given: $25.5 billion for FY 93

Application Information: Contact the Employment Security Department for your state.

Deadline: N/A

Contact: Jack C. Barthwell, III, Director
Department of Labor
Michigan Employment Security Commission
7310 Woodward Avenue
Detroit, MI 48202
(313) 876-5500

EMPLOYMENT AND TRAINING ASSISTANCE—DISLOCATED WORKERS

Employment and Training Administration, Department of Labor
200 Constitution Avenue, NW
Washington, DC 20210
(202) 535-0577

Description: Federal grants given to state and local programs to assist workers through training and employment services. These are workers who have been terminated or laid off, or who have received notice of such, and are not likely to return to their previous occupation or industry, or who are long-term unemployed. Targeted individuals include those affected by mass layoffs and natural disasters.

$ Given: Total nationwide of $571.1 million for FY 93

Application Information: Inquire at Employment Security Office listed below.

Deadline: N/A

Contact: Jack C. Barthwell, III, Director
Department of Labor
Michigan Employment Security Commission
7310 Woodward Avenue
Detroit, MI 48202
(313) 876-5500

WOMEN'S SPECIAL EMPLOYMENT ASSISTANCE

Office of Administrative Management
Women's Bureau
Room S3305
Office of the Secretary, Department of Labor
Washington, DC 20210
(202) 523-6606
Description: Provides advisory services and counseling, and disseminates technical information to help the employment opportunities of women—especially in the realm of nontraditional women's jobs and jobs in new technologies.
$ Given: N/A
Application Information: Write to Women's Bureau in your region listed below.
Deadline: N/A
Contact: Sandra K. Frank, Regional Administrator
Region V, Women's Bureau
Department of Labor
230 South Dearborn Street
Room 1022
Chicago, IL 60604
(312) 353-6985

EMERGENCY LOANS

Farmers Home Administration
Department of Agriculture
14th Street Independence Avenue, SW
Washington, DC 20250
(202) 690-1533
Description: Provides loans to family farmers (either owner or tenant), ranchers, and aquaculture operators to cover losses resulting from natural or other major disasters. Recipients must be unable to obtain credit from other sources.
$ Given: $81.4 million est. FY 92. Average size for FY 92 was est. $42,300.
Application Information: Consult local telephone directory under United States Government, Department of Agriculture, for Farmers Home Administration Office.
Deadline: N/A

Contact: Farmers Home Administration
Manly Miles Building
1405 South Harrison Road
Room 209
East Lansing, MI 48823
(517) 337-6631

ECONOMIC INJURY DISASTER LOANS

Office of Disaster Assistance
Small Business Administration
409 3rd Street, SW
Washington, DC 20416
(202) 205-6734
Description: Provides loans to small businesses suffering economic damage under presidential, Small Business Administration, and/or Department of Agriculture declared disaster. Must be a small business or agricultural concern, be located within declared disaster area, and be unable to obtain credit elsewhere.
$ Given: $60 million for FY 92. During FY 91, 1,076 loans were made.
Application Information: Refer to local Disaster Area Office of the Small Business Administration.
Deadline: N/A
Contact: Small Business Administration, Region V
Federal Building
300 South Riverside Plaza
Room 1975
Chicago, IL 60606-6611
(312) 353-0359

MINNESOTA

EMPLOYMENT SERVICE

United States Employment Service
Employment and Training Administration, Department of Labor
Washington, DC 20210
(202) 535-0157
Description: Provides placement services for job seekers and employers. These include services to special applicant groups, such as veterans, the handicapped, youth, minority, and older workers; a

computerized interstate job listing; and other labor market
information.
$ Given: FY 93 est. $821.6 million
Application Information: Contact the Employment Security
Department for your state.
Deadline: N/A
Contact: R. Jane Brown, Commissioner
                Department of Jobs and Training
                390 North Robert Street
                St. Paul, MN 55101
                (612) 296-3711

UNEMPLOYMENT INSURANCE

Unemployment Insurance Service
Employment and Training Administration, Department of Labor
Washington, DC 20210
(202) 523-7831
Description: Provides unemployment insurance for workers whose
employers have contributed to state unemployment funds, federal
civilian employees, ex-service persons, those who have become
unemployed as a result of product imports, and those whose
unemployment comes under the purview of a presidentially declared
disaster.
$ Given: $25.5 billion for FY 93
Application Information: Contact the Employment Security
Department for your state.
Deadline: N/A
Contact: R. Jane Brown, Commissioner
                Department of Jobs and Training
                390 North Robert Street
                St. Paul, MN 55101
                (612) 296-3711

EMPLOYMENT AND TRAINING ASSISTANCE—DISLOCATED WORKERS

Employment and Training Administration, Department of Labor
200 Constitution Avenue, NW
Washington, DC 20210
(202) 535-0577
Description: Federal grants given to state and local programs to
assist workers through training and employment services. These are
workers who have been terminated or laid off, or who have received

notice of such, and are not likely to return to their previous occupation or industry, or who are long-term unemployed. Targeted individuals include those affected by mass layoffs and natural disasters.

$ Given: Total nationwide of $571.1 million for FY 93

Application Information: Inquire at Employment Security Office listed below.

Deadline: N/A

Contact: R. Jane Brown, Commissioner
Department of Jobs and Training
390 North Robert Street
St. Paul, MN 55101
(612) 296-3711

WOMEN'S SPECIAL EMPLOYMENT ASSISTANCE

Office of Administrative Management
Women's Bureau
Room S3305
Office of the Secretary, Department of Labor
Washington, DC 20210
(202) 523-6606

Description: Provides advisory services and counseling, and disseminates technical information to help the employment opportunities of women—especially in the realm of nontraditional women's jobs and jobs in new technologies.

$ Given: N/A

Application Information: Write to Women's Bureau in your region listed below.

Deadline: N/A

Contact: Sandra K. Frank, Regional Administrator
Region V, Women's Bureau
Department of Labor
230 South Dearborn Street
Room 1022
Chicago, IL 60604
(312) 353-6985

EMERGENCY LOANS

Farmers Home Administration
Department of Agriculture
14th Street Independence Avenue, SW
Washington, DC 20250
(202) 690-1533
Description: Provides loans to family farmers (either owner or tenant), ranchers, and aquaculture operators to cover losses resulting from natural or other major disasters. Recipients must be unable to obtain credit from other sources.
$ Given: $81.4 million est. FY 92. Average size for FY 92 was est. $42,300.
Application Information: Consult local telephone directory under United States Government, Department of Agriculture, for Farmers Home Administration Office.
Deadline: N/A
Contact: Farmers Home Administration
410 Farm Credit Building
375 Jackson Street
St. Paul, MN 55101
(612) 290-3842

ECONOMIC INJURY DISASTER LOANS

Office of Disaster Assistance
Small Business Administration
409 3rd Street, SW
Washington, DC 20416
(202) 205-6734
Description: Provides loans to small businesses suffering economic damage under presidential, Small Business Administration, and/or Department of Agriculture declared disaster. Must be a small business or agricultural concern, be located within declared disaster area, and be unable to obtain credit elsewhere.
$ Given: $60 million for FY 92. During FY 91, 1,076 loans were made.
Application Information: Refer to local Disaster Area Office of the Small Business Administration.
Deadline: N/A

Contact: Small Business Administration, Region V
Federal Building
300 South Riverside Plaza
Room 1975
Chicago, IL 60606-6611
(312) 353-0359

MISSISSIPPI

EMPLOYMENT SERVICE

United States Employment Service
Employment and Training Administration, Department of Labor
Washington, DC 20210
(202) 535-0157
Description: Provides placement services for job seekers and employers. These include services to special applicant groups, such as veterans, the handicapped, youth, minority, and older workers; a computerized interstate job listing; and other labor market information.
$ Given: FY 93 est. $821.6 million
Application Information: Contact the Employment Security Department for your state.
Deadline: N/A
Contact: Linda Ross Aldy, Executive Director
Employment Security Commission
P.O. Box 1699
1520 West Capital Street
Jackson, MS 39215-1699
(601) 961-7400

UNEMPLOYMENT INSURANCE

Unemployment Insurance Service
Employment and Training Administration, Department of Labor
Washington, DC 20210
(202) 523-7831
Description: Provides unemployment insurance for workers whose employers have contributed to state unemployment funds, federal civilian employees, ex-service persons, those who have become unemployed as a result of product imports, and those whose unemployment comes under the purview of a presidentially declared disaster.

$ Given: $25.5 billion for FY 93
Application Information: Contact the Employment Security Department for your state.
Deadline: N/A
Contact: Linda Ross Aldy, Executive Director
Employment Security Commission
P.O. Box 1699
1520 West Capital Street
Jackson, MS 39215-1699
(601) 961-7400

EMPLOYMENT AND TRAINING ASSISTANCE—DISLOCATED WORKERS

Employment and Training Administration, Department of Labor
200 Constitution Avenue, NW
Washington, DC 20210
(202) 535-0577
Description: Federal grants given to state and local programs to assist workers through training and employment services. These are workers who have been terminated or laid off, or who have received notice of such, and are not likely to return to their previous occupation or industry, or who are long-term unemployed. Targeted individuals include those affected by mass layoffs and natural disasters.
$ Given: Total nationwide of $571.1 million for FY 93
Application Information: Inquire at Employment Security Office listed below.
Deadline: N/A
Contact: Linda Ross Aldy, Executive Director
Employment Security Commission
P.O. Box 1699
1520 West Capital Street
Jackson, MS 39215-1699
(601) 961-7400

WOMEN'S SPECIAL EMPLOYMENT ASSISTANCE

Office of Administrative Management
Women's Bureau
Room S3305
Office of the Secretary, Department of Labor
Washington, DC 20210
(202) 523-6606

Description: Provides advisory services and counseling, and disseminates technical information to help the employment opportunities of women—especially in the realm of nontraditional women's jobs and jobs in new technologies.
$ Given: N/A
Application Information: Write to Women's Bureau in your region listed below.
Deadline: N/A
Contact: Delores L. Crockett, Regional Administrator
               Region IV, Women's Bureau
               Department of Labor
               1371 Peachtree Street, NE
               Room 323
               Atlanta, GA 30367
               (404) 347-4461

EMERGENCY LOANS

Farmers Home Administration
Department of Agriculture
14th Street Independence Avenue, SW
Washington, DC 20250
(202) 690-1533
Description: Provides loans to family farmers (either owner or tenant), ranchers, and aquaculture operators to cover losses resulting from natural or other major disasters. Recipients must be unable to obtain credit from other sources.
$ Given: $81.4 million est. FY 92. Average size for FY 92 was est. $42,300.
Application Information: Consult local telephone directory under United States Government, Department of Agriculture, for Farmers Home Administration Office.
Deadline: N/A
Contact: Farmers Home Administration
               Federal Building
               Suite 831
               100 West Capitol
               Jackson, MS 39269
               (601) 965-4316

ECONOMIC INJURY DISASTER LOANS

Office of Disaster Assistance
Small Business Administration
409 3rd Street, SW
Washington, DC 20416
(202) 205-6734
Description: Provides loans to small businesses suffering economic damage under presidential, Small Business Administration, and/or Department of Agriculture declared disaster. Must be a small business or agricultural concern, be located within declared disaster area, and be unable to obtain credit elsewhere.
$ Given: $60 million for FY 92. During FY 91, 1,076 loans were made.
Application Information: Refer to local Disaster Area Office of the Small Business Administration.
Deadline: N/A
Contact: Small Business Administration, Region IV
1375 Peachtree Street, NE
Fifth Floor
Atlanta, GA 30367-8102
(404) 347-2797

MISSOURI

EMPLOYMENT SERVICE

United States Employment Service
Employment and Training Administration, Department of Labor
Washington, DC 20210
(202) 535-0157
Description: Provides placement services for job seekers and employers. These include services to special applicant groups, such as veterans, the handicapped, youth, minority, and older workers; a computerized interstate job listing; and other labor market information.
$ Given: FY 93 est. $821.6 million
Application Information: Contact the Employment Security Department for your state.
Deadline: N/A

Contact: Tom Deuschle, Director
Department of Labor and Industrial Relations
Division of Employment Security
421 East Dunklin Street
P.O. Box 59
Jefferson City, MO 65101
(314) 751-3976

UNEMPLOYMENT INSURANCE

Unemployment Insurance Service
Employment and Training Administration, Department of Labor
Washington, DC 20210
(202) 523-7831
Description: Provides unemployment insurance for workers whose employers have contributed to state unemployment funds, federal civilian employees, ex-service persons, those who have become unemployed as a result of product imports, and those whose unemployment comes under the purview of a presidentially declared disaster.
$ Given: $25.5 billion for FY 93
Application Information: Contact the Employment Security Department for your state.
Deadline: N/A
Contact: Tom Deuschle, Director
Department of Labor and Industrial Relations
Division of Employment Security
421 East Dunklin Street
P.O. Box 59
Jefferson City, MO 65101
(314) 751-3976

EMPLOYMENT AND TRAINING ASSISTANCE—DISLOCATED WORKERS

Employment and Training Administration, Department of Labor
200 Constitution Avenue, NW
Washington, DC 20210
(202) 535-0577
Description: Federal grants given to state and local programs to assist workers through training and employment services. These are workers who have been terminated or laid off, or who have received notice of such, and are not likely to return to their previous occupation or industry, or who are long-term unemployed. Targeted

individuals include those affected by mass layoffs and natural disasters.

$ Given: Total nationwide of $571.1 million for FY 93

Application Information: Inquire at Employment Security Office listed below.

Deadline: N/A

Contact: Tom Deuschle, Director
Department of Labor and Industrial Relations
Division of Employment Security
421 East Dunklin Street
P.O. Box 59
Jefferson City, MO 65101
(314) 751-3976

WOMEN'S SPECIAL EMPLOYMENT ASSISTANCE

Office of Administrative Management
Women's Bureau
Room S3305
Office of the Secretary, Department of Labor
Washington, DC 20210
(202) 523-6606

Description: Provides advisory services and counseling, and disseminates technical information to help the employment opportunities of women—especially in the realm of nontraditional women's jobs and jobs in new technologies.

$ Given: N/A

Application Information: Write to Women's Bureau in your region listed below.

Deadline: N/A

Contact: Rose A. Kemp, Regional Administrator
Region VII, Women's Bureau
Department of Labor
Federal Building
Room 2511
911 Walnut Street
Kansas City, MO 64106
(816) 426-6108

EMERGENCY LOANS

Farmers Home Administration
Department of Agriculture
14th Street Independence Avenue, SW
Washington, DC 20250
(202) 690-1533
Description: Provides loans to family farmers (either owner or tenant), ranchers, and aquaculture operators to cover losses resulting from natural or other major disasters. Recipients must be unable to obtain credit from other sources.
$ Given: $81.4 million est. FY 92. Average size for FY 92 was est. $42,300.
Application Information: Consult local telephone directory under United States Government, Department of Agriculture, for Farmers Home Administration Office.
Deadline: N/A
Contact: Farmers Home Administration
601 Business Loop, 70 West
Parkade Center
Suite 235
Columbia, MO 65203
(314) 876-0976

ECONOMIC INJURY DISASTER LOANS

Office of Disaster Assistance
Small Business Administration
409 3rd Street, SW
Washington, DC 20416
(202) 205-6734
Description: Provides loans to small businesses suffering economic damage under presidential, Small Business Administration, and/or Department of Agriculture declared disaster. Must be a small business or agricultural concern, be located within declared disaster area, and be unable to obtain credit elsewhere.
$ Given: $60 million for FY 92. During FY 91, 1,076 loans were made.
Application Information: Refer to local Disaster Area Office of the Small Business Administration.
Deadline: N/A

Contact: Small Business Administration, Region VII
911 Walnut Street
Thirteenth Floor
Kansas City, MO 64106
(816) 426-3609

MONTANA

EMPLOYMENT SERVICE

United States Employment Service
Employment and Training Administration, Department of Labor
Washington, DC 20210
(202) 535-0157
Description: Provides placement services for job seekers and employers. These include services to special applicant groups, such as veterans, the handicapped, youth, minority, and older workers; a computerized interstate job listing; and other labor market information.
$ Given: FY 93 est. $821.6 million
Application Information: Contact the Employment Security Department for your state.
Deadline: N/A
Contact: Mario A. Micone, Commissioner
Department of Labor and Industry
P.O. Box 1728
Helena, MT 59624
(406) 444-3555

UNEMPLOYMENT INSURANCE

Unemployment Insurance Service
Employment and Training Administration, Department of Labor
Washington, DC 20210
(202) 523-7831
Description: Provides unemployment insurance for workers whose employers have contributed to state unemployment funds, federal civilian employees, ex-service persons, those who have become unemployed as a result of product imports, and those whose unemployment comes under the purview of a presidentially declared disaster.
$ Given: $25.5 billion for FY 93

Application Information: Contact the Employment Security Department for your state.
Deadline: N/A
Contact: Mario A. Micone, Commissioner
              Department of Labor and Industry
              P.O. Box 1728
              Helena, MT 59624
              (406) 444-3555

EMPLOYMENT AND TRAINING ASSISTANCE—DISLOCATED WORKERS

Employment and Training Administration, Department of Labor
200 Constitution Avenue, NW
Washington, DC 20210
(202) 535-0577
Description: Federal grants given to state and local programs to assist workers through training and employment services. These are workers who have been terminated or laid off, or who have received notice of such, and are not likely to return to their previous occupation or industry, or who are long-term unemployed. Targeted individuals include those affected by mass layoffs and natural disasters.
$ Given: Total nationwide of $571.1 million for FY 93
Application Information: Inquire at Employment Security Office listed below.
Deadline: N/A
Contact: Mario A. Micone, Commissioner
              Department of Labor and Industry
              P.O. Box 1728
              Helena, MT 59624
              (406) 444-3555

WOMEN'S SPECIAL EMPLOYMENT ASSISTANCE

Office of Administrative Management
Women's Bureau
Room S3305
Office of the Secretary, Department of Labor ·
Washington, DC 20210
(202) 523-6606
Description: Provides advisory services and counseling, and disseminates technical information to help the employment

opportunities of women—especially in the realm of nontraditional women's jobs and jobs in new technologies.

$ Given: N/A

Application Information: Write to Women's Bureau in your region listed below.

Deadline: N/A

Contact: Oleta Crain, Regional Administrator
Region VIII, Women's Bureau
Department of Labor
Federal Office Building
Room 1452
1801 California Street
Suite 905
Denver, CO 80202-2614
(303) 391-6755

EMERGENCY LOANS

Farmers Home Administration
Department of Agriculture
14th Street Independence Avenue, SW
Washington, DC 20250
(202) 690-1533

Description: Provides loans to family farmers (either owner or tenant), ranchers, and aquaculture operators to cover losses resulting from natural or other major disasters. Recipients must be unable to obtain credit from other sources.

$ Given: $81.4 million est. FY 92. Average size for FY 92 was est. $42,300.

Application Information: Consult local telephone directory under United States Government, Department of Agriculture, for Farmers Home Administration Office.

Deadline: N/A

Contact: Farmers Home Administration
900 Technology Boulevard
Suite B
P.O. Box 850
Bozeman, MT 59771
(406) 585-2500

ECONOMIC INJURY DISASTER LOANS

Office of Disaster Assistance
Small Business Administration
409 3rd Street, SW
Washington, DC 20416
(202) 205-6734

Description: Provides loans to small businesses suffering economic damage under presidential, Small Business Administration, and/or Department of Agriculture declared disaster. Must be a small business or agricultural concern, be located within declared disaster area, and be unable to obtain credit elsewhere.

$ Given: $60 million for FY 92. During FY 91, 1,076 loans were made.

Application Information: Refer to local Disaster Area Office of the Small Business Administration.

Deadline: N/A

Contact: Small Business Administration, Region VIII
999 18th Street
Suite 701
Denver, CO 80202
(303) 294-7001

NEBRASKA

EMPLOYMENT SERVICE

United States Employment Service
Employment and Training Administration, Department of Labor
Washington, DC 20210
(202) 535-0157

Description: Provides placement services for job seekers and employers. These include services to special applicant groups, such as veterans, the handicapped, youth, minority, and older workers; a computerized interstate job listing; and other labor market information.

$ Given: FY 93 est. $821.6 million

Application Information: Contact the Employment Security Department for your state.

Deadline: N/A

Contact: Dan Dolan, Commissioner of Labor
Department of Labor
550 South 16th Street
P.O. Box 94600
Lincoln, NE 68509-4600
(402) 471-3405

UNEMPLOYMENT INSURANCE

Unemployment Insurance Service
Employment and Training Administration, Department of Labor
Washington, DC 20210
(202) 523-7831
Description: Provides unemployment insurance for workers whose
employers have contributed to state unemployment funds, federal
civilian employees, ex-service persons, those who have become
unemployed as a result of product imports, and those whose
unemployment comes under the purview of a presidentially declared
disaster.
$ Given: $25.5 billion for FY 93
Application Information: Contact the Employment Security
Department for your state.
Deadline: N/A
Contact: Dan Dolan, Commissioner of Labor
Department of Labor
550 South 16th Street
P.O. Box 94600
Lincoln, NE 68509-4600
(402) 471-3405

EMPLOYMENT AND TRAINING ASSISTANCE—DISLOCATED WORKERS

Employment and Training Administration, Department of Labor
200 Constitution Avenue, NW
Washington, DC 20210
(202) 535-0577
Description: Federal grants given to state and local programs to
assist workers through training and employment services. These are
workers who have been terminated or laid off, or who have received
notice of such, and are not likely to return to their previous
occupation or industry, or who are long-term unemployed. Targeted
individuals include those affected by mass layoffs and natural
disasters.

$ Given: Total nationwide of $571.1 million for FY 93
Application Information: Inquire at Employment Security Office listed below.
Deadline: N/A
Contact: Dan Dolan, Commissioner of Labor
Department of Labor
550 South 16th Street
P.O. Box 94600
Lincoln, NE 68509-4600
(402) 471-3405

WOMEN'S SPECIAL EMPLOYMENT ASSISTANCE

Office of Administrative Management
Women's Bureau
Room S3305
Office of the Secretary, Department of Labor
Washington, DC 20210
(202) 523-6606
Description: Provides advisory services and counseling, and disseminates technical information to help the employment opportunities of women—especially in the realm of nontraditional women's jobs and jobs in new technologies.
$ Given: N/A
Application Information: Write to Women's Bureau in your region listed below.
Deadline: N/A
Contact: Rose A. Kemp, Regional Administrator
Region VII, Women's Bureau
Department of Labor
Federal Building
Room 2511
911 Walnut Street
Kansas City, MO 64106
(816) 426-6108

EMERGENCY LOANS

Farmers Home Administration
Department of Agriculture
14th Street Independence Avenue, SW
Washington, DC 20250
(202) 690-1533

Description: Provides loans to family farmers (either owner or tenant), ranchers, and aquaculture operators to cover losses resulting from natural or other major disasters. Recipients must be unable to obtain credit from other sources.

$ Given: $81.4 million est. FY 92. Average size for FY 92 was est. $42,300.

Application Information: Consult local telephone directory under United States Government, Department of Agriculture, for Farmers Home Administration Office.

Deadline: N/A

Contact: Farmers Home Administration
Federal Building
Room 308
100 Centennial Mall North
Lincoln, NE 68508
(402) 437-5551

ECONOMIC INJURY DISASTER LOANS

Office of Disaster Assistance
Small Business Administration
409 3rd Street, SW
Washington, DC 20416
(202) 205-6734

Description: Provides loans to small businesses suffering economic damage under presidential, Small Business Administration, and/or Department of Agriculture declared disaster. Must be a small business or agricultural concern, be located within declared disaster area, and be unable to obtain credit elsewhere.

$ Given: $60 million for FY 92. During FY 91, 1,076 loans were made.

Application Information: Refer to local Disaster Area Office of the Small Business Administration.

Deadline: N/A

Contact: Small Business Administration, Region VII
911 Walnut Street
Thirteenth Floor
Kansas City, MO 64106
(816) 426-3609

NEVADA

EMPLOYMENT SERVICE

United States Employment Service
Employment and Training Administration, Department of Labor
Washington, DC 20210
(202) 535-0157
Description: Provides placement services for job seekers and employers. These include services to special applicant groups, such as veterans, the handicapped, youth, minority, and older workers; a computerized interstate job listing; and other labor market information.
$ Given: FY 93 est. $821.6 million
Application Information: Contact the Employment Security Department for your state.
Deadline: N/A
Contact: Stanley P. Jones, Executive Director
Department of Employment Security
500 East Third Street
Carson City, NV 89713
(702) 885-4635

UNEMPLOYMENT INSURANCE

Unemployment Insurance Service
Employment and Training Administration, Department of Labor
Washington, DC 20210
(202) 523-7831
Description: Provides unemployment insurance for workers whose employers have contributed to state unemployment funds, federal civilian employees, ex-service persons, those who have become unemployed as a result of product imports, and those whose unemployment comes under the purview of a presidentially declared disaster.
$ Given: $25.5 billion for FY 93
Application Information: Contact the Employment Security Department for your state.
Deadline: N/A
Contact: Stanley P. Jones, Executive Director
Department of Employment Security
500 East Third Street
Carson City, NV 89713
(702) 885-4635

EMPLOYMENT AND TRAINING ASSISTANCE—DISLOCATED WORKERS

Employment and Training Administration, Department of Labor
200 Constitution Avenue, NW
Washington, DC 20210
(202) 535-0577
Description: Federal grants given to state and local programs to assist workers through training and employment services. These are workers who have been terminated or laid off, or who have received notice of such, and are not likely to return to their previous occupation or industry, or who are long-term unemployed. Targeted individuals include those affected by mass layoffs and natural disasters.
$ Given: Total nationwide of $571.1 million for FY 93
Application Information: Inquire at Employment Security Office listed below.
Deadline: N/A
Contact: Stanley P. Jones, Executive Director
Department of Employment Security
500 East Third Street
Carson City, NV 89713
(702) 885-4635

WOMEN'S SPECIAL EMPLOYMENT ASSISTANCE

Office of Administrative Management
Women's Bureau
Room S3305
Office of the Secretary, Department of Labor
Washington, DC 20210
(202) 523-6606
Description: Provides advisory services and counseling, and disseminates technical information to help the employment opportunities of women—especially in the realm of nontraditional women's jobs and jobs in new technologies.
$ Given: N/A
Application Information: Write to Women's Bureau in your region listed below.
Deadline: N/A

Contact: Rose A. Kemp, Regional Administrator
Region VII, Women's Bureau
Department of Labor
Federal Building
Room 2511
911 Walnut Street
Kansas City, MO 64106
(816) 426-6108

EMERGENCY LOANS

Farmers Home Administration
Department of Agriculture
14th Street Independence Avenue, SW
Washington, DC 20250
(202) 690-1533
Description: Provides loans to family farmers (either owner or tenant), ranchers, and aquaculture operators to cover losses resulting from natural or other major disasters. Recipients must be unable to obtain credit from other sources.
$ Given: $81.4 million est. FY 92. Average size for FY 92 was est. $42,300.
Application Information: Consult local telephone directory under United States Government, Department of Agriculture, for Farmers Home Administration Office.
Deadline: N/A
Contact: Farmers Home Administration
194 West Main Street
Suite F
Woodland, CA 95695-2915
(916) 666-3382

ECONOMIC INJURY DISASTER LOANS

Office of Disaster Assistance
Small Business Administration
409 3rd Street, SW
Washington, DC 20416
(202) 205-6734
Description: Provides loans to small businesses suffering economic damage under presidential, Small Business Administration, and/or Department of Agriculture declared disaster. Must be a small

business or agricultural concern, be located within declared disaster area, and be unable to obtain credit elsewhere.

$ Given: $60 million for FY 92. During FY 91, 1,076 loans were made.

Application Information: Refer to local Disaster Area Office of the Small Business Administration.

Deadline: N/A

Contact: Small Business Administration, Region IX
71 Stevenson Street
Twentieth Floor
San Francisco, CA 94105-2939
(415) 744-6402

NEW HAMPSHIRE

EMPLOYMENT SERVICE

United States Employment Service
Employment and Training Administration, Department of Labor
Washington, DC 20210
(202) 535-0157

Description: Provides placement services for job seekers and employers. These include services to special applicant groups, such as veterans, the handicapped, youth, minority, and older workers; a computerized interstate job listing; and other labor market information.

$ Given: FY 93 est. $821.6 million

Application Information: Contact the Employment Security Department for your state.

Deadline: N/A

Contact: John Ratoff, Commissioner
Department of Employment Security
32 South Main Street
Room 204
Concord, NH 03301
(603) 224-3311, Ext. 211

UNEMPLOYMENT INSURANCE

Unemployment Insurance Service
Employment and Training Administration, Department of Labor
Washington, DC 20210
(202) 523-7831

Description: Provides unemployment insurance for workers whose employers have contributed to state unemployment funds, federal civilian employees, ex-service persons, those who have become unemployed as a result of product imports, and those whose unemployment comes under the purview of a presidentially declared disaster.

$ Given: $25.5 billion for FY 93

Application Information: Contact the Employment Security Department for your state.

Deadline: N/A

Contact: John Ratoff, Commissioner
Department of Employment Security
32 South Main Street
Room 204
Concord, NH 03301
(603) 224-3311, Ext. 211

EMPLOYMENT AND TRAINING ASSISTANCE—DISLOCATED WORKERS

Employment and Training Administration, Department of Labor
200 Constitution Avenue, NW
Washington, DC 20210
(202) 535-0577

Description: Federal grants given to state and local programs to assist workers through training and employment services. These are workers who have been terminated or laid off, or who have received notice of such, and are not likely to return to their previous occupation or industry, or who are long-term unemployed. Targeted individuals include those affected by mass layoffs and natural disasters.

$ Given: Total nationwide of $571.1 million for FY 93

Application Information: Inquire at Employment Security Office listed below.

Deadline: N/A

Contact: John Ratoff, Commissioner
Department of Employment Security
32 South Main Street
Room 204
Concord, NH 03301
(603) 224-3311, Ext. 211

WOMEN'S SPECIAL EMPLOYMENT ASSISTANCE

Office of Administrative Management
Women's Bureau
Room S3305
Office of the Secretary, Department of Labor
Washington, DC 20210
(202) 523-6606

Description: Provides advisory services and counseling, and disseminates technical information to help the employment opportunities of women—especially in the realm of nontraditional women's jobs and jobs in new technologies.
$ Given: N/A
Application Information: Write to Women's Bureau in your region listed below.
Deadline: N/A
Contact: Martha Izzi, Regional Administrator
Region I, Women's Bureau
Department of Labor
One Congress Street
Boston, MA 02214
(617) 565-1988

EMERGENCY LOANS

Farmers Home Administration
Department of Agriculture
14th Street Independence Avenue, SW
Washington, DC 20250
(202) 690-1533

Description: Provides loans to family farmers (either owner or tenant), ranchers, and aquaculture operators to cover losses resulting from natural or other major disasters. Recipients must be unable to obtain credit from other sources.
$ Given: $81.4 million est. FY 92. Average size for FY 92 was est. $42,300.
Application Information: Consult local telephone directory under United States Government, Department of Agriculture, for Farmers Home Administration Office.
Deadline: N/A

Contact: Farmers Home Administration
City Center
Third Floor
89 Main Street
Montpelier, VT 05602
(802) 223-2371

ECONOMIC INJURY DISASTER LOANS

Office of Disaster Assistance
Small Business Administration
409 3rd Street, SW
Washington, DC 20416
(202) 205-6734
Description: Provides loans to small businesses suffering economic damage under presidential, Small Business Administration, and/or Department of Agriculture declared disaster. Must be a small business or agricultural concern, be located within declared disaster area, and be unable to obtain credit elsewhere.
$ Given: $60 million for FY 92. During FY 91, 1,076 loans were made.
Application Information: Refer to local Disaster Area Office of the Small Business Administration.
Deadline: N/A
Contact: Small Business Administration, Region I
155 Federal Street
Ninth Floor
Boston, MA 02110
(617) 451-2023

NEW JERSEY

EMPLOYMENT SERVICE

United States Employment Service
Employment and Training Administration, Department of Labor
Washington, DC 20210
(202) 535-0157
Description: Provides placement services for job seekers and employers. These include services to special applicant groups, such as veterans, the handicapped, youth, minority, and older workers; a computerized interstate job listing; and other labor market information.

$ Given: FY 93 est. $821.6 million
Application Information: Contact the Employment Security
Department for your state.
Deadline: N/A
Contact: Raymond L. Bramucci, Commissioner
              Department of Labor
              John Fitch Plaza
              Trenton, NJ 08625
              (609) 292-2323

UNEMPLOYMENT INSURANCE

Unemployment Insurance Service
Employment and Training Administration, Department of Labor
Washington, DC 20210
(202) 523-7831
Description: Provides unemployment insurance for workers whose
employers have contributed to state unemployment funds, federal
civilian employees, ex-service persons, those who have become
unemployed as a result of product imports, and those whose
unemployment comes under the purview of a presidentially declared
disaster.
$ Given: $25.5 billion for FY 93
Application Information: Contact the Employment Security
Department for your state.
Deadline: N/A
Contact: Raymond L. Bramucci, Commissioner
              Department of Labor
              John Fitch Plaza
              Trenton, NJ 08625
              (609) 292-2323

EMPLOYMENT AND TRAINING ASSISTANCE—DISLOCATED WORKERS

Employment and Training Administration, Department of Labor
200 Constitution Avenue, NW
Washington, DC 20210
(202) 535-0577
Description: Federal grants given to state and local programs to
assist workers through training and employment services. These are
workers who have been terminated or laid off, or who have received
notice of such, and are not likely to return to their previous
occupation or industry, or who are long-term unemployed. Targeted

individuals include those affected by mass layoffs and natural disasters.

$ Given: Total nationwide of $571.1 million for FY 93

Application Information: Inquire at Employment Security Office listed below.

Deadline: N/A

Contact: Raymond L. Bramucci, Commissioner
Department of Labor
John Fitch Plaza
Trenton, NJ 08625
(609) 292-2323

WOMEN'S SPECIAL EMPLOYMENT ASSISTANCE

Office of Administrative Management
Women's Bureau
Room S3305
Office of the Secretary, Department of Labor
Washington, DC 20210
(202) 523-6606

Description: Provides advisory services and counseling, and disseminates technical information to help the employment opportunities of women—especially in the realm of nontraditional women's jobs and jobs in new technologies.

$ Given: N/A

Application Information: Write to Women's Bureau in your region listed below.

Deadline: N/A

Contact: Mary C. Murphree, Regional Administrator
Region II, Women's Bureau
Department of Labor
201 Varick Street
Room 601
New York, NY 10014
(212) 337-2389

EMERGENCY LOANS

Farmers Home Administration
Department of Agriculture
14th Street Independence Avenue, SW
Washington, DC 20250
(202) 690-1533

Description: Provides loans to family farmers (either owner or tenant), ranchers, and aquaculture operators to cover losses resulting from natural or other major disasters. Recipients must be unable to obtain credit from other sources.

$ Given: $81.4 million est. FY 92. Average size for FY 92 was est. $42,300.

Application Information: Consult local telephone directory under United States Government, Department of Agriculture, for Farmers Home Administration Office.

Deadline: N/A

Contact: Farmers Home Administration
Tarnsfield and Woodlane Roads
Tarnsfield Plaza
Suite 22
Mt. Holly, NJ 08060
(609) 265-3600

ECONOMIC INJURY DISASTER LOANS

Office of Disaster Assistance
Small Business Administration
409 3rd Street, SW
Washington, DC 20416
(202) 205-6734

Description: Provides loans to small businesses suffering economic damage under presidential, Small Business Administration, and/or Department of Agriculture declared disaster. Must be a small business or agricultural concern, be located within declared disaster area, and be unable to obtain credit elsewhere.

$ Given: $60 million for FY 92. During FY 91, 1,076 loans were made.

Application Information: Refer to local Disaster Area Office of the Small Business Administration.

Deadline: N/A

Contact: Small Business Administration, Region II
26 Federal Plaza
Room 31-08
New York, NY 10278
(212) 264-7772

NEW MEXICO

EMPLOYMENT SERVICE

United States Employment Service
Employment and Training Administration, Department of Labor
Washington, DC 20210
(202) 535-0157
Description: Provides placement services for job seekers and employers. These include services to special applicant groups, such as veterans, the handicapped, youth, minority, and older workers; a computerized interstate job listing; and other labor market information.
$ Given: FY 93 est. $821.6 million
Application Information: Contact the Employment Security Department for your state.
Deadline: N/A
Contact: Patrick G. Baca, Secretary of Labor
Employment Security Department
P.O. Box 1928
Albuquerque, NM 87103
(505) 841-8409

UNEMPLOYMENT INSURANCE

Unemployment Insurance Service
Employment and Training Administration, Department of Labor
Washington, DC 20210
(202) 523-7831
Description: Provides unemployment insurance for workers whose employers have contributed to state unemployment funds, federal civilian employees, ex-service persons, those who have become unemployed as a result of product imports, and those whose unemployment comes under the purview of a presidentially declared disaster.
$ Given: $25.5 billion for FY 93
Application Information: Contact the Employment Security Department for your state.
Deadline: N/A

Contact: Patrick G. Baca, Secretary of Labor
Employment Security Department
P.O. Box 1928
Albuquerque, NM 87103
(505) 841-8409

EMPLOYMENT AND TRAINING ASSISTANCE—DISLOCATED WORKERS

Employment and Training Administration, Department of Labor
200 Constitution Avenue, NW
Washington, DC 20210
(202) 535-0577
Description: Federal grants given to state and local programs to assist workers through training and employment services. These are workers who have been terminated or laid off, or who have received notice of such, and are not likely to return to their previous occupation or industry, or who are long-term unemployed. Targeted individuals include those affected by mass layoffs and natural disasters.
$ Given: Total nationwide of $571.1 million for FY 93
Application Information: Inquire at Employment Security Office listed below.
Deadline: N/A
Contact: Patrick G. Baca, Secretary of Labor
Employment Security Department
P.O. Box 1928
Albuquerque, NM 87103
(505) 841-8409

WOMEN'S SPECIAL EMPLOYMENT ASSISTANCE

Office of Administrative Management
Women's Bureau
Room S3305
Office of the Secretary, Department of Labor
Washington, DC 20210
(202) 523-6606
Description: Provides advisory services and counseling, and disseminates technical information to help the employment opportunities of women—especially in the realm of nontraditional women's jobs and jobs in new technologies.
$ Given: N/A

Application Information: Write to Women's Bureau in your region listed below.

Deadline: N/A

Contact: Evelyn Smith, Regional Administrator
Region VI, Women's Bureau
Department of Labor
Federal Building
Suite 731
525 Griffin Street
Dallas, TX 75202
(214) 767-6985

EMERGENCY LOANS

Farmers Home Administration
Department of Agriculture
14th Street Independence Avenue, SW
Washington, DC 20250
(202) 690-1533

Description: Provides loans to family farmers (either owner or tenant), ranchers, and aquaculture operators to cover losses resulting from natural or other major disasters. Recipients must be unable to obtain credit from other sources.

$ Given: $81.4 million est. FY 92. Average size for FY 92 was est. $42,300.

Application Information: Consult local telephone directory under United States Government, Department of Agriculture, for Farmers Home Administration Office.

Deadline: N/A

Contact: Farmers Home Administration
Federal Building
Room 3414
517 Gold Avenue, SW
Albuquerque, NM 87102
(505) 766-2462

ECONOMIC INJURY DISASTER LOANS

Office of Disaster Assistance
Small Business Administration
409 3rd Street, SW
Washington, DC 20416
(202) 205-6734

Description: Provides loans to small businesses suffering economic damage under presidential, Small Business Administration, and/or Department of Agriculture declared disaster. Must be a small business or agricultural concern, be located within declared disaster area, and be unable to obtain credit elsewhere.

$ Given: $60 million for FY 92. During FY 91, 1,076 loans were made.

Application Information: Refer to local Disaster Area Office of the Small Business Administration.

Deadline: N/A

Contact: Small Business Administration, Region VI
8625 King George Drive
Building C
Dallas, TX 75235-3391
(214) 767-7643

NEW YORK

EMPLOYMENT SERVICE

United States Employment Service
Employment and Training Administration, Department of Labor
Washington, DC 20210
(202) 535-0157

Description: Provides placement services for job seekers and employers. These include services to special applicant groups, such as veterans, the handicapped, youth, minority, and older workers; a computerized interstate job listing; and other labor market information.

$ Given: FY 93 est. $821.6 million

Application Information: Contact the Employment Security Department for your state.

Deadline: N/A

Contact: Virgil Hodges, Deputy Commissioner
Department of Labor
State Office Campus
Building 12
Albany, NY 12240
(518) 457-0206

UNEMPLOYMENT INSURANCE

Unemployment Insurance Service
Employment and Training Administration, Department of Labor
Washington, DC 20210
(202) 523-7831
Description: Provides unemployment insurance for workers whose employers have contributed to state unemployment funds, federal civilian employees, ex-service persons, those who have become unemployed as a result of product imports, and those whose unemployment comes under the purview of a presidentially declared disaster.
$ Given: $25.5 billion for FY 93
Application Information: Contact the Employment Security Department for your state.
Deadline: N/A
Contact: Virgil Hodges, Deputy Commissioner
              Department of Labor
              State Office Campus
              Building 12
              Albany, NY 12240
              (518) 457-0206

EMPLOYMENT AND TRAINING ASSISTANCE—DISLOCATED WORKERS

Employment and Training Administration, Department of Labor
200 Constitution Avenue, NW
Washington, DC 20210
(202) 535-0577
Description: Federal grants given to state and local programs to assist workers through training and employment services. These are workers who have been terminated or laid off, or who have received notice of such, and are not likely to return to their previous occupation or industry, or who are long-term unemployed. Targeted individuals include those affected by mass layoffs and natural disasters.
$ Given: Total nationwide of $571.1 million for FY 93
Application Information: Inquire at Employment Security Office listed below.
Deadline: N/A

Contact: Virgil Hodges, Deputy Commissioner
Department of Labor
State Office Campus
Building 12
Albany, NY 12240
(518) 457-0206

WOMEN'S SPECIAL EMPLOYMENT ASSISTANCE
Office of Administrative Management
Women's Bureau
Room S3305
Office of the Secretary, Department of Labor
Washington, DC 20210
(202) 523-6606
Description: Provides advisory services and counseling, and disseminates technical information to help the employment opportunities of women—especially in the realm of nontraditional women's jobs and jobs in new technologies.
$ Given: N/A
Application Information: Write to Women's Bureau in your region listed below.
Deadline: N/A
Contact: Mary C. Murphree, Regional Administrator
Region II, Women's Bureau
Department of Labor
201 Varick Street
Room 601
New York, NY 10014
(212) 337-2389

EMERGENCY LOANS
Farmers Home Administration
Department of Agriculture
14th Street Independence Avenue, SW
Washington, DC 20250
(202) 690-1533
Description: Provides loans to family farmers (either owner or tenant), ranchers, and aquaculture operators to cover losses resulting from natural or other major disasters. Recipients must be unable to obtain credit from other sources.
$ Given: $81.4 million est. FY 92. Average size for FY 92 was est. $42,300.

Application Information: Consult local telephone directory under United States Government, Department of Agriculture, for Farmers Home Administration Office.

Deadline: N/A

Contact: Farmers Home Administration
Federal Building
100 South Clinton Street
Room 871
Syracuse, NY 13261-7318
(315) 423-5290

ECONOMIC INJURY DISASTER LOANS

Office of Disaster Assistance
Small Business Administration
409 3rd Street, SW
Washington, DC 20416
(202) 205-6734

Description: Provides loans to small businesses suffering economic damage under presidential, Small Business Administration, and/or Department of Agriculture declared disaster. Must be a small business or agricultural concern, be located within declared disaster area, and be unable to obtain credit elsewhere.

$ Given: $60 million for FY 92. During FY 91, 1,076 loans were made.

Application Information: Refer to local Disaster Area Office of the Small Business Administration.

Deadline: N/A

Contact: Small Business Administration, Region II
26 Federal Plaza
Room 31-08
New York, NY 10278
(212) 264-7772

NORTH CAROLINA

EMPLOYMENT SERVICE

United States Employment Service
Employment and Training Administration, Department of Labor
Washington, DC 20210
(202) 535-0157

Description: Provides placement services for job seekers and employers. These include services to special applicant groups, such as veterans, the handicapped, youth, minority, and older workers; a computerized interstate job listing; and other labor market information.

$ Given: FY 93 est. $821.6 million

Application Information: Contact the Employment Security Department for your state.

Deadline: N/A

Contact: Ann Q. Duncan, Chair
Employment Security Division
P.O. Box 25903
700 Wade Avenue
Raleigh, NC 27611
(919) 733-7546

UNEMPLOYMENT INSURANCE

Unemployment Insurance Service
Employment and Training Administration, Department of Labor
Washington, DC 20210
(202) 523-7831

Description: Provides unemployment insurance for workers whose employers have contributed to state unemployment funds, federal civilian employees, ex-service persons, those who have become unemployed as a result of product imports, and those whose unemployment comes under the purview of a presidentially declared disaster.

$ Given: $25.5 billion for FY 93

Application Information: Contact the Employment Security Department for your state.

Deadline: N/A

Contact: Ann Q. Duncan, Chair
Employment Security Division
P.O. Box 25903
700 Wade Avenue
Raleigh, NC 27611
(919) 733-7546

EMPLOYMENT AND TRAINING ASSISTANCE—DISLOCATED WORKERS

Employment and Training Administration, Department of Labor
200 Constitution Avenue, NW
Washington, DC 20210
(202) 535-0577

Description: Federal grants given to state and local programs to assist workers through training and employment services. These are workers who have been terminated or laid off, or who have received notice of such, and are not likely to return to their previous occupation or industry, or who are long-term unemployed. Targeted individuals include those affected by mass layoffs and natural disasters.

$ Given: Total nationwide of $571.1 million for FY 93

Application Information: Inquire at Employment Security Office listed below.

Deadline: N/A

Contact: Ann Q. Duncan, Chair
Employment Security Division
P.O. Box 25903
700 Wade Avenue
Raleigh, NC 27611
(919) 733-7546

WOMEN'S SPECIAL EMPLOYMENT ASSISTANCE

Office of Administrative Management
Women's Bureau
Room S3305
Office of the Secretary, Department of Labor
Washington, DC 20210
(202) 523-6606

Description: Provides advisory services and counseling, and disseminates technical information to help the employment opportunities of women—especially in the realm of nontraditional women's jobs and jobs in new technologies.

$ Given: N/A

Application Information: Write to Women's Bureau in your region listed below.

Deadline: N/A

Contact: Delores L. Crockett, Regional Administrator
Region IV, Women's Bureau
Department of Labor
1371 Peachtree Street, NE
Room 323
Atlanta, GA 30367
(404) 347-4461

EMERGENCY LOANS
Farmers Home Administration
Department of Agriculture
14th Street Independence Avenue, SW
Washington, DC 20250
(202) 690-1533
Description: Provides loans to family farmers (either owner or tenant), ranchers, and aquaculture operators to cover losses resulting from natural or other major disasters. Recipients must be unable to obtain credit from other sources.
$ Given: $81.4 million est. FY 92. Average size for FY 92 was est. $42,300.
Application Information: Consult local telephone directory under United States Government, Department of Agriculture, for Farmers Home Administration Office.
Deadline: N/A
Contact: Farmers Home Administration
4405 South Bland Road
Suite 260
Raleigh, NC 27609
(919) 790-2731

ECONOMIC INJURY DISASTER LOANS
Office of Disaster Assistance
Small Business Administration
409 3rd Street, SW
Washington, DC 20416
(202) 205-6734
Description: Provides loans to small businesses suffering economic damage under presidential, Small Business Administration, and/or Department of Agriculture declared disaster. Must be a small business or agricultural concern, be located within declared disaster area, and be unable to obtain credit elsewhere.
$ Given: $60 million for FY 92. During FY 91, 1,076 loans were made.
Application Information: Refer to local Disaster Area Office of the Small Business Administration.
Deadline: N/A

Contact: Small Business Administration, Region IV
1375 Peachtree Street, NE
Fifth Floor
Atlanta, GA 30367-8102
(404) 347-2797

NORTH DAKOTA

EMPLOYMENT SERVICE

United States Employment Service
Employment and Training Administration, Department of Labor
Washington, DC 20210
(202) 535-0157
Description: Provides placement services for job seekers and employers. These include services to special applicant groups, such as veterans, the handicapped, youth, minority, and older workers; a computerized interstate job listing; and other labor market information.
$ Given: FY 93 est. $821.6 million
Application Information: Contact the Employment Security Department for your state.
Deadline: N/A
Contact: Michael V. Deisz, Executive Director
Job Service North Dakota
P.O. Box 1537
1000 East Divide Avenue
Bismark, ND 58501/2
(701) 224-2836

UNEMPLOYMENT INSURANCE

Unemployment Insurance Service
Employment and Training Administration, Department of Labor
Washington, DC 20210
(202) 523-7831
Description: Provides unemployment insurance for workers whose employers have contributed to state unemployment funds, federal civilian employees, ex-service persons, those who have become unemployed as a result of product imports, and those whose unemployment comes under the purview of a presidentially declared disaster.
$ Given: $25.5 billion for FY 93

Application Information: Contact the Employment Security Department for your state.
Deadline: N/A
Contact: Michael V. Deisz, Executive Director
                Job Service North Dakota
                P.O. Box 1537
                1000 East Divide Avenue
                Bismark, ND 58501/2
                (701) 224-2836

EMPLOYMENT AND TRAINING ASSISTANCE—DISLOCATED WORKERS

Employment and Training Administration, Department of Labor
200 Constitution Avenue, NW
Washington, DC 20210
(202) 535-0577
Description: Federal grants given to state and local programs to assist workers through training and employment services. These are workers who have been terminated or laid off, or who have received notice of such, and are not likely to return to their previous occupation or industry, or who are long-term unemployed. Targeted individuals include those affected by mass layoffs and natural disasters.
$ Given: Total nationwide of $571.1 million for FY 93
Application Information: Inquire at Employment Security Office listed below.
Deadline: N/A
Contact: Michael V. Deisz, Executive Director
                Job Service North Dakota
                P.O. Box 1537
                1000 East Divide Avenue
                Bismark, ND 58501/2
                (701) 224-2836

WOMEN'S SPECIAL EMPLOYMENT ASSISTANCE

Office of Administrative Management
Women's Bureau
Room S3305
Office of the Secretary, Department of Labor
Washington, DC 20210
(202) 523-6606

Description: Provides advisory services and counseling, and disseminates technical information to help the employment opportunities of women—especially in the realm of nontraditional women's jobs and jobs in new technologies.

$ Given: N/A

Application Information: Write to Women's Bureau in your region listed below.

Deadline: N/A

Contact: Oleta Crain, Regional Administrator
Region VIII, Women's Bureau
Department of Labor
Federal Office Building
Room 1452
1801 California Street
Suite 905
Denver, CO 80202-2614
(303) 391-6755

EMERGENCY LOANS

Farmers Home Administration
Department of Agriculture
14th Street Independence Avenue, SW
Washington, DC 20250
(202) 690-1533

Description: Provides loans to family farmers (either owner or tenant), ranchers, and aquaculture operators to cover losses resulting from natural or other major disasters. Recipients must be unable to obtain credit from other sources.

$ Given: $81.4 million est. FY 92. Average size for FY 92 was est. $42,300.

Application Information: Consult local telephone directory under United States Government, Department of Agriculture, for Farmers Home Administration Office.

Deadline: N/A

Contact: Farmers Home Administration
Federal Building
Room 208
Third and Rosser
P.O. Box 1737
Bismark, ND 58502
(701) 250-4781

ECONOMIC INJURY DISASTER LOANS

Office of Disaster Assistance
Small Business Administration
409 3rd Street, SW
Washington, DC 20416
(202) 205-6734
Description: Provides loans to small businesses suffering economic damage under presidential, Small Business Administration, and/or Department of Agriculture declared disaster. Must be a small business or agricultural concern, be located within declared disaster area, and be unable to obtain credit elsewhere.
$ Given: $60 million for FY 92. During FY 91, 1,076 loans were made.
Application Information: Refer to local Disaster Area Office of the Small Business Administration.
Deadline: N/A
Contact: Small Business Administration, Region VIII
999 18th Street
Suite 701
Denver, CO 80202
(303) 294-7001

OHIO

EMPLOYMENT SERVICE

United States Employment Service
Employment and Training Administration, Department of Labor
Washington, DC 20210
(202) 535-0157
Description: Provides placement services for job seekers and employers. These include services to special applicant groups, such as veterans, the handicapped, youth, minority, and older workers; a computerized interstate job listing; and other labor market information.
$ Given: FY 93 est. $821.6 million
Application Information: Contact the Employment Security Department for your state.
Deadline: N/A

Contact: James Conrad, Administrator
Bureau of Employment Services
145 South Front Street
P.O. Box 1618
Columbus, OH 43216
(614) 466-2100

UNEMPLOYMENT INSURANCE

Unemployment Insurance Service
Employment and Training Administration, Department of Labor
Washington, DC 20210
(202) 523-7831
Description: Provides unemployment insurance for workers whose employers have contributed to state unemployment funds, federal civilian employees, ex-service persons, those who have become unemployed as a result of product imports, and those whose unemployment comes under the purview of a presidentially declared disaster.
$ Given: $25.5 billion for FY 93
Application Information: Contact the Employment Security Department for your state.
Deadline: N/A
Contact: James Conrad, Administrator
Bureau of Employment Services
145 South Front Street
P.O. Box 1618
Columbus, OH 43216
(614) 466-2100

EMPLOYMENT AND TRAINING ASSISTANCE—DISLOCATED WORKERS

Employment and Training Administration, Department of Labor
200 Constitution Avenue, NW
Washington, DC 20210
(202) 535-0577
Description: Federal grants given to state and local programs to assist workers through training and employment services. These are workers who have been terminated or laid off, or who have received notice of such, and are not likely to return to their previous occupation or industry, or who are long-term unemployed. Targeted individuals include those affected by mass layoffs and natural disasters.

$ Given: Total nationwide of $571.1 million for FY 93
Application Information: Inquire at Employment Security Office
listed below.
Deadline: N/A
Contact: James Conrad, Administrator
Bureau of Employment Services
145 South Front Street
P.O. Box 1618
Columbus, OH 43216
(614) 466-2100

WOMEN'S SPECIAL EMPLOYMENT ASSISTANCE
Office of Administrative Management
Women's Bureau
Room S3305
Office of the Secretary, Department of Labor
Washington, DC 20210
(202) 523-6606
Description: Provides advisory services and counseling, and
disseminates technical information to help the employment
opportunities of women—especially in the realm of nontraditional
women's jobs and jobs in new technologies.
$ Given: N/A
Application Information: Write to Women's Bureau in your region
listed below.
Deadline: N/A
Contact: Sandra K. Frank, Regional Administrator
Region V, Women's Bureau
Department of Labor
230 South Dearborn Street
Room 1022
Chicago, IL 60604
(312) 353-6985

EMERGENCY LOANS
Farmers Home Administration
Department of Agriculture
14th Street Independence Avenue, SW
Washington, DC 20250
(202) 690-1533
Description: Provides loans to family farmers (either owner or
tenant), ranchers, and aquaculture operators to cover losses

resulting from natural or other major disasters. Recipients must be unable to obtain credit from other sources.

$ Given: $81.4 million est. FY 92. Average size for FY 92 was est. $42,300.

Application Information: Consult local telephone directory under United States Government, Department of Agriculture, for Farmers Home Administration Office.

Deadline: N/A

Contact: Farmers Home Administration
Federal Building
Room 507
200 North High Street
Columbus, OH 43215
(614) 469-5606

ECONOMIC INJURY DISASTER LOANS

Office of Disaster Assistance
Small Business Administration
409 3rd Street, SW
Washington, DC 20416
(202) 205-6734

Description: Provides loans to small businesses suffering economic damage under presidential, Small Business Administration, and/or Department of Agriculture declared disaster. Must be a small business or agricultural concern, be located within declared disaster area, and be unable to obtain credit elsewhere.

$ Given: $60 million for FY 92. During FY 91, 1,076 loans were made.

Application Information: Refer to local Disaster Area Office of the Small Business Administration.

Deadline: N/A

Contact: Small Business Administration, Region V
Federal Building
300 South Riverside Plaza
Room 1975
Chicago, IL 60606-6611
(312) 353-0359

OKLAHOMA

EMPLOYMENT SERVICE

United States Employment Service
Employment and Training Administration, Department of Labor
Washington, DC 20210
(202) 535-0157
Description: Provides placement services for job seekers and employers. These include services to special applicant groups, such as veterans, the handicapped, youth, minority, and older workers; a computerized interstate job listing; and other labor market information.
$ Given: FY 93 est. $821.6 million
Application Information: Contact the Employment Security Department for your state.
Deadline: N/A
Contact: Bob Funston, Executive Director
Employment Security Commission
Will Rogers Memorial Office Building
Oklahoma City, OK 73105
(405) 557-7256

UNEMPLOYMENT INSURANCE

Unemployment Insurance Service
Employment and Training Administration, Department of Labor
Washington, DC 20210
(202) 523-7831
Description: Provides unemployment insurance for workers whose employers have contributed to state unemployment funds, federal civilian employees, ex-service persons, those who have become unemployed as a result of product imports, and those whose unemployment comes under the purview of a presidentially declared disaster.
$ Given: $25.5 billion for FY 93
Application Information: Contact the Employment Security Department for your state.
Deadline: N/A
Contact: Bob Funston, Executive Director
Employment Security Commission
Will Rogers Memorial Office Building
Oklahoma City, OK 73105
(405) 557-7256

Federal Grants

EMPLOYMENT AND TRAINING ASSISTANCE—DISLOCATED WORKERS

Employment and Training Administration, Department of Labor
200 Constitution Avenue, NW
Washington, DC 20210
(202) 535-0577

Description: Federal grants given to state and local programs to assist workers through training and employment services. These are workers who have been terminated or laid off, or who have received notice of such, and are not likely to return to their previous occupation or industry, or who are long-term unemployed. Targeted individuals include those affected by mass layoffs and natural disasters.

$ Given: Total nationwide of $571.1 million for FY 93

Application Information: Inquire at Employment Security Office listed below.

Deadline: N/A

Contact: Bob Funston, Executive Director
Employment Security Commission
Will Rogers Memorial Office Building
Oklahoma City, OK 73105
(405) 557-7256

WOMEN'S SPECIAL EMPLOYMENT ASSISTANCE

Office of Administrative Management
Women's Bureau
Room S3305
Office of the Secretary, Department of Labor
Washington, DC 20210
(202) 523-6606

Description: Provides advisory services and counseling, and disseminates technical information to help the employment opportunities of women—especially in the realm of nontraditional women's jobs and jobs in new technologies.

$ Given: N/A

Application Information: Write to Women's Bureau in your region listed below.

Deadline: N/A

Contact: Evelyn Smith, Regional Administrator
Region VI, Women's Bureau
Department of Labor
Federal Building
Suite 731
525 Griffin Street
Dallas, TX 75202
(214) 767-6985

EMERGENCY LOANS

Farmers Home Administration
Department of Agriculture
14th Street Independence Avenue, SW
Washington, DC 20250
(202) 690-1533

Description: Provides loans to family farmers (either owner or tenant), ranchers, and aquaculture operators to cover losses resulting from natural or other major disasters. Recipients must be unable to obtain credit from other sources.

$ Given: $81.4 million est. FY 92. Average size for FY 92 was est. $42,300.

Application Information: Consult local telephone directory under United States Government, Department of Agriculture, for Farmers Home Administration Office.

Deadline: N/A

Contact: Farmers Home Administration
USDA Agricultural Center Office Building
Stillwater, OK 74074
(405) 624-4250

ECONOMIC INJURY DISASTER LOANS

Office of Disaster Assistance
Small Business Administration
409 3rd Street, SW
Washington, DC 20416
(202) 205-6734

Description: Provides loans to small businesses suffering economic damage under presidential, Small Business Administration, and/or Department of Agriculture declared disaster. Must be a small business or agricultural concern, be located within declared disaster area, and be unable to obtain credit elsewhere.

$ Given: $60 million for FY 92. During FY 91, 1,076 loans were made.

Application Information: Refer to local Disaster Area Office of the Small Business Administration.

Deadline: N/A

Contact: Small Business Administration, Region VI
8625 King George Drive
Building C
Dallas, TX 75235-3391
(214) 767-7643

OREGON

EMPLOYMENT SERVICE

United States Employment Service
Employment and Training Administration, Department of Labor
Washington, DC 20210
(202) 535-0157

Description: Provides placement services for job seekers and employers. These include services to special applicant groups, such as veterans, the handicapped, youth, minority, and older workers; a computerized interstate job listing; and other labor market information.

$ Given: FY 93 est. $821.6 million

Application Information: Contact the Employment Security Department for your state.

Deadline: N/A

Contact: Pamela A. Mattson, Administrator
Employment Division
Department of Human Resources
875 Union Street, NE
Salem, OR 97311
(503) 378-3208

UNEMPLOYMENT INSURANCE

Unemployment Insurance Service
Employment and Training Administration, Department of Labor
Washington, DC 20210
(202) 523-7831

Description: Provides unemployment insurance for workers whose employers have contributed to state unemployment funds, federal

civilian employees, ex-service persons, those who have become unemployed as a result of product imports, and those whose unemployment comes under the purview of a presidentially declared disaster.

$ Given: $25.5 billion for FY 93

Application Information: Contact the Employment Security Department for your state.

Deadline: N/A

Contact: Pamela A. Mattson, Administrator
Employment Division
Department of Human Resources
875 Union Street, NE
Salem, OR 97311
(503) 378-3208

EMPLOYMENT AND TRAINING ASSISTANCE—DISLOCATED WORKERS

Employment and Training Administration, Department of Labor
200 Constitution Avenue, NW
Washington, DC 20210
(202) 535-0577

Description: Federal grants given to state and local programs to assist workers through training and employment services. These are workers who have been terminated or laid off, or who have received notice of such, and are not likely to return to their previous occupation or industry, or who are long-term unemployed. Targeted individuals include those affected by mass layoffs and natural disasters.

$ Given: Total nationwide of $571.1 million for FY 93

Application Information: Inquire at Employment Security Office listed below.

Deadline: N/A

Contact: Pamela A. Mattson, Administrator
Employment Division
Department of Human Resources
875 Union Street, NE
Salem, OR 97311
(503) 378-3208

WOMEN'S SPECIAL EMPLOYMENT ASSISTANCE

Office of Administrative Management
Women's Bureau
Room S3305
Office of the Secretary, Department of Labor
Washington, DC 20210
(202) 523-6606

Description: Provides advisory services and counseling, and disseminates technical information to help the employment opportunities of women—especially in the realm of nontraditional women's jobs and jobs in new technologies.

$ Given: N/A

Application Information: Write to Women's Bureau in your region listed below.

Deadline: N/A

Contact: Regional Administrator
         Region X, Women's Bureau
         Department of Labor
         1111 Third Avenue
         Room 885
         Seattle, WA 98101-3211
         (206) 553-1534

EMERGENCY LOANS

Farmers Home Administration
Department of Agriculture
14th Street Independence Avenue, SW
Washington, DC 20250
(202) 690-1533

Description: Provides loans to family farmers (either owner or tenant), ranchers, and aquaculture operators to cover losses resulting from natural or other major disasters. Recipients must be unable to obtain credit from other sources.

$ Given: $81.4 million est. FY 92. Average size for FY 92 was est. $42,300.

Application Information: Consult local telephone directory under United States Government, Department of Agriculture, for Farmers Home Administration Office.

Deadline: N/A

Contact: Farmers Home Administration
Federal Building
Room 1590
1220 SW 3rd Avenue
Portland, OR 97204
(503) 326-2731

ECONOMIC INJURY DISASTER LOANS

Office of Disaster Assistance
Small Business Administration
409 3rd Street, SW
Washington, DC 20416
(202) 205-6734
Description: Provides loans to small businesses suffering economic damage under presidential, Small Business Administration, and/or Department of Agriculture declared disaster. Must be a small business or agricultural concern, be located within declared disaster area, and be unable to obtain credit elsewhere.
$ Given: $60 million for FY 92. During FY 91, 1,076 loans were made.
Application Information: Refer to local Disaster Area Office of the Small Business Administration.
Deadline: N/A
Contact: Small Business Administration, Region X
2615 4th Avenue
Room 440
Seattle, WA 98121
(206) 442-5676

PENNSYLVANIA

EMPLOYMENT SERVICE

United States Employment Service
Employment and Training Administration, Department of Labor
Washington, DC 20210
(202) 535-0157
Description: Provides placement services for job seekers and employers. These include services to special applicant groups, such as veterans, the handicapped, youth, minority, and older workers; a computerized interstate job listing; and other labor market information.

$ Given: FY 93 est. $821.6 million
Application Information: Contact the Employment Security
Department for your state.
Deadline: N/A
Contact: Thomas Foley, Secretary
              Department of Labor and Industry
              1700 Labor and Industry Building
              7th and Forster Streets
              Harrisburg, PA 17120
              (717) 787-1745

UNEMPLOYMENT INSURANCE
Unemployment Insurance Service
Employment and Training Administration, Department of Labor
Washington, DC 20210
(202) 523-7831
Description: Provides unemployment insurance for workers whose
employers have contributed to state unemployment funds, federal
civilian employees, ex-service persons, those who have become
unemployed as a result of product imports, and those whose
unemployment comes under the purview of a presidentially declared
disaster.
$ Given: $25.5 billion for FY 93
Application Information: Contact the Employment Security
Department for your state.
Deadline: N/A
Contact: Thomas Foley, Secretary
              Department of Labor and Industry
              1700 Labor and Industry Building
              7th and Forster Streets
              Harrisburg, PA 17120
              (717) 787-1745

EMPLOYMENT AND TRAINING ASSISTANCE—DISLOCATED WORKERS

Employment and Training Administration, Department of Labor
200 Constitution Avenue, NW
Washington, DC 20210
(202) 535-0577
Description: Federal grants given to state and local programs to
assist workers through training and employment services. These are
workers who have been terminated or laid off, or who have received

notice of such, and are not likely to return to their previous occupation or industry, or who are long-term unemployed. Targeted individuals include those affected by mass layoffs and natural disasters.

$ Given: Total nationwide of $571.1 million for FY 93
Application Information: Inquire at Employment Security Office listed below.
Deadline: N/A
Contact: Thomas Foley, Secretary
Department of Labor and Industry
1700 Labor and Industry Building
7th and Forster Streets
Harrisburg, PA 17120
(717) 787-1745

WOMEN'S SPECIAL EMPLOYMENT ASSISTANCE

Office of Administrative Management
Women's Bureau
Room S3305
Office of the Secretary, Department of Labor
Washington, DC 20210
(202) 523-6606

Description: Provides advisory services and counseling, and disseminates technical information to help the employment opportunities of women—especially in the realm of nontraditional women's jobs and jobs in new technologies.
$ Given: N/A
Application Information: Write to Women's Bureau in your region listed below.
Deadline: N/A
Contact: Regional Administrator
Region III, Women's Bureau
Department of Labor
Gateway Building
Room 13280
3535 Market Street
Philadelphia, PA 19104
(215) 596-1184

EMERGENCY LOANS

Farmers Home Administration
Department of Agriculture
14th Street Independence Avenue, SW
Washington, DC 20250
(202) 690-1533
Description: Provides loans to family farmers (either owner or tenant), ranchers, and aquaculture operators to cover losses resulting from natural or other major disasters. Recipients must be unable to obtain credit from other sources.
$ Given: $81.4 million est. FY 92. Average size for FY 92 was est. $42,300.
Application Information: Consult local telephone directory under United States Government, Department of Agriculture, for Farmers Home Administration Office.
Deadline: N/A
Contact: Farmers Home Administration
One Credit Union Place
Suite 330
Harrisburg, PA 17110-2996
(717) 782-4476

ECONOMIC INJURY DISASTER LOANS

Office of Disaster Assistance
Small Business Administration
409 3rd Street, SW
Washington, DC 20416
(202) 205-6734
Description: Provides loans to small businesses suffering economic damage under presidential, Small Business Administration, and/or Department of Agriculture declared disaster. Must be a small business or agricultural concern, be located within declared disaster area, and be unable to obtain credit elsewhere.
$ Given: $60 million for FY 92. During FY 91, 1,076 loans were made.
Application Information: Refer to local Disaster Area Office of the Small Business Administration.
Deadline: N/A

Contact: Small Business Administration, Region III
475 Allendale Road
Suite 201
King of Prussia, PA 19406
(215) 962-3700

PUERTO RICO

EMPLOYMENT SERVICE

United States Employment Service
Employment and Training Administration, Department of Labor
Washington, DC 20210
(202) 535-0157
Description: Provides placement services for job seekers and employers. These include services to special applicant groups, such as veterans, the handicapped, youth, minority, and older workers; a computerized interstate job listing; and other labor market information.
$ Given: FY 93 est. $821.6 million
Application Information: Contact the Employment Security Department for your state.
Deadline: N/A
Contact: Luy N. Delgado Zayas, Secretary of Labor
Bureau of Employment Security
505 Munoz Rivera Avenue
Hato Rey, PR 00918
(809) 753-0550

UNEMPLOYMENT INSURANCE

Unemployment Insurance Service
Employment and Training Administration, Department of Labor
Washington, DC 20210
(202) 523-7831
Description: Provides unemployment insurance for workers whose employers have contributed to state unemployment funds, federal civilian employees, ex-service persons, those who have become unemployed as a result of product imports, and those whose unemployment comes under the purview of a presidentially declared disaster.
$ Given: $25.5 billion for FY 93

Application Information: Contact the Employment Security Department for your state.
Deadline: N/A
Contact: Luy N. Delgado Zayas, Secretary of Labor
Bureau of Employment Security
505 Munoz Rivera Avenue
Hato Rey, PR 00918
(809) 753-0550

EMPLOYMENT AND TRAINING ASSISTANCE—DISLOCATED WORKERS

Employment and Training Administration, Department of Labor
200 Constitution Avenue, NW
Washington, DC 20210
(202) 535-0577
Description: Federal grants given to state and local programs to assist workers through training and employment services. These are workers who have been terminated or laid off, or who have received notice of such, and are not likely to return to their previous occupation or industry, or who are long-term unemployed. Targeted individuals include those affected by mass layoffs and natural disasters.
$ Given: Total nationwide of $571.1 million for FY 93
Application Information: Inquire at Employment Security Office listed below.
Deadline: N/A
Contact: Luy N. Delgado Zayas, Secretary of Labor
Bureau of Employment Security
505 Munoz Rivera Avenue
Hato Rey, PR 00918
(809) 753-0550

WOMEN'S SPECIAL EMPLOYMENT ASSISTANCE

Office of Administrative Management
Women's Bureau
Room S3305
Office of the Secretary, Department of Labor
Washington, DC 20210
(202) 523-6606
Description: Provides advisory services and counseling, and disseminates technical information to help the employment

opportunities of women—especially in the realm of nontraditional women's jobs and jobs in new technologies.

$ Given: N/A

Application Information: Write to Women's Bureau in your region listed below.

Deadline: N/A

Contact: Mary C. Murphree, Regional Administrator
Region II, Women's Bureau
Department of Labor
201 Varick Street
Room 601
New York, NY 10014
(212) 337-2389

EMERGENCY LOANS

Farmers Home Administration
Department of Agriculture
14th Street Independence Avenue, SW
Washington, DC 20250
(202) 690-1533

Description: Provides loans to family farmers (either owner or tenant), ranchers, and aquaculture operators to cover losses resulting from natural or other major disasters. Recipients must be unable to obtain credit from other sources.

$ Given: $81.4 million est. FY 92. Average size for FY 92 was est. $42,300.

Application Information: Consult local telephone directory under United States Government, Department of Agriculture, for Farmers Home Administration Office.

Deadline: N/A

Contact: Farmers Home Administration
New San Juan Center Building
Room 501
159 Carlos E. Chardon Street
G.P.O. Box 6106G
Hato Rey, PR 00918-5481
(809) 766-5095

ECONOMIC INJURY DISASTER LOANS

Office of Disaster Assistance
Small Business Administration
409 3rd Street, SW
Washington, DC 20416
(202) 205-6734
Description: Provides loans to small businesses suffering economic damage under presidential, Small Business Administration, and/or Department of Agriculture declared disaster. Must be a small business or agricultural concern, be located within declared disaster area, and be unable to obtain credit elsewhere.
$ Given: $60 million for FY 92. During FY 91, 1,076 loans were made.
Application Information: Refer to local Disaster Area Office of the Small Business Administration.
Deadline: N/A
Contact: Small Business Administration, Region II
26 Federal Plaza
Room 31-08
New York, NY 10278
(212) 264-7772

RHODE ISLAND

EMPLOYMENT SERVICE

United States Employment Service
Employment and Training Administration, Department of Labor
Washington, DC 20210
(202) 535-0157
Description: Provides placement services for job seekers and employers. These include services to special applicant groups, such as veterans, the handicapped, youth, minority, and older workers; a computerized interstate job listing; and other labor market information.
$ Given: FY 93 est. $821.6 million
Application Information: Contact the Employment Security Department for your state.
Deadline: N/A

Contact: John M. Robinson, Director
Department of Employment Security and Training
24 101 Friendship Street
Providence, RI 02903-3740
(401) 277-3732

UNEMPLOYMENT INSURANCE

Unemployment Insurance Service
Employment and Training Administration, Department of Labor
Washington, DC 20210
(202) 523-7831
Description: Provides unemployment insurance for workers whose employers have contributed to state unemployment funds, federal civilian employees, ex-service persons, those who have become unemployed as a result of product imports, and those whose unemployment comes under the purview of a presidentially declared disaster.
$ Given: $25.5 billion for FY 93
Application Information: Contact the Employment Security Department for your state.
Deadline: N/A
Contact: John M. Robinson, Director
Department of Employment Security and Training
24 101 Friendship Street
Providence, RI 02903-3740
(401) 277-3732

EMPLOYMENT AND TRAINING ASSISTANCE—DISLOCATED WORKERS

Employment and Training Administration, Department of Labor
200 Constitution Avenue, NW
Washington, DC 20210
(202) 535-0577
Description: Federal grants given to state and local programs to assist workers through training and employment services. These are workers who have been terminated or laid off, or who have received notice of such, and are not likely to return to their previous occupation or industry, or who are long-term unemployed. Targeted individuals include those affected by mass layoffs and natural disasters.
$ Given: Total nationwide of $571.1 million for FY 93

Application Information: Inquire at Employment Security Office listed below.
Deadline: N/A
Contact: John M. Robinson, Director
Department of Employment Security and Training
24 101 Friendship Street
Providence, RI 02903-3740
(401) 277-3732

WOMEN'S SPECIAL EMPLOYMENT ASSISTANCE
Office of Administrative Management
Women's Bureau
Room S3305
Office of the Secretary, Department of Labor
Washington, DC 20210
(202) 523-6606
Description: Provides advisory services and counseling, and disseminates technical information to help the employment opportunities of women—especially in the realm of nontraditional women's jobs and jobs in new technologies.
$ Given: N/A
Application Information: Write to Women's Bureau in your region listed below.
Deadline: N/A
Contact: Martha Izzi, Regional Administrator
Region I, Women's Bureau
Department of Labor
One Congress Street
Boston, MA 02214
(617) 565-1988

EMERGENCY LOANS
Farmers Home Administration
Department of Agriculture
14th Street Independence Avenue, SW
Washington, DC 20250
(202) 690-1533
Description: Provides loans to family farmers (either owner or tenant), ranchers, and aquaculture operators to cover losses resulting from natural or other major disasters. Recipients must be unable to obtain credit from other sources.

$ Given: $81.4 million est. FY 92. Average size for FY 92 was est. $42,300.
Application Information: Consult local telephone directory under United States Government, Department of Agriculture, for Farmers Home Administration Office.
Deadline: N/A
Contact: Farmers Home Administration
451 West Street
Amherst, MA 01002
(413) 253-4300

ECONOMIC INJURY DISASTER LOANS

Office of Disaster Assistance
Small Business Administration
409 3rd Street, SW
Washington, DC 20416
(202) 205-6734
Description: Provides loans to small businesses suffering economic damage under presidential, Small Business Administration, and/or Department of Agriculture declared disaster. Must be a small business or agricultural concern, be located within declared disaster area, and be unable to obtain credit elsewhere.
$ Given: $60 million for FY 92. During FY 91, 1,076 loans were made.
Application Information: Refer to local Disaster Area Office of the Small Business Administration.
Deadline: N/A
Contact: Small Business Administration, Region I
155 Federal Street
Ninth Floor
Boston, MA 02110
(617) 451-2023

SOUTH CAROLINA

EMPLOYMENT SERVICE

United States Employment Service
Employment and Training Administration, Department of Labor
Washington, DC 20210
(202) 535-0157

Description: Provides placement services for job seekers and employers. These include services to special applicant groups, such as veterans, the handicapped, youth, minority, and older workers; a computerized interstate job listing; and other labor market information.

$ Given: FY 93 est. $821.6 million

Application Information: Contact the Employment Security Department for your state.

Deadline: N/A

Contact: Robert E. David, Executive Director
Employment Security Commission
P.O. Box 995
1550 Gadsen Street
Columbia, SC 29202
(803) 737-2617

UNEMPLOYMENT INSURANCE

Unemployment Insurance Service

Employment and Training Administration, Department of Labor
Washington, DC 20210
(202) 523-7831

Description: Provides unemployment insurance for workers whose employers have contributed to state unemployment funds, federal civilian employees, ex-service persons, those who have become unemployed as a result of product imports, and those whose unemployment comes under the purview of a presidentially declared disaster.

$ Given: $25.5 billion for FY 93

Application Information: Contact the Employment Security Department for your state.

Deadline: N/A

Contact: Robert E. David, Executive Director
Employment Security Commission
P.O. Box 995
1550 Gadsen Street
Columbia, SC 29202
(803) 737-2617

EMPLOYMENT AND TRAINING ASSISTANCE—DISLOCATED WORKERS

Employment and Training Administration, Department of Labor
200 Constitution Avenue, NW
Washington, DC 20210
(202) 535-0577

Description: Federal grants given to state and local programs to assist workers through training and employment services. These are workers who have been terminated or laid off, or who have received notice of such, and are not likely to return to their previous occupation or industry, or who are long-term unemployed. Targeted individuals include those affected by mass layoffs and natural disasters.

$ Given: Total nationwide of $571.1 million for FY 93

Application Information: Inquire at Employment Security Office listed below.

Deadline: N/A

Contact: Robert E. David, Executive Director
Employment Security Commission
P.O. Box 995
1550 Gadsen Street
Columbia, SC 29202
(803) 737-2617

WOMEN'S SPECIAL EMPLOYMENT ASSISTANCE

Office of Administrative Management
Women's Bureau
Room S3305
Office of the Secretary, Department of Labor
Washington, DC 20210
(202) 523-6606

Description: Provides advisory services and counseling, and disseminates technical information to help the employment opportunities of women—especially in the realm of nontraditional women's jobs and jobs in new technologies.

$ Given: N/A

Application Information: Write to Women's Bureau in your region listed below.

Deadline: N/A

Contact: Delores L. Crockett, Regional Administrator
Region IV, Women's Bureau
Department of Labor
1371 Peachtree Street, NE
Room 323
Atlanta, GA 30367
(404) 347-4461

EMERGENCY LOANS

Farmers Home Administration
Department of Agriculture
14th Street Independence Avenue, SW
Washington, DC 20250
(202) 690-1533
Description: Provides loans to family farmers (either owner or tenant), ranchers, and aquaculture operators to cover losses resulting from natural or other major disasters. Recipients must be unable to obtain credit from other sources.
$ Given: $81.4 million est. FY 92. Average size for FY 92 was est. $42,300.
Application Information: Consult local telephone directory under United States Government, Department of Agriculture, for Farmers Home Administration Office.
Deadline: N/A
Contact: Farmers Home Administration
Strom Thurmond Federal Building
1835 Assembly Street
Room 1007
Columbia, SC 29201
(803) 765-5163

ECONOMIC INJURY DISASTER LOANS

Office of Disaster Assistance
Small Business Administration
409 3rd Street, SW
Washington, DC 20416
(202) 205-6734
Description: Provides loans to small businesses suffering economic damage under presidential, Small Business Administration, and/or Department of Agriculture declared disaster. Must be a small business or agricultural concern, be located within declared disaster area, and be unable to obtain credit elsewhere.

$ Given: $60 million for FY 92. During FY 91, 1,076 loans were made.

Application Information: Refer to local Disaster Area Office of the Small Business Administration.

Deadline: N/A

Contact: Small Business Administration, Region IV
1375 Peachtree Street, NE
Fifth Floor
Atlanta, GA 30367-8102
(404) 347-2797

SOUTH DAKOTA

EMPLOYMENT SERVICE

United States Employment Service
Employment and Training Administration, Department of Labor
Washington, DC 20210
(202) 535-0157

Description: Provides placement services for job seekers and employers. These include services to special applicant groups, such as veterans, the handicapped, youth, minority, and older workers; a computerized interstate job listing; and other labor market information.

$ Given: FY 93 est. $821.6 million

Application Information: Contact the Employment Security Department for your state.

Deadline: N/A

Contact: Peter de Hueck, Secretary
Department of Labor
Kneip Building
700 Governors Drive
Pierre, SD 57501-2277
(605) 773-3101

UNEMPLOYMENT INSURANCE

Unemployment Insurance Service
Employment and Training Administration, Department of Labor
Washington, DC 20210
(202) 523-7831

Description: Provides unemployment insurance for workers whose employers have contributed to state unemployment funds, federal

civilian employees, ex-service persons, those who have become unemployed as a result of product imports, and those whose unemployment comes under the purview of a presidentially declared disaster.

$ Given: $25.5 billion for FY 93

Application Information: Contact the Employment Security Department for your state.

Deadline: N/A

Contact: Peter de Hueck, Secretary
Department of Labor
Kneip Building
700 Governors Drive
Pierre, SD 57501-2277
(605) 773-3101

EMPLOYMENT AND TRAINING ASSISTANCE—DISLOCATED WORKERS

Employment and Training Administration, Department of Labor
200 Constitution Avenue, NW
Washington, DC 20210
(202) 535-0577

Description: Federal grants given to state and local programs to assist workers through training and employment services. These are workers who have been terminated or laid off, or who have received notice of such, and are not likely to return to their previous occupation or industry, or who are long-term unemployed. Targeted individuals include those affected by mass layoffs and natural disasters.

$ Given: Total nationwide of $571.1 million for FY 93

Application Information: Inquire at Employment Security Office listed below.

Deadline: N/A

Contact: Peter de Hueck, Secretary
Department of Labor
Kneip Building
700 Governors Drive
Pierre, SD 57501-2277
(605) 773-3101

WOMEN'S SPECIAL EMPLOYMENT ASSISTANCE

Office of Administrative Management
Women's Bureau
Room S3305
Office of the Secretary, Department of Labor
Washington, DC 20210
(202) 523-6606

Description: Provides advisory services and counseling, and disseminates technical information to help the employment opportunities of women—especially in the realm of nontraditional women's jobs and jobs in new technologies.

$ Given: N/A

Application Information: Write to Women's Bureau in your region listed below.

Deadline: N/A

Contact: Oleta Crain, Regional Administrator
              Region VIII, Women's Bureau
              Department of Labor
              Federal Office Building
              Room 1452
              1801 California Street
              Suite 905
              Denver, CO 80202-2614
              (303) 391-6755

EMERGENCY LOANS

Farmers Home Administration
Department of Agriculture
14th Street Independence Avenue, SW
Washington, DC 20250
(202) 690-1533

Description: Provides loans to family farmers (either owner or tenant), ranchers, and aquaculture operators to cover losses resulting from natural or other major disasters. Recipients must be unable to obtain credit from other sources.

$ Given: $81.4 million est. FY 92. Average size for FY 92 was est. $42,300.

Application Information: Consult local telephone directory under United States Government, Department of Agriculture, for Farmers Home Administration Office.

Deadline: N/A

Contact: Farmers Home Administration
Huron Federal Building
Room 308
200 Fourth Street, SW
Huron, SD 57350
(605) 353-1430

ECONOMIC INJURY DISASTER LOANS

Office of Disaster Assistance
Small Business Administration
409 3rd Street, SW
Washington, DC 20416
(202) 205-6734
Description: Provides loans to small businesses suffering economic damage under presidential, Small Business Administration, and/or Department of Agriculture declared disaster. Must be a small business or agricultural concern, be located within declared disaster area, and be unable to obtain credit elsewhere.
$ Given: $60 million for FY 92. During FY 91, 1,076 loans were made.
Application Information: Refer to local Disaster Area Office of the Small Business Administration.
Deadline: N/A
Contact: Small Business Administration, Region VIII
999 18th Street
Suite 701
Denver, CO 80202
(303) 294-7001

TENNESSEE

EMPLOYMENT SERVICE

United States Employment Service
Employment and Training Administration, Department of Labor
Washington, DC 20210
(202) 535-0157
Description: Provides placement services for job seekers and employers. These include services to special applicant groups, such as veterans, the handicapped, youth, minority, and older workers; a computerized interstate job listing; and other labor market information.

$ Given: FY 93 est. $821.6 million
Application Information: Contact the Employment Security Department for your state.
Deadline: N/A
Contact: James A. Davenport, Commissioner
Department of Employment Security
Volunteer Plaza Building
Twelfth Floor
500 James Robertson Parkway
Nashville, TN 37245-0001
(615) 741-2131

UNEMPLOYMENT INSURANCE

Unemployment Insurance Service
Employment and Training Administration, Department of Labor
Washington, DC 20210
(202) 523-7831
Description: Provides unemployment insurance for workers whose employers have contributed to state unemployment funds, federal civilian employees, ex-service persons, those who have become unemployed as a result of product imports, and those whose unemployment comes under the purview of a presidentially declared disaster.
$ Given: $25.5 billion for FY 93
Application Information: Contact the Employment Security Department for your state.
Deadline: N/A
Contact: James A. Davenport, Commissioner
Department of Employment Security
Volunteer Plaza Building
Twelfth Floor
500 James Robertson Parkway
Nashville, TN 37245-0001
(615) 741-2131

EMPLOYMENT AND TRAINING ASSISTANCE—DISLOCATED WORKERS

Employment and Training Administration, Department of Labor
200 Constitution Avenue, NW
Washington, DC 20210
(202) 535-0577

Description: Federal grants given to state and local programs to assist workers through training and employment services. These are workers who have been terminated or laid off, or who have received notice of such, and are not likely to return to their previous occupation or industry, or who are long-term unemployed. Targeted individuals include those affected by mass layoffs and natural disasters.

$ Given: Total nationwide of $571.1 million for FY 93

Application Information: Inquire at Employment Security Office listed below.

Deadline: N/A

Contact: James A. Davenport, Commissioner
Department of Employment Security
Volunteer Plaza Building
Twelfth Floor
500 James Robertson Parkway
Nashville, TN 37245-0001
(615) 741-2131

WOMEN'S SPECIAL EMPLOYMENT ASSISTANCE

Office of Administrative Management
Women's Bureau
Room S3305
Office of the Secretary, Department of Labor
Washington, DC 20210
(202) 523-6606

Description: Provides advisory services and counseling, and disseminates technical information to help the employment opportunities of women—especially in the realm of nontraditional women's jobs and jobs in new technologies.

$ Given: N/A

Application Information: Write to Women's Bureau in your region listed below.

Deadline: N/A

Contact: Delores L. Crockett, Regional Administrator
Region IV, Women's Bureau
Department of Labor
1371 Peachtree Street, NE
Room 323
Atlanta, GA 30367
(404) 347-4461

EMERGENCY LOANS

Farmers Home Administration
Department of Agriculture
14th Street Independence Avenue, SW
Washington, DC 20250
(202) 690-1533

Description: Provides loans to family farmers (either owner or tenant), ranchers, and aquaculture operators to cover losses resulting from natural or other major disasters. Recipients must be unable to obtain credit from other sources.

$ Given: $81.4 million est. FY 92. Average size for FY 92 was est. $42,300.

Application Information: Consult local telephone directory under United States Government, Department of Agriculture, for Farmers Home Administration Office.

Deadline: N/A

Contact: Farmers Home Administration
3322 West End Avenue
Suite 300
Nashville, TN 37203-1071
(615) 736-7341

ECONOMIC INJURY DISASTER LOANS

Office of Disaster Assistance
Small Business Administration
409 3rd Street, SW
Washington, DC 20416
(202) 205-6734

Description: Provides loans to small businesses suffering economic damage under presidential, Small Business Administration, and/or Department of Agriculture declared disaster. Must be a small business or agricultural concern, be located within declared disaster area, and be unable to obtain credit elsewhere.

$ Given: $60 million for FY 92. During FY 91, 1,076 loans were made.

Application Information: Refer to local Disaster Area Office of the Small Business Administration.

Deadline: N/A

Contact: Small Business Administration, Region IV
1375 Peachtree Street, NE
Fifth Floor
Atlanta, GA 30367-8102
(404) 347-2797

TEXAS

EMPLOYMENT SERVICE

United States Employment Service
Employment and Training Administration, Department of Labor
Washington, DC 20210
(202) 535-0157
Description: Provides placement services for job seekers and employers. These include services to special applicant groups, such as veterans, the handicapped, youth, minority, and older workers; a computerized interstate job listing; and other labor market information.
$ Given: FY 93 est. $821.6 million
Application Information: Contact the Employment Security Department for your state.
Deadline: N/A
Contact: William Grossenbacher, Administrator
Texas Employment Commission
638 TEC Building
15th and Congress Avenue
Austin, TX 78778
(512) 463-2652

UNEMPLOYMENT INSURANCE

Unemployment Insurance Service
Employment and Training Administration, Department of Labor
Washington, DC 20210
(202) 523-7831
Description: Provides unemployment insurance for workers whose employers have contributed to state unemployment funds, federal civilian employees, ex-service persons, those who have become unemployed as a result of product imports, and those whose unemployment comes under the purview of a presidentially declared disaster.
$ Given: $25.5 billion for FY 93

Application Information: Contact the Employment Security
Department for your state.
Deadline: N/A
Contact: William Grossenbacher, Administrator
               Texas Employment Commission
               638 TEC Building
               15th and Congress Avenue
               Austin, TX 78778
               (512) 463-2652

EMPLOYMENT AND TRAINING ASSISTANCE—DISLOCATED WORKERS

Employment and Training Administration, Department of Labor
200 Constitution Avenue, NW
Washington, DC 20210
(202) 535-0577
Description: Federal grants given to state and local programs to
assist workers through training and employment services. These are
workers who have been terminated or laid off, or who have received
notice of such, and are not likely to return to their previous
occupation or industry, or who are long-term unemployed. Targeted
individuals include those affected by mass layoffs and natural
disasters.
$ Given: Total nationwide of $571.1 million for FY 93
Application Information: Inquire at Employment Security Office
listed below.
Deadline: N/A
Contact: William Grossenbacher, Administrator
               Texas Employment Commission
               638 TEC Building
               15th and Congress Avenue
               Austin, TX 78778
               (512) 463-2652

WOMEN'S SPECIAL EMPLOYMENT ASSISTANCE

Office of Administrative Management
Women's Bureau
Room S3305
Office of the Secretary, Department of Labor
Washington, DC 20210
(202) 523-6606

Description: Provides advisory services and counseling, and disseminates technical information to help the employment opportunities of women—especially in the realm of nontraditional women's jobs and jobs in new technologies.
$ Given: N/A
Application Information: Write to Women's Bureau in your region listed below.
Deadline: N/A
Contact: Evelyn Smith, Regional Administrator
        Region VI, Women's Bureau
        Department of Labor
        Federal Building
        Suite 731
        525 Griffin Street
        Dallas, TX 75202
        (214) 767-6985

EMERGENCY LOANS

Farmers Home Administration
Department of Agriculture
14th Street Independence Avenue, SW
Washington, DC 20250
(202) 690-1533
Description: Provides loans to family farmers (either owner or tenant), ranchers, and aquaculture operators to cover losses resulting from natural or other major disasters. Recipients must be unable to obtain credit from other sources.
$ Given: $81.4 million est. FY 92. Average size for FY 92 was est. $42,300.
Application Information: Consult local telephone directory under United States Government, Department of Agriculture, for Farmers Home Administration Office.
Deadline: N/A
Contact: Farmers Home Administration
        Federal Building
        Suite 102
        101 South Main
        Temple, TX 76501
        (817) 524-4063

ECONOMIC INJURY DISASTER LOANS

Office of Disaster Assistance
Small Business Administration
409 3rd Street, SW
Washington, DC 20416
(202) 205-6734
Description: Provides loans to small businesses suffering economic damage under presidential, Small Business Administration, and/or Department of Agriculture declared disaster. Must be a small business or agricultural concern, be located within declared disaster area, and be unable to obtain credit elsewhere.
$ Given: $60 million for FY 92. During FY 91, 1,076 loans were made.
Application Information: Refer to local Disaster Area Office of the Small Business Administration.
Deadline: N/A
Contact: Small Business Administration, Region VI
8625 King George Drive
Building C
Dallas, TX 75235-3391
(214) 767-7643

UTAH

EMPLOYMENT SERVICE

United States Employment Service
Employment and Training Administration, Department of Labor
Washington, DC 20210
(202) 535-0157
Description: Provides placement services for job seekers and employers. These include services to special applicant groups, such as veterans, the handicapped, youth, minority, and older workers; a computerized interstate job listing; and other labor market information.
$ Given: FY 93 est. $821.6 million
Application Information: Contact the Employment Security Department for your state.
Deadline: N/A

Contact: Floyd G. Astin, Administrator
Department of Employment Security and Training
P.O. Box 11249
174 Social Hall Avenue
Salt Lake City, UT 84147-0249
(801) 533-2201

UNEMPLOYMENT INSURANCE

Unemployment Insurance Service
Employment and Training Administration, Department of Labor
Washington, DC 20210
(202) 523-7831
Description: Provides unemployment insurance for workers whose employers have contributed to state unemployment funds, federal civilian employees, ex-service persons, those who have become unemployed as a result of product imports, and those whose unemployment comes under the purview of a presidentially declared disaster.
$ Given: $25.5 billion for FY 93
Application Information: Contact the Employment Security Department for your state.
Deadline: N/A
Contact: Floyd G. Astin, Administrator
Department of Employment Security and Training
P.O. Box 11249
174 Social Hall Avenue
Salt Lake City, UT 84147-0249
(801) 533-2201

EMPLOYMENT AND TRAINING ASSISTANCE—DISLOCATED WORKERS

Employment and Training Administration, Department of Labor
200 Constitution Avenue, NW
Washington, DC 20210
(202) 535-0577
Description: Federal grants given to state and local programs to assist workers through training and employment services. These are workers who have been terminated or laid off, or who have received notice of such, and are not likely to return to their previous occupation or industry, or who are long-term unemployed. Targeted individuals include those affected by mass layoffs and natural disasters.

$ Given: Total nationwide of $571.1 million for FY 93
Application Information: Inquire at Employment Security Office listed below.
Deadline: N/A
Contact: Floyd G. Astin, Administrator
    Department of Employment Security and Training
    P.O. Box 11249
    174 Social Hall Avenue
    Salt Lake City, UT 84147-0249
    (801) 533-2201

WOMEN'S SPECIAL EMPLOYMENT ASSISTANCE

Office of Administrative Management
Women's Bureau
Room S3305
Office of the Secretary, Department of Labor
Washington, DC 20210
(202) 523-6606
Description: Provides advisory services and counseling, and disseminates technical information to help the employment opportunities of women—especially in the realm of nontraditional women's jobs and jobs in new technologies.
$ Given: N/A
Application Information: Write to Women's Bureau in your region listed below.
Deadline: N/A
Contact: Oleta Crain, Regional Administrator
    Region VIII, Women's Bureau
    Department of Labor
    Federal Office Building
    Room 1452
    1801 California Street
    Suite 905
    Denver, CO 80202-2614
    (303) 391-6755

EMERGENCY LOANS

Farmers Home Administration
Department of Agriculture
14th Street Independence Avenue, SW
Washington, DC 20250
(202) 690-1533

Description: Provides loans to family farmers (either owner or tenant), ranchers, and aquaculture operators to cover losses resulting from natural or other major disasters. Recipients must be unable to obtain credit from other sources.

$ Given: $81.4 million est. FY 92. Average size for FY 92 was est. $42,300.

Application Information: Consult local telephone directory under United States Government, Department of Agriculture, for Farmers Home Administration Office.

Deadline: N/A

Contact: Farmers Home Administration
                Federal Building
                Room 5438
                125 South State Street
                Salt Lake City, UT 84138
                (801) 524-4063

ECONOMIC INJURY DISASTER LOANS

Office of Disaster Assistance
Small Business Administration
409 3rd Street, SW
Washington, DC 20416
(202) 205-6734

Description: Provides loans to small businesses suffering economic damage under presidential, Small Business Administration, and/or Department of Agriculture declared disaster. Must be a small business or agricultural concern, be located within declared disaster area, and be unable to obtain credit elsewhere.

$ Given: $60 million for FY 92. During FY 91, 1,076 loans were made.

Application Information: Refer to local Disaster Area Office of the Small Business Administration.

Deadline: N/A

Contact: Small Business Administration, Region VIII
999 18th Street
Suite 701
Denver, CO 80202
(303) 294-7001

VERMONT

EMPLOYMENT SERVICE

United States Employment Service
Employment and Training Administration, Department of Labor
Washington, DC 20210
(202) 535-0157
Description: Provides placement services for job seekers and employers. These include services to special applicant groups, such as veterans, the handicapped, youth, minority, and older workers; a computerized interstate job listing; and other labor market information.
$ Given: FY 93 est. $821.6 million
Application Information: Contact the Employment Security Department for your state.
Deadline: N/A
Contact: Patricia Thomas, Commissioner
Department of Employment Security and Training
P.O. Box 488
5 Green Mountain Drive
Montpelier, VT 05602
(802) 229-0311

UNEMPLOYMENT INSURANCE

Unemployment Insurance Service
Employment and Training Administration, Department of Labor
Washington, DC 20210
(202) 523-7831
Description: Provides unemployment insurance for workers whose employers have contributed to state unemployment funds, federal civilian employees, ex-service persons, those who have become unemployed as a result of product imports, and those whose unemployment comes under the purview of a presidentially declared disaster.
$ Given: $25.5 billion for FY 93

Application Information: Contact the Employment Security Department for your state.
Deadline: N/A
Contact: Patricia Thomas, Commissioner
Department of Employment Security and Training
P.O. Box 488
5 Green Mountain Drive
Montpelier, VT 05602
(802) 229-0311

EMPLOYMENT AND TRAINING ASSISTANCE—DISLOCATED WORKERS

Employment and Training Administration, Department of Labor
200 Constitution Avenue, NW
Washington, DC 20210
(202) 535-0577
Description: Federal grants given to state and local programs to assist workers through training and employment services. These are workers who have been terminated or laid off, or who have received notice of such, and are not likely to return to their previous occupation or industry, or who are long-term unemployed. Targeted individuals include those affected by mass layoffs and natural disasters.
$ Given: Total nationwide of $571.1 million for FY 93
Application Information: Inquire at Employment Security Office listed below.
Deadline: N/A
Contact: Patricia Thomas, Commissioner
Department of Employment Security and Training
P.O. Box 488
5 Green Mountain Drive
Montpelier, VT 05602
(802) 229-0311

WOMEN'S SPECIAL EMPLOYMENT ASSISTANCE

Office of Administrative Management
Women's Bureau
Room S3305
Office of the Secretary, Department of Labor
Washington, DC 20210
(202) 523-6606

Description: Provides advisory services and counseling, and disseminates technical information to help the employment opportunities of women—especially in the realm of nontraditional women's jobs and jobs in new technologies.

$ Given: N/A

Application Information: Write to Women's Bureau in your region listed below.

Deadline: N/A

Contact: Martha Izzi, Regional Administrator
            Region I, Women's Bureau
            Department of Labor
            One Congress Street
            Boston, MA 02214
            (617) 565-1988

EMERGENCY LOANS

Farmers Home Administration
Department of Agriculture
14th Street Independence Avenue, SW
Washington, DC 20250
(202) 690-1533

Description: Provides loans to family farmers (either owner or tenant), ranchers, and aquaculture operators to cover losses resulting from natural or other major disasters. Recipients must be unable to obtain credit from other sources.

$ Given: $81.4 million est. FY 92. Average size for FY 92 was est. $42,300.

Application Information: Consult local telephone directory under United States Government, Department of Agriculture, for Farmers Home Administration Office.

Deadline: N/A

Contact: Farmers Home Administration
            City Center
            Third Floor
            89 Main Street
            Montpelier, VT 05602
            (802) 223-2371

ECONOMIC INJURY DISASTER LOANS
Office of Disaster Assistance
Small Business Administration
409 3rd Street, SW
Washington, DC 20416
(202) 205-6734
Description: Provides loans to small businesses suffering economic damage under presidential, Small Business Administration, and/or Department of Agriculture declared disaster. Must be a small business or agricultural concern, be located within declared disaster area, and be unable to obtain credit elsewhere.
$ Given: $60 million for FY 92. During FY 91, 1,076 loans were made.
Application Information: Refer to local Disaster Area Office of the Small Business Administration.
Deadline: N/A
Contact: Small Business Administration, Region I
155 Federal Street
Ninth Floor
Boston, MA 02110
(617) 451-2023

VIRGINIA

EMPLOYMENT SERVICE
United States Employment Service
Employment and Training Administration, Department of Labor
Washington, DC 20210
(202) 535-0157
Description: Provides placement services for job seekers and employers. These include services to special applicant groups, such as veterans, the handicapped, youth, minority, and older workers; a computerized interstate job listing; and other labor market information.
$ Given: FY 93 est. $821.6 million
Application Information: Contact the Employment Security Department for your state.
Deadline: N/A

Contact: Ralph G. Cantrell, Commissioner
Virginia Employment Commission
P.O. Box 1358
Richmond, VA 23211
(804) 786-3011

UNEMPLOYMENT INSURANCE
Unemployment Insurance Service
Employment and Training Administration, Department of Labor
Washington, DC 20210
(202) 523-7831
Description: Provides unemployment insurance for workers whose employers have contributed to state unemployment funds, federal civilian employees, ex-service persons, those who have become unemployed as a result of product imports, and those whose unemployment comes under the purview of a presidentially declared disaster.
$ Given: $25.5 billion for FY 93
Application Information: Contact the Employment Security Department for your state.
Deadline: N/A
Contact: Ralph G. Cantrell, Commissioner
Virginia Employment Commission
P.O. Box 1358
Richmond, VA 23211
(804) 786-3011

EMPLOYMENT AND TRAINING ASSISTANCE—DISLOCATED WORKERS
Employment and Training Administration, Department of Labor
200 Constitution Avenue, NW
Washington, DC 20210
(202) 535-0577
Description: Federal grants given to state and local programs to assist workers through training and employment services. These are workers who have been terminated or laid off, or who have received notice of such, and are not likely to return to their previous occupation or industry, or who are long-term unemployed. Targeted individuals include those affected by mass layoffs and natural disasters.
$ Given: Total nationwide of $571.1 million for FY 93

Application Information: Inquire at Employment Security Office listed below.
Deadline: N/A
Contact: Ralph G. Cantrell, Commissioner
Virginia Employment Commission
P.O. Box 1358
Richmond, VA 23211
(804) 786-3011

WOMEN'S SPECIAL EMPLOYMENT ASSISTANCE
Office of Administrative Management
Women's Bureau
Room S3305
Office of the Secretary, Department of Labor
Washington, DC 20210
(202) 523-6606
Description: Provides advisory services and counseling, and disseminates technical information to help the employment opportunities of women—especially in the realm of nontraditional women's jobs and jobs in new technologies.
$ Given: N/A
Application Information: Write to Women's Bureau in your region listed below.
Deadline: N/A
Contact: Regional Administrator
Region III, Women's Bureau
Department of Labor
Gateway Building
Room 13280
3535 Market Street
Philadelphia, PA 19104
(215) 596-1184

EMERGENCY LOANS
Farmers Home Administration
Department of Agriculture
14th Street Independence Avenue, SW
Washington, DC 20250
(202) 690-1533
Description: Provides loans to family farmers (either owner or tenant), ranchers, and aquaculture operators to cover losses

resulting from natural or other major disasters. Recipients must be unable to obtain credit from other sources.
$ Given: $81.4 million est. FY 92. Average size for FY 92 was est. $42,300.
Application Information: Consult local telephone directory under United States Government, Department of Agriculture, for Farmers Home Administration Office.
Deadline: N/A
Contact: Farmers Home Administration
Federal Building
Room 8213
400 North 8th Street
Richmond, VA 23240
(804) 771-2451

ECONOMIC INJURY DISASTER LOANS
Office of Disaster Assistance
Small Business Administration
409 3rd Street, SW
Washington, DC 20416
(202) 205-6734
Description: Provides loans to small businesses suffering economic damage under presidential, Small Business Administration, and/or Department of Agriculture declared disaster. Must be a small business or agricultural concern, be located within declared disaster area, and be unable to obtain credit elsewhere.
$ Given: $60 million for FY 92. During FY 91, 1,076 loans were made.
Application Information: Refer to local Disaster Area Office of the Small Business Administration.
Deadline: N/A
Contact: Small Business Administration, Region III
475 Allendale Road
Suite 201
King of Prussia, PA 19406
(215) 962-3700

VIRGIN ISLANDS

EMPLOYMENT SERVICE

United States Employment Service
Employment and Training Administration, Department of Labor
Washington, DC 20210
(202) 535-0157
Description: Provides placement services for job seekers and employers. These include services to special applicant groups, such as veterans, the handicapped, youth, minority, and older workers; a computerized interstate job listing; and other labor market information.
$ Given: FY 93 est. $821.6 million
Application Information: Contact the Employment Security Department for your state.
Deadline: N/A
Contact: Carol M. Burke, Assistant Commissioner
          Employment Security Agency
          Virgin Islands Department of Labor
          78 Queen Street, Christiansted
          St. Croix, VI 00820
          (809) 773-5114

UNEMPLOYMENT INSURANCE

Unemployment Insurance Service
Employment and Training Administration, Department of Labor
Washington, DC 20210
(202) 523-7831
Description: Provides unemployment insurance for workers whose employers have contributed to state unemployment funds, federal civilian employees, ex-service persons, those who have become unemployed as a result of product imports, and those whose unemployment comes under the purview of a presidentially declared disaster.
$ Given: $25.5 billion for FY 93
Application Information: Contact the Employment Security Department for your state.
Deadline: N/A

Contact: Carol M. Burke, Assistant Commissioner
Employment Security Agency
Virgin Islands Department of Labor
78 Queen Street, Christiansted
St. Croix, VI 00820
(809) 773-5114

EMPLOYMENT AND TRAINING ASSISTANCE—DISLOCATED WORKERS

Employment and Training Administration, Department of Labor
200 Constitution Avenue, NW
Washington, DC 20210
(202) 535-0577
Description: Federal grants given to state and local programs to assist workers through training and employment services. These are workers who have been terminated or laid off, or who have received notice of such, and are not likely to return to their previous occupation or industry, or who are long-term unemployed. Targeted individuals include those affected by mass layoffs and natural disasters.
$ Given: Total nationwide of $571.1 million for FY 93
Application Information: Inquire at Employment Security Office listed below.
Deadline: N/A
Contact: Carol M. Burke, Assistant Commissioner
Employment Security Agency
Virgin Islands Department of Labor
78 Queen Street, Christiansted
St. Croix, VI 00820
(809) 773-5114

WOMEN'S SPECIAL EMPLOYMENT ASSISTANCE

Office of Administrative Management
Women's Bureau
Room S3305
Office of the Secretary, Department of Labor
Washington, DC 20210
(202) 523-6606
Description: Provides advisory services and counseling, and disseminates technical information to help the employment opportunities of women—especially in the realm of nontraditional women's jobs and jobs in new technologies.

$ Given: N/A

Application Information: Write to Women's Bureau in your region listed below.

Deadline: N/A

Contact: Mary C. Murphree, Regional Administrator
Region II, Women's Bureau
Department of Labor
201 Varick Street
Room 601
New York, NY 10014
(212) 337-2389

EMERGENCY LOANS

Farmers Home Administration
Department of Agriculture
14th Street Independence Avenue, SW
Washington, DC 20250
(202) 690-1533

Description: Provides loans to family farmers (either owner or tenant), ranchers, and aquaculture operators to cover losses resulting from natural or other major disasters. Recipients must be unable to obtain credit from other sources.

$ Given: $81.4 million est. FY 92. Average size for FY 92 was est. $42,300.

Application Information: Consult local telephone directory under United States Government, Department of Agriculture, for Farmers Home Administration Office.

Deadline: N/A

Contact: Farmers Home Administration
City Center
Third Floor
89 Main Street
Montpelier, VT 05602
(802) 223-2371

ECONOMIC INJURY DISASTER LOANS

Office of Disaster Assistance
Small Business Administration
409 3rd Street, SW
Washington, DC 20416
(202) 205-6734

Description: Provides loans to small businesses suffering economic damage under presidential, Small Business Administration, and/or Department of Agriculture declared disaster. Must be a small business or agricultural concern, be located within declared disaster area, and be unable to obtain credit elsewhere.
$ Given: $60 million for FY 92. During FY 91, 1,076 loans were made.
Application Information: Refer to local Disaster Area Office of the Small Business Administration.
Deadline: N/A
Contact: Small Business Administration, Region II
26 Federal Plaza
Room 31-08
New York, NY 10278
(212) 264-7772

WASHINGTON

EMPLOYMENT SERVICE

United States Employment Service
Employment and Training Administration, Department of Labor
Washington, DC 20210
(202) 535-0157
Description: Provides placement services for job seekers and employers. These include services to special applicant groups, such as veterans, the handicapped, youth, minority, and older workers; a computerized interstate job listing; and other labor market information.
$ Given: FY 93 est. $821.6 million
Application Information: Contact the Employment Security Department for your state.
Deadline: N/A
Contact: Isiah Turner, Commissioner
Employment Security Department
212 Maple Park
P.O. Box 367
Olympia, WA 98504
(206) 753-5114

UNEMPLOYMENT INSURANCE

Unemployment Insurance Service
Employment and Training Administration, Department of Labor
Washington, DC 20210
(202) 523-7831

Description: Provides unemployment insurance for workers whose employers have contributed to state unemployment funds, federal civilian employees, ex-service persons, those who have become unemployed as a result of product imports, and those whose unemployment comes under the purview of a presidentially declared disaster.

$ Given: $25.5 billion for FY 93

Application Information: Contact the Employment Security Department for your state.

Deadline: N/A

Contact: Isiah Turner, Commissioner
Employment Security Department
212 Maple Park
P.O. Box 367
Olympia, WA 98504
(206) 753-5114

EMPLOYMENT AND TRAINING ASSISTANCE—DISLOCATED WORKERS

Employment and Training Administration, Department of Labor
200 Constitution Avenue, NW
Washington, DC 20210
(202) 535-0577

Description: Federal grants given to state and local programs to assist workers through training and employment services. These are workers who have been terminated or laid off, or who have received notice of such, and are not likely to return to their previous occupation or industry, or who are long-term unemployed. Targeted individuals include those affected by mass layoffs and natural disasters.

$ Given: Total nationwide of $571.1 million for FY 93

Application Information: Inquire at Employment Security Office listed below.

Deadline: N/A

Contact: Isiah Turner, Commissioner
Employment Security Department
212 Maple Park
P.O. Box 367
Olympia, WA 98504
(206) 753-5114

WOMEN'S SPECIAL EMPLOYMENT ASSISTANCE
Office of Administrative Management
Women's Bureau
Room S3305
Office of the Secretary, Department of Labor
Washington, DC 20210
(202) 523-6606
Description: Provides advisory services and counseling, and disseminates technical information to help the employment opportunities of women—especially in the realm of nontraditional women's jobs and jobs in new technologies.
$ Given: N/A
Application Information: Write to Women's Bureau in your region listed below.
Deadline: N/A
Contact: Regional Administrator
Region X, Women's Bureau
Department of Labor
1111 Third Avenue
Room 885
Seattle, WA 98101-3211
(206) 553-1534

EMERGENCY LOANS
Farmers Home Administration
Department of Agriculture
14th Street Independence Avenue, SW
Washington, DC 20250
(202) 690-1533
Description: Provides loans to family farmers (either owner or tenant), ranchers, and aquaculture operators to cover losses resulting from natural or other major disasters. Recipients must be unable to obtain credit from other sources.
$ Given: $81.4 million est. FY 92. Average size for FY 92 was est. $42,300.

Application Information: Consult local telephone directory under United States Government, Department of Agriculture for Farmers Home Administration Office.
Deadline: N/A
Contact: Farmers Home Administration
Federal Building
Room 319
P.O. Box 2427
Wenatchee, WA 98807
(509) 662-4352

ECONOMIC INJURY DISASTER LOANS

Office of Disaster Assistance
Small Business Administration
409 3rd Street, SW
Washington, DC 20416
(202) 205-6734
Description: Provides loans to small businesses suffering economic damage under presidential, Small Business Administration, and/or Department of Agriculture declared disaster. Must be a small business or agricultural concern, be located within declared disaster area, and be unable to obtain credit elsewhere.
$ Given: $60 million for FY 92. During FY 91, 1,076 loans were made.
Application Information: Refer to local Disaster Area Office of the Small Business Administration.
Deadline: N/A
Contact: Small Business Administration, Region X
2615 4th Avenue
Room 440
Seattle, WA 98121
(206) 442-5676

WEST VIRGINIA

EMPLOYMENT SERVICE

United States Employment Service
Employment and Training Administration, Department of Labor
Washington, DC 20210
(202) 535-0157

Description: Provides placement services for job seekers and employers. These include services to special applicant groups, such as veterans, the handicapped, youth, minority, and older workers; a computerized interstate job listing; and other labor market information.

$ Given: FY 93 est. $821.6 million

Application Information: Contact the Employment Security Department for your state.

Deadline: N/A

Contact: Andrew N. Richardson, Commissioner
Bureau of Employment Programs
State Office Building
112 California Avenue
Charleston, WV 25305
(304) 348-2630

UNEMPLOYMENT INSURANCE

Unemployment Insurance Service
Employment and Training Administration, Department of Labor
Washington, DC 20210
(202) 523-7831

Description: Provides unemployment insurance for workers whose employers have contributed to state unemployment funds, federal civilian employees, ex-service persons, those who have become unemployed as a result of product imports, and those whose unemployment comes under the purview of a presidentially declared disaster.

$ Given: $25.5 billion for FY 93

Application Information: Contact the Employment Security Department for your state.

Deadline: N/A

Contact: Andrew N. Richardson, Commissioner
Bureau of Employment Programs
State Office Building
112 California Avenue
Charleston, WV 25305
(304) 348-2630

EMPLOYMENT AND TRAINING ASSISTANCE—DISLOCATED WORKERS

Employment and Training Administration, Department of Labor
200 Constitution Avenue, NW
Washington, DC 20210
(202) 535-0577

Description: Federal grants given to state and local programs to assist workers through training and employment services. These are workers who have been terminated or laid off, or who have received notice of such, and are not likely to return to their previous occupation or industry, or who are long-term unemployed. Targeted individuals include those affected by mass layoffs and natural disasters.

$ Given: Total nationwide of $571.1 million for FY 93

Application Information: Inquire at Employment Security Office listed below.

Deadline: N/A

Contact: Andrew N. Richardson, Commissioner
Bureau of Employment Programs
State Office Building
112 California Avenue
Charleston, WV 25305
(304) 348-2630

WOMEN'S SPECIAL EMPLOYMENT ASSISTANCE

Office of Administrative Management
Women's Bureau
Room S3305
Office of the Secretary, Department of Labor
Washington, DC 20210
(202) 523-6606

Description: Provides advisory services and counseling, and disseminates technical information to help the employment opportunities of women—especially in the realm of nontraditional women's jobs and jobs in new technologies.

$ Given: N/A

Application Information: Write to Women's Bureau in your region listed below.

Deadline: N/A

Contact: Regional Administrator
Region III, Women's Bureau
Department of Labor
Gateway Building
Room 13280
3535 Market Street
Philadelphia, PA 19104
(215) 596-1184

EMERGENCY LOANS

Farmers Home Administration
Department of Agriculture
14th Street Independence Avenue, SW
Washington, DC 20250
(202) 690-1533
Description: Provides loans to family farmers (either owner or tenant), ranchers, and aquaculture operators to cover losses resulting from natural or other major disasters. Recipients must be unable to obtain credit from other sources.
$ Given: $81.4 million est. FY 92. Average size for FY 92 was est. $42,300.
Application Information: Consult local telephone directory under United States Government, Department of Agriculture, for Farmers Home Administration Office.
Deadline: N/A
Contact: Farmers Home Administration
75 High Street
P.O. Box 678
Morgantown, WV 26505
(304) 291-4791

ECONOMIC INJURY DISASTER LOANS

Office of Disaster Assistance
Small Business Administration
409 3rd Street, SW
Washington, DC 20416
(202) 205-6734
Description: Provides loans to small businesses suffering economic damage under presidential, Small Business Administration, and/or Department of Agriculture declared disaster. Must be a small business or agricultural concern, be located within declared disaster area, and be unable to obtain credit elsewhere.

$ Given: $60 million for FY 92. During FY 91, 1,076 loans were made.
Application Information: Refer to local Disaster Area Office of the Small Business Administration.
Deadline: N/A
Contact: Small Business Administration, Region III
475 Allendale Road
Suite 201
King of Prussia, PA 19406
(215) 962-3700

WISCONSIN

EMPLOYMENT SERVICE

United States Employment Service
Employment and Training Administration, Department of Labor
Washington, DC 20210
(202) 535-0157
Description: Provides placement services for job seekers and employers. These include services to special applicant groups, such as veterans, the handicapped, youth, minority, and older workers; a computerized interstate job listing; and other labor market information.
$ Given: FY 93 est. $821.6 million
Application Information: Contact the Employment Security Department for your state.
Deadline: N/A
Contact: Gerald Whitburn, Secretary
Department of Industry, Labor and Human Relations
P.O. Box 7946
201 East Washington Avenue
Madison, WI 53707
(608) 266-7552

UNEMPLOYMENT INSURANCE
Unemployment Insurance Service
Employment and Training Administration, Department of Labor
Washington, DC 20210
(202) 523-7831
Description: Provides unemployment insurance for workers whose employers have contributed to state unemployment funds, federal

civilian employees, ex-service persons, those who have become unemployed as a result of product imports, and those whose unemployment comes under the purview of a presidentially declared disaster.

$ Given: $25.5 billion for FY 93

Application Information: Contact the Employment Security Department for your state.

Deadline: N/A

Contact: Gerald Whitburn, Secretary
Department of Industry, Labor and Human Relations
P.O. Box 7946
201 East Washington Avenue
Madison, WI 53707
(608) 266-7552

EMPLOYMENT AND TRAINING ASSISTANCE—DISLOCATED WORKERS

Employment and Training Administration, Department of Labor
200 Constitution Avenue, NW
Washington, DC 20210
(202) 535-0577

Description: Federal grants given to state and local programs to assist workers through training and employment services. These are workers who have been terminated or laid off, or who have received notice of such, and are not likely to return to their previous occupation or industry, or who are long-term unemployed. Targeted individuals include those affected by mass layoffs and natural disasters.

$ Given: Total nationwide of $571.1 million for FY 93

Application Information: Inquire at Employment Security Office listed below.

Deadline: N/A

Contact: Gerald Whitburn, Secretary
Department of Industry, Labor and Human Relations
P.O. Box 7946
201 East Washington Avenue
Madison, WI 53707
(608) 266-7552

WOMEN'S SPECIAL EMPLOYMENT ASSISTANCE

Office of Administrative Management
Women's Bureau
Room S3305
Office of the Secretary, Department of Labor
Washington, DC 20210
(202) 523-6606

Description: Provides advisory services and counseling, and disseminates technical information to help the employment opportunities of women—especially in the realm of nontraditional women's jobs and jobs in new technologies.

$ Given: N/A

Application Information: Write to Women's Bureau in your region listed below.

Deadline: N/A

Contact: Sandra K. Frank, Regional Administrator
            Region V, Women's Bureau
            Department of Labor
            230 South Dearborn Street
            Room 1022
            Chicago, IL 60604
            (312) 353-6985

EMERGENCY LOANS

Farmers Home Administration
Department of Agriculture
14th Street Independence Avenue, SW
Washington, DC 20250
(202) 690-1533

Description: Provides loans to family farmers (either owner or tenant), ranchers, and aquaculture operators to cover losses resulting from natural or other major disasters. Recipients must be unable to obtain credit from other sources.

$ Given: $81.4 million est. FY 92. Average size for FY 92 was est. $42,300.

Application Information: Consult local telephone directory under United States Government, Department of Agriculture, for Farmers Home Administration Office.

Deadline: N/A

Contact: Farmers Home Administration
4949 Kirschling Court
Stevens Point, WI 54481
(715) 345-7600

ECONOMIC INJURY DISASTER LOANS

Office of Disaster Assistance
Small Business Administration
409 3rd Street, SW
Washington, DC 20416
(202) 205-6734

Description: Provides loans to small businesses suffering economic damage under presidential, Small Business Administration, and/or Department of Agriculture declared disaster. Must be a small business or agricultural concern, be located within declared disaster area, and be unable to obtain credit elsewhere.

$ Given: $60 million for FY 92. During FY 91, 1,076 loans were made.

Application Information: Refer to local Disaster Area Office of the Small Business Administration.

Deadline: N/A

Contact: Small Business Administration, Region V
Federal Building
300 South Riverside Plaza
Room 1975
Chicago, IL 60606-6611
(312) 353-0359

WYOMING

EMPLOYMENT SERVICE

United States Employment Service
Employment and Training Administration, Department of Labor
Washington, DC 20210
(202) 535-0157

Description: Provides placement services for job seekers and employers. These include services to special applicant groups, such as veterans, the handicapped, youth, minority, and older workers; a computerized interstate job listing; and other labor market information.

$ Given: FY 93 est. $821.6 million

Application Information: Contact the Employment Security
Department for your state.
Deadline: N/A
Contact: Dick Sadler, Executive Director
Employment Security Commission
P.O. Box 2760
Center and Midwest Streets
Casper, WY 82602
(307) 235-3650

UNEMPLOYMENT INSURANCE

Unemployment Insurance Service
Employment and Training Administration, Department of Labor
Washington, DC 20210
(202) 523-7831
Description: Provides unemployment insurance for workers whose
employers have contributed to state unemployment funds, federal
civilian employees, ex-service persons, those who have become
unemployed as a result of product imports, and those whose
unemployment comes under the purview of a presidentially declared
disaster.
$ Given: $25.5 billion for FY 93
Application Information: Contact the Employment Security
Department for your state.
Deadline: N/A
Contact: Dick Sadler, Executive Director
Employment Security Commission
P.O. Box 2760
Center and Midwest Streets
Casper, WY 82602
(307) 235-3650

EMPLOYMENT AND TRAINING ASSISTANCE—DISLOCATED WORKERS

Employment and Training Administration, Department of Labor
200 Constitution Avenue, NW
Washington, DC 20210
(202) 535-0577
Description: Federal grants given to state and local programs to
assist workers through training and employment services. These are
workers who have been terminated or laid off, or who have received
notice of such, and are not likely to return to their previous

occupation or industry, or who are long-term unemployed. Targeted individuals include those affected by mass layoffs and natural disasters.

$ Given: Total nationwide of $571.1 million for FY 93

Application Information: Inquire at Employment Security Office listed below.

Deadline: N/A

Contact: Dick Sadler, Executive Director
Employment Security Commission
P.O. Box 2760
Center and Midwest Streets
Casper, WY 82602
(307) 235-3650

WOMEN'S SPECIAL EMPLOYMENT ASSISTANCE

Office of Administrative Management
Women's Bureau
Room S3305
Office of the Secretary, Department of Labor
Washington, DC 20210
(202) 523-6606

Description: Provides advisory services and counseling, and disseminates technical information to help the employment opportunities of women—especially in the realm of nontraditional women's jobs and jobs in new technologies.

$ Given: N/A

Application Information: Write to Women's Bureau in your region listed below.

Deadline: N/A

Contact: Oleta Crain, Regional Administrator
Region VIII, Women's Bureau
Department of Labor
Federal Office Building
Room 1452
1801 California Street
Suite 905
Denver, CO 80202-2614
(303) 391-6755

Federal Grants

EMERGENCY LOANS

Farmers Home Administration
Department of Agriculture
14th Street Independence Avenue, SW
Washington, DC 20250
(202) 690-1533
Description: Provides loans to family farmers (either owner or tenant), ranchers, and aquaculture operators to cover losses resulting from natural or other major disasters. Recipients must be unable to obtain credit from other sources.
$ Given: $81.4 million est. FY 92. Average size for FY 92 was est. $42,300.
Application Information: Consult local telephone directory under United States Government, Department of Agriculture, for Farmers Home Administration Office.
Deadline: N/A
Contact: Farmers Home Administration
Federal Building / Room 1005
100 East B Street
P.O. Box 820
Casper, WY 82602
(307) 261-5271

ECONOMIC INJURY DISASTER LOANS

Office of Disaster Assistance
Small Business Administration
409 3rd Street, SW
Washington, DC 20416
(202) 205-6734
Description: Provides loans to small businesses suffering economic damage under presidential, Small Business Administration, and/or Department of Agriculture declared disaster. Must be a small business or agricultural concern, be located within declared disaster area, and be unable to obtain credit elsewhere.
$ Given: $60 million for FY 92. During FY 91, 1,076 loans were made.
Application Information: Refer to local Disaster Area Office of the Small Business Administration.
Deadline: N/A
Contact: Small Business Administration, Region VIII
999 18th Street
Suite 701
Denver, CO 80202
(303) 294-7001

Index

Index

Index

Index

Index